Stephen Arthurs was born in T
potter until 1998 when he began
have appeared in the National Post, the Vancouver Sun, the Edmonton Journal, the Calgary Herald, the Ottawa Citizen, the Montreal Gazette, and the Kingston Whig-Standard.

He lives on Hornby Island in British Columbia with his wife Robyn.

To John & Betty
Merry Christmas 2003
Love
Stephen & Robyn

STARTING
TO
WANDER

Living and Travelling in Central Mexico

STEPHEN ARTHURS

Glyphon Books

STARTING TO WANDER

Enquiries and orders may be sent to: glyphonbooks@yahoo.com

National Library of Canada Cataloguing in Publication
Arthurs, Stephen, 1951-
Starting to wander : living and travelling in Central Mexico / Stephen Arthurs.

Includes bibliographical references.
ISBN 0-9733262-0-4
1. Arthurs, Stephen, 1951- --Journeys--Mexico. 2. San Miguel de Allende (Mexico)--Description and travel. 3. Mexico--Description and travel.
I. Title.
F1391.S26A77 2003 917.2'41 C2003-910973-9

Author's Note

In the interest of privacy, some of the names, biographical details, and actions of the people described in this book are fictional.

Where dollar amounts have been mentioned, they refer to U.S., not Canadian, dollars.

My sincere thanks to Gloria Herbert for her valued assistance. I also owe a huge debt of gratitude to three very remarkable women: Robyn Richards, Ananda Arthurs, and Grace Scott Arthurs. To all of them, thank you.

To Robyn

Chapter 1

Our deciding to move to Mexico for five months in November of 2000 didn't just come out of the blue. It had its genesis in a three-week holiday we spent there several years before. There were many episodes from that short holiday that influenced our decision about whether or not to return for a longer stay. Some nudged us towards the idea and some nudged us away. Here are five of them.

The first time we ventured forth into the heart of Mexico in 1997, our plane had just touched its nose down on the Mexico City Airport runway, when Robyn threw up.

It wasn't because of the landing, which had been a very gentle Japanese Air Line kind of thing, and it wasn't because of the flight, which had been a smooth and pleasant one. Oh, it was tempting to blame Mexico, with its reputation as the perpetrator of so much gastrointestinal discomfort against newly arrived guests, but considering we hadn't even stepped outside the aircraft yet, that hardly seemed fair. No, it was probably just some flu bug she brought with her from Canada, but it *was* a rather inauspicious beginning to our trip.

We gathered up our packs from the overhead compartments, along with a handful of JAL air-sickness bags, and went out and hopped onto a bus to Cuernavaca. We were operating on the assumption that it would be cleaner, safer, and cheaper to spend our first night somewhere beyond the pollution of Mexico City. We had just settled down in our seats, and were getting ready to watch silly men being crushed by falling pianos in *Home Alone 2*, when Robyn threw up again.

Now although Robyn is a mere wisp of a woman, at times she can be really quite formidable, giving people her dreaded ***look*** when they don't measure up or when they – God help them – tick her off. This is what I call "Big Robyn." But she also has a very sad, limp-rag-doll persona that pops up once in a while when she gets tired or sick. I call it "Little Robyn," and after throwing up several more times on that bus ride, until all she could do was dry heave, she became itsy-bitsy, teeny-weeny Little Robyn, practically disappearing altogether. I tried to lighten the mood a little by suggesting that we could always turn around and go straight back to Canada. But when she replied, "Not right now. Ask me again in half an hour, though," I realized our holiday was in serious jeopardy.

When we got off the bus, it was nighttime in Cuernavaca, and it was as if we were stepping out of one nicely ordered universe, and straight into another of total chaos. We were swept away from the bus in a tide of people and managed to barely squirm our way out of the mass only then to be pounced upon by a swarm of hectoring taxi drivers eagerly offering their services. There was a frenzied cacophony of noise and lights from cars, buses, and motor scooters swooshing past us on all sides, along with an incessant badgering of voices saying, "Taxi! Taxi! Taxi!" The air smelt of diesel fumes and fried pork and I was desperately trying not to get separated from Robyn. Finally, standing at the curb, I asked one of the drivers if he knew where Hotel Juarez was. I had spent a long time analyzing my guidebook to come up with this name, and, being somewhat proud of my selection, I had been expecting the taxista to say something like, "Ah, I can tell you're a seasoned traveller my friend. That is a fine choice. High standards at an affordable price. Excellent choice, excellent. Since you are so knowledgeable, perhaps you could suggest a good restaurant for me and my wife? We have an anniversary coming up . . ."

Instead he said no, he'd never heard of it.

"Do you have the address?" he said.

"Of course, it's right here in my . . ."

Guidebook? Guidebook is in pack. Pack is . . .

Oh . . my . . God! Our packs are still on the bus! I used to play the position of wide receiver on our high school football team, a job tailor-made for the fleet of foot, but I was never really motivated to achieve my maximum potential. I always ran much faster when I was being chased by dogs, neighbours, and older brothers. Terror really is the best motivater. While I stood there feeling as if I had just been dropped into the midst of a carnival spook-show ride, complete with flashing lights, blaring horns, and creepy smells, I realized that every vestige of comfort that we, and especially Robyn, were likely to need that night was now probably being carried off proudly and smugly by some poor beggar that I had neglected to give a peso to when he held out his frail little hand just a few brief moments before.

I was motivated. God was I motivated! I must have reached the bus in three seconds flat. Heart pounding in my throat, sweat streaming down my face, leaving a trail of perplexed Mexicans behind me, I reached the platform that our bus had pulled into and, not wanting to even dare to look for fear of what I wouldn't see, I peered with dread down along the side of our bus towards the mid-section where the cargo doors were located. The platform, which moments earlier had been bustling with activity, was now completely devoid of people. I began to feel physically sick. My stomach felt like a rapidly deflating balloon, and it seemed likely that my worst fears were about to unfold. Then, almost as if manifested through sheer willpower, the shapes of two little bundles gradually differentiated themselves from the Rorschach test of shadows that were obscuring the back wheel. They looked absolutely glorious sitting there quietly waiting on that greasy asphalt pavement, such good, well-behaved little backpacks. And although I wanted to turn around and hug each and every kind and gentle Mexican who had not stolen our luggage, I thought better of it, and just tried to settle down and wipe that huge idiotic smile from my very flushed face before I freaked out any more poor souls. Perhaps, I thought, my frazzled state was just a result of not yet having adjusted to the thin air at this altitude. Yeah, that was probably it.

As casually as possible, I walked over and snatched up our packs and then scooted quickly back to Robyn and the cabby. After a brief riffling through the guidebook, and a momentary pause while I gazed aghast at the unpronounceable street name, I took a deep breath and asked him to take us to Netzahualcoyotl 19, please.

The driver dropped us off at a locked door on a dimly lit street full of old and crumbling colonial buildings. When I asked him if he was sure it was the right place, he shrugged, pushed the buzzer for me, and made his getaway – rather too quickly I thought.

Some moments later, the door opened up an inch or so, and through the crack a rather bewildered young man of about seventeen with something in his mouth stared blankly at me.

"Do you have a room," I said in my lousy but functional Spanish.

"Mm hm," he mumbled as he opened the door a little further.

We walked into the dark hallway and he closed the giant door behind us with a somewhat ominous and resounding *clunka-clunk*. Being thrown into a dungeon probably makes a sound like that, I thought. Once inside, I was able to get a better look at the fellow and I saw what it was he had in his mouth. It was a toothbrush, sticking out like a long skinny cigar from his firmly shut mouth, and there was toothpaste leaking out all around his lips.

Nice. Then he led us forever down a long narrow hallway, stepped around to his right, and took up his position behind a fairly respectable-looking hotel front desk. At this point, being rather more accustomed to the Canadian way of doing things, I expected the toothbrush to come out, followed perhaps by a "Isn't the searing heat a lovely change after six months of snow?" or at least a Mexican equivalent.

But he didn't say anything at all. Just stood there staring at me. I looked at Robyn. No help there. Still very Little Robyn. I looked back at the young man. Still nothing. Definitely some cultural thing happening here. Young guy does finally manage a smile, which isn't easy while you're chewing on a toothbrush with a mouth full of toothpaste, but it looked as if I was going to have to do most of the talking.

"Do you have a room with two beds?" I enquired.

He nodded and then motioned for us to follow him down the hallway. He led us up a long, long flight of very narrow, very dark stairs. If the ground floor of this place resembled a medieval dungeon, we were now clearly headed for the Tower. The little staircase twisted and contorted as in a surrealistic painting, never passing anything that looked like a room, and there was not a single sign of another occupant in the place.

We finally stopped in front of a door. He unlocked it and led us inside.

The room looked like a jail cell. Robyn flopped onto one of the beds and I could tell from her vacant look that she wasn't planning to get up.

"Oh this will be just fine," she said with a little smile. "If you don't like it, just find something nice for yourself and close my door on your way out. I've decided to die here, okay honey?"

Sigh.

I followed our host out onto the staircase, and closed the door behind me. I had serious reservations about the room.

"Is it quiet around here at night, señor?"

Before answering, the young man took the toothbrush out of his foamy mouth, stuck his head out a nearby window, and spat out a mighty wad of saliva and toothpaste amalgam. With one ear cocked towards the window, he waited in frozen silence for a second or two until the loud resounding *splat* confirmed that his emissary to the outside world had completed its three-story descent unimpeded.

For me, this was the crowning moment to a truly horrible day. The rest of that night is, thankfully, a bit of a blur. After only ninety minutes in Mexico, Robyn had become terribly sick, I had come frighteningly close to losing all our luggage, and now, with uncanny precision, I had managed to locate the most revolting hotel on the face of the earth. This very definitely qualified as one mighty big nudge away from taking the big leap.

The next morning, I decided to head off in search of a better hotel while Robyn tried to sleep herself back to life.

Down at street level, the morning air was spring-like, cool and fresh, and the streets were alive with that going-to-work energy that a new day usually brings with it. Mothers and fathers and brothers and sisters were totally dedicated to the task of getting the children off to school. The sounds of children playing on the school grounds blended together with the chirpy sounds of thousands of birds in the many treed plazas around the city to produce a delightful and cheery background noise like the babble of a happily enchanted brook. The young children literally bounced down the cobbled sidewalks hand in hand with a mom or an older brother, and then paused briefly at the small street vendors' stalls along the way to buy some little toy or piece of candy.

I eventually found the hotel I was looking for, the Colonial, also recommended by my now very suspect guidebook. But this one was a gem. It was like a miniature version of a grand hotel. Beautiful, tall arcades surrounded a pretty little garden-courtyard complete with a little stone fountain. The person in attendance was an attractive Indian woman called Victoria (pronounced "beektoria" in Mexico). She was busy washing sheets and the office was closed but she said since the owner didn't come by very often, she would try to get in to find me a room key. She couldn't even show me a room without getting into the office because the stairway access to the upstairs rooms was inside the office as well. Victoria smiled demurely and pointed to a small arched opening in the office doorway that sort of resembled a ticket window at a movie theatre. I wasn't sure what she had planned or if her plans were for me or for her, but a moment later all was made clear. As she hiked up her skirt part way, she gave me a turn-around-please motion with her fingers. I respectfully averted my eyes as any considerate Canadian would do, and then proceeded to use my excellent peripheral vision to take full advantage of the situation. Furtively, I watched as Victoria's skirt came all the way up to her waist and she then started to pull herself, head first, through the little opening. For a few very special moments I had a clear view, peripherally of course, of her fine and ample rear end, which lodged itself, stuck itself in fact, in that narrow opening, one that I'm sure was never intended to function as an entrance. Come on girl, pull! I certainly don't want to have to get in there and push, and I hate to even think how a Mexican fire department might handle an emergency situation like this one.

Anyway, after popping out the other side like a champagne cork, a very twinkly and somewhat flushed Victoria then opened the door from the inside. I'm sure I was a little flushed myself. Our mutually embarrassed smiles were like gentle little cross-cultural acknowledgements that fate had generously bestowed on the two of us one of its very best vaudeville routines ever; to me those smiles were indicative that for a few brief moments, the two sides of the canyon between us had been pulled close enough together for each of us to take a nice leisurely stroll across.

The room was beautiful and clean and I took it on the spot. Later, after we hauled our stuff over from the Hotel Juárez, Robyn declared that the new room was absolutely lovely. Then she promptly threw up. A christening of sorts I suppose. After a few moments, Robyn started to laugh. Oh God, now she's delirious.

"You know," she started thoughtfully, "all this vomiting is actually beginning to seem a little funny. When we get home we can show our pictures to our friends and say, 'This one is a picture of Robyn throwing up at the Cortés Palace. And this one, we just love this one, here she is throwing up beside that amazing pyramid at Xochicalco.' "

This was a dangerous point in the conversation. If I laughed, there was every possibility, still very Little Robyn might burst into tears and call a cab for a fast ride back to the airport, and then it would be home again in five hours.

"Ah, lighten up, Stephen," she said with a friendly little push. "Hey, we could write a book . . . We could call it *Mexico on Five Barfs a Day*."

Sensing it was finally safe to step into the water, I laughed, and gave her a great big hug. Count this as one very tentative nudge forward.

That afternoon we headed off on our first real tourism jaunt to the Catedral de la Asunción. It was built by the Franciscans during the time of Cortés in 1526, and is an excellent example of the early fortress-style churches built in the days when the natives were not exactly friendly. The small bevel-sided window slits are usually more associated with castles than churches, but defence was no doubt an important consideration in the early days of New Spain.

Once inside, we sat down in one of the pews and let the cool, dark air soothe and surround us. At the front of the cathedral, on our side of the altar was a wonderfully elegant and quite mystical arrangement that hung from the ceiling effectively filling up a small portion of that vast empty space created by the barrel-vaulted roof. Seven large glass bowls fitted with wicks and filled with oil were sparkling and flickering up there in the dark void, giving the church a truly magical atmosphere. Like some sorcerer's apprentice, there was a man standing on a ladder, pushing and pulling the bowls up and down with a long stick to trim their wicks or otherwise attend to their needs. To me he looked like a puppeteer animating the heavens. The bowls were hanging at various heights, scattered randomly like flickering stars, and all the while that giant mythological being was fussing over them.

Robyn spoke softly in my ear, “I think I’ll just sit here all day, watching those bowls.”

It’s always tempting to ridicule the Roman Catholic Church. And the Church establishment does have a lot to answer for (the Crusades and the Inquisition being two of the more obvious lapses in judgement), but from what I could see all around me, the deep devotion of these people was not something to be mocked; it was something to be celebrated. Everything I had read on the subject indicated to me that the Mexican people had evolved one of the nicest blends of faith-based traditions that you’d ever find anywhere; that through their festivals and pilgrimages they expressed a gentle and deep devotion to the importance of goodness and kindness in their lives. Their fearless blending of Indian and Christian myths intrigued me, and I wanted to just breathe it all in for a while. Three weeks just wasn’t enough time. One more nudge towards the abyss.

One man who was not at all shy to express his disdain for the Church and its transgressions was Diego Rivera, the acclaimed muralist. Since Robyn was feeling pretty good after the cool, dark, soothing vibes of the cathedral, we decided to head over to the nearby Palacio de Cortés, where some of Rivera’s finest murals can be viewed.

The theme of Rivera’s Cuernavaca murals was very blunt: *Human Barbarism in the Name of Profit and Religion* – no shades of grey in this man’s work. I found them to be absolutely stunning. But at the same time they were unnerving. There was a peculiar contrapuntal mix of feelings that swirled around inside them. His themes were deeply rooted in the brutal clashes between rich and poor that have occurred throughout Mexican history, but his style was quite innocent and child-like, and this created a disconcerting rift between theme and style. I found myself playfully seeking out hidden images and faces in the large murals as if I were searching for Lowly Worm in a Richard Scarry book, only then to be suddenly clobbered by the cruelty depicted in his work.

On our way out of the museum, we stumbled onto an exhibit containing displays of some of Mexico's greatest national treasures – a copy of the Constitution, an original flag from the War of Independence, and a large bell – so we decided to take a look.

We entered the room and were directed by a sign to turn sharply left. On doing so we were immediately confronted by two short men dressed in helmets and dark green army fatigues brandishing submachine guns. They looked intent on drilling holes right through us, if not with their guns, then certainly with their threatening eyes. These guys were extremely serious fighter-dudes.

Trying to ratchet down the sense of hostility in the room a little, I said, "Oh, hi there . . . Wow, nice boots."

The ***look*** from Robyn. It was a good sign actually, meant she was coming to life again. She pointed over to a little notice on the bell. It said, "No Tocar," meaning "Don't Touch."

Robyn and I frowned at one another with our very best this-is-serious-and I'm-trying-not-to-laugh expressions.

"I don't think they need the sign do you?" whispered Robyn sideways under her breath while keeping a very straight face.

"I think one machine gun says it all," I replied.

The contrasting values of different cultures fascinate me, and the thought of having the opportunity to immerse ourselves in a culture as complex as Mexico's for a significant period of time was definitely another nudge towards the edge. I'm not sure what we do with our national treasures in Canada, but we sure as hell don't do this. I'm not sure we have any actually. No, that's not true. Beside the highway there near Duncan, B.C., stands the world's largest hockey stick – the thing's over 200 feet long – surely a national treasure if ever there was one. Come to think of it, I guess maybe that would be worth mowing down a few dozen crazed hockey fanatics for.

After a quick glance around, we figured it wasn't worth dying for, and we walked out.

We spent only a couple more days in Cuernavaca. Whatever

Robyn had picked up before we left home, be it flu or food poisoning or whatever, was clearly losing its grip on her, and, good sport that she was, she was ready to carry on with the holiday. So we packed up our things once again and struck out for the next stop on our journey, Taxco, a small, very quaint, colonial town two hours away by bus.

Thanks, in part, to a very goofy 1950s Mexican movie called something like *The Revenge of the Aztec Mummies*, the trip passed by quite quickly, and we soon found ourselves at the edge of tiny little Taxco, a village which like the road that brings you to it, clings precariously to the side of a very precipitous mountain.

After leafing through our guidebook on the bus, I learned that, as befits a village perched high on a mountain in the Sierra Madre, Taxco has had its ups and downs. Rather than subject you to a lengthy description of the history of Taxco, suffice it to say it was a silver-mining town that had exactly three ups and three downs between the years of 1529 and 1929, at which time it had one final up thanks to an American, William Spratling, who helped establish it as Mexico's pre-eminent silver-smithing town.

The importance of Spratling and others like him is that they were the first wave of foreigners to come to Mexico with the intention of establishing expat artist colonies there. And now these so-called colonies are in themselves interesting places to visit, partly for their unique gringo culture and partly, as with Taxco and San Miguel de Allende, for their rich Mexican culture as well.

It's hard to know whether these influxes of new blood have been good or bad for Mexico. Spratling helped initiate an economic boom in Taxco with his innovative and popular new jewellery designs, but he was also described as a charlatan, a hustler and a relentless self-aggrandizer. His friendships with the likes of William Faulkner and Sherwood Anderson led to Taxco becoming a steamy cauldron for the evolution of new ideas from the many writers and painters who came to live there. But according to one such writer, Rodney Gallop, who was there in the late Thirties, "It remains uncertain whether they are painters who have gone there to drink, or drinkers who have gone there to paint."

Our guidebook said that we should head uphill from the bus depot and that we would thereby encounter the bottom edge of the town of Taxco and its famous mercado or market. Since heading downhill would have taken us over a steep precipice and splattered us onto the stony bottom of a deep chasm, we decided to take the clever guidebook's advice. After the dust had settled from our bus's departure, we crossed the street and headed directly uphill.

There is no north, south, east, or west in Taxco, just uphill and downhill. Bewildered by the multitude of fruit and candy stalls before us, we decided against looking for an entrance to the market and instead, like true adventurers, we simply barged through the stalls as best we could.

Before we could say "Huitzilopochtli" (the Aztec god of war), we found ourselves in the middle of a human maelstrom. Suddenly, we were swept up into a river of people flowing uphill towards the centre of town. You don't want to fight a riptide like that, you'll only risk injury or exhaustion. It's better if you think of it as an exercise in letting go, and just sit back and enjoy the sights while the stream carries you merrily along like an overly enthusiastic friend. On one side of us colours were busting out of a chaotic display of scarves like great slashes of vivid colour painted with large brush strokes by a precocious child. On the other side, ripe red billiard-ball tomatoes were stacked with dizzying complexity into geometric heaps that made pyramids out of spheres. We flew past a dimly lit nook and glimpsed a long line of patient customers all waiting beside an ancient, conveyor-type contraption with multiple gears and chains that was spawning tortillas by the thousands like some giant mechanical ant.

Robyn and I smiled at one another as we were drawn farther and farther up along this gravity-defying river through this three-dimensional maze called the mercado. There was a wonderful counterbalancing sub-plot to all of this chaos, namely, the gentleness of the people all around us. The force of the current was overwhelmingly strong, but it was also slow and relaxed – a lot like Mexican society, I thought. We in the rest of North America have an incredible longing to belong, having pretty much lost any sense of collective identity in our own countries. But the pulse of some ancient bond that glues the culture together still seemed to be beating hard there. Surprisingly, they were letting us join in and share that sense of belonging with them. For a little while – it felt like our own.

That was the final nudge. It became clear to me then and there in that marvellous river of people that I had to make an effort to get a better understanding of this complicated and confusing culture. I had to go deeper. And I also realized I had reached a point in my life where I was looking for a new source of enrichment. I was in need of a change. In the words of Larry Diamond, Tom Robbins' stockbroker turned mystic from *Half Asleep in Frog Pajamas*, "If the sea teaches us humility, the desert teaches us patience," and that ride through the Taxco market made it clear to me that after listening to the ocean for twenty-five years, a move to the desert was long overdue.

The time frame for such a trip was settled for me when, in the first four months of the year 2000, I was in the worst and most constant pain that I'd ever experienced in my life, pain from a degenerative disc in my back. Seeing with the clarity that such an experience can often bestow, I realized that it was probably a question of now or never. When I started to heal sometime in May of that year, Robyn and I started to plan our trip.

There is a type of traveller you may encounter in Mexico called an old hand. These are people who have been coming to Mexico for thirty or forty years, never pay more than five dollars for a room, eat food only from the most unhygienic of street vendors, look like more emaciated and grey-haired versions of Mick Jagger, and think they know absolutely everything there is to know about Mexico – provided it involves ordering a beer or where to find some really good weed. These folks used to tell us that our experiences in coastal Mexico were trivial compared to what a person could find in the interior, in "real" Mexico. We resented this, as you might expect, since our experiences on the coast – real or unreal – seemed quite profound to us. So I have always hesitated to comment on the differences between the coast and the interior when speaking about Mexico. However, at the risk of being labelled an old hand myself, a fate worse than death to me, I must unfortunately tell you this: the fact is, you don't see the real Mexico unless you head for the interior; that's where the heart of the country is.

Sorry, but it's true. And you can't imagine how hard it is for me to admit how right all those brainless jerkheads were all along.

So, on the Day of the Dead, November 2, 2000, two very alive people found themselves at the Vancouver International Airport heading off for a five-month sojourn into the heart of Mexico. And if the Taxco trip had shaken up my plans a little for quietly living out the rest of my life on safe and sane little Hornby Island, this next trip was about to do major and irreversible damage.

Chapter 2

As we passed through the doors into the Vancouver International Airport around seven o'clock that morning, I finally felt completely free from the weight of all the organizing and planning that had been required to get us there. Everything I needed to exist for the next five months I was carrying with me, and I veritably bounced along the smooth tile floor of that terminal like an astronaut playing on the surface of the moon.

Our cat Dodi was happily ensconced with Robyn's brother where she would be fawned over constantly by his eleven-year-old son, and where she would finally be worshipped with the sort of obsequious devotion she no doubt thought she deserved. We set things up so that Robyn's eighty-seven-year-old dad who lives next door would receive two visits a day from the local homecare service, and saw to it that all of his bills as well as ours were put on automatic withdrawal. Friends had agreed to drop in and check up on our house; precious possessions were moved out entirely so they could at least be stolen from someone else's place while we were gone; all insurance premiums were prepaid; and arrangements were made for our mail to be delivered to our good friend Paul who had the unenviable task of trying to sort out the minuscule amount of wheat from the great heaps of worthless chaff.

Leaving home for five months really is the most irresponsible thing to do. "What if I die while you're in Mexico?" exclaimed my mother. This is a trick question by the way; there is no answer to it. Just smile and reassure your mother that it won't happen like that. The truth, which is that her death could just as easily happen while you're taking a leak off your back porch, is not something she wants to contemplate. As we headed over to the check-in with our small carry-on suitcases rolling easily behind us, we were quite giddy with happiness. There was nothing burdensome ahead of us, just an empty slate of time to be filled in with new and exotic adventures. Heaven must feel like this, I thought – unencumbered, simplified, full of hope, and empowered by the guilt-free use of credit cards.

We had spent the previous night in a motel near the airport that must have been a lovely place back in the Fifties when I suspect it was built. (Not in the prettiest part of town exactly – on the way there we had a charming view of a man standing on the top edge of a two-story building gazing down at the pavement where he had just thrown a dead seagull and a strap-on penis.) Last time we stayed there it was called the Stay N Save or the Sleep N Weep or the You Snooze You Lose – I can't remember exactly – but since that time they had changed their name to Ye Olde Trendy and Posh Inn, or something like that, in a desperate lurch towards trying to give the place a little class. And to be fair, these folks were making a concerted effort to improve things. For instance, unable to entirely rid our room of its Moose Jaw-pub smell of smoke and spilt beer, they appear to have hosed it down with a deodorizer reminiscent of taxicab air fresheners. And instead of one chintzy abstract painting on the wall above the beds, they now had *two* chintzy abstract paintings on the wall above the beds – a matched set of identical ones, as we soon discovered after careful scrutiny. Now just how cute is that? As for the ongoing demolition of whole huge sections of the hotel, well, it lent a certain dark and edgy Art Wrecko ambience to the place, so all in all it wasn't a complete loss.

After a quick and easy check-in with Japan Airlines, we headed over to the food court for a bite to eat and a much-needed coffee. Not a morning person, I tend to stumble around mumbling incongruities and knocking into things until I get my coffee. No doubt with a very stunned expression on my face, I stood gazing up at the names of the various food booths and became increasingly horrified at the thought of having to eat chicken teriyaki, french fries, and Orange Julius for breakfast. I kept looking for the sign that said,

"Breakfast Here Numbskull," but alas, there wasn't one.

Eventually, I discerned a little sandwich counter advertising a breakfast special, and so I marched confidently up to it. I lifted the edges of my mouth as far as they would go at that early hour of the day and formed a slightly crooked smile that probably made me look as if I'd just had my mouth frozen by the dentist. I then declared forthrightly, "One breakfast special please."

Across the counter stood a very short and quite friendly Chinese fellow who pointed to the sign above his head which indicated that there were four variations to the breakfast special, all served on an English muffin. Completely unprepared for this sudden challenge, like a student asked to actually show the teacher the homework he didn't do, I just stared at his sign blankly.

"Hambacon?" he said, trying to help.

I squinted at him as if I were trying in vain to read an eye chart. My thoughts were, "What in God's name do you mean by that!?" But there was just enough brain activity going on inside my head to de-activate the little internal switch that was always wanting to blurt out such things. Did he mean I could have ham and bacon on a muffin and no egg? Did he mean I could have my egg with either ham or bacon? Or was he asking if I wanted my egg with both ham and bacon? It was tempting to just say yes and hope for the best, but I was fearful that one false step at this crucial juncture in our first day of travel might lead to some horrendous catastrophe later on.

There was a painfully long pause as I tried to get my morning, pre-coffee brain to move my lips and say something somewhat coherent. *Rr-rr-rr . . . Rr-rr-rr* went my brain like a car trying in vain to start when its battery is half-dead. Come on baby, you can do it, come on baby.

And then I sensed a stirring in the pile of leaves that was my cognitive functioning apparatus: all the variations include the egg and the muffin. Why of course! And you get to choose from a selection of extras! Brilliant! Not wanting to get charged extra for choosing too many extras, I answered just, "Ham, please."

"Hamgood," he said quickly and efficiently.

At that moment, with the pressure off momentarily, I began to suspect that maybe this little guy working away busily behind the counter wasn't really a lunch counter cook after all but someone who was developing a new form of language called Quickspeak made up entirely of two-word combinations. I listened carefully as a woman customer moved up beside me and addressed him.

"Do you have tea?" she said.

"Teaya," was his rapid-fire response.

"Ah hah! That's it!" I blurted out, quickly clapping my hand against my mouth to shut it up.

She moved back from the counter a little, sensing danger I suspect, and rather than ask our little Chinese friend to repeat whatever it was he'd said, she opted for silence as her safest course.

He turned to me and said, "Buttermayonnaise?"

Definitely getting the hang of it now and wanting to impress the woman with my newfound skill, I confidently replied, "Mayonnaiseplease."

I brought my breakfast back to our table where Robyn had been guarding our carry-on bags and then she went to the same counter. When she got back, she sat down and with a big smile on her face started to tell me all about the cute guy at the sandwich place.

"This is how our conversation went," she said.

"I'd like a glass of milk, please."

"Smalllarge?"

"Oh, large, please. I'll take the biggest you can give me. I'll take the whole cow if you have it."

"Takecow," he fired back.

Robyn's eyes gleamed as she leaned across the table towards me.

"Isn't that a hoot?" she said.

"Is-hoot," I replied.

One person at a time, that little Chinese man was quietly changing the world.

My eyes wandered idly around the cafeteria for a few lazy moments after finishing my muffin and then ground to a halt on a large family of people who were spilling out of their table which had only been designed to hold the basic Canadian nuclear family of precisely 3.72 people.

It took me a moment to be sure, I was a little out of practice, but I finally concluded that – they had to be Mexicans.

One of the reasons it was hard to tell was because there was a smattering of Canadian-type clothing spread amongst the group. Perhaps part of the family was living here now. But their Mexican-ness leaked out all around them anyway. The whole family was doting over the baby in the group who was being passed from person to person like a giant ice-cream cone of which everyone was entitled to several nuzzles and multiple licks. And there was a twenty-year-old girl, not the mother, who, although she wore a baseball cap and jeans much as any other young Canadian woman might do, was distinctly Mexican. And it wasn't because she looked Hispanic. In a multi-cultural country like Canada, that really isn't enough to place anybody. The real clues were in the details.

First of all, she had clearly, and unapologetically I might add, spent a good deal of time that morning carefully applying make-up to her face, and as a reward for her efforts, she looked positively stunning. The baseball cap wasn't just flung carelessly onto her head. She had taken the time to pull her carefully combed, dark and lustrous hair through the hole at the back of the cap, and tie it with a nice dark blue velvety hair tie. Her jeans were new and a perfect fit; her fingernails were long and painted a snazzy silver colour; and she was wearing simple but pretty earrings.

Mexican culture always seems to transcend foreign influences. Instead of being absorbed into another culture, they appropriate foreign influences for their own purposes. They don't dress like Americans when they go around in baseball caps and jeans, they dress like Mexicans who have been given a few new toys to use in Mexican ways. Mexican culture has succeeded in beating back a tremendous cultural assault from the Americans in a way it was never able to do with its soldiers on the battlefield. Chalk up one for the little guys, I say.

I like to think of Mexico as a storehouse of traditional human values, like a seed bank for the preservation of old seed stock that can be dipped into if we ever find that the path we've taken in the modern world leads us to disaster. The young Mexican woman in the airport was carrying with her the remnants of things like old-fashioned romance, respect for the family unit, and dignified public behaviour; and someday we may just need a bag of that stuff.

This tendency of Mexico to absorb the cultures of its invaders while remaining fundamentally the same at its core has been going on in Mexico for a very long time.

In 1253 A.D., the Aztecs, also known as the Mexica, came to the central valley of Mexico from the north, just as we had done. The Aztecs were one in a long chain of Indian peoples who, over the centuries, had travelled down from the drought-prone northern parts of Mexico and raided the more resource-rich regions of the south. (This plundering by barbarians from the north seems to have been a common occurrence in other parts of the world as well. The Romans were plundered from the north, as were the Greeks, and the Chinese.) Conquering the region around Mexico City landed them a particularly valuable prize because the water from five contiguous lakes made it especially feasible for large settled populations to survive and flourish there.

But it seems that in every case where a barbarian group conquered the established civilization, the new invading group evolved to a higher cultural level than before by taking on many of the characteristics of the conquered people. The barbarians got more than just a new piece of land: they got a whole new civilization free in every bag. Walmart may eventually conquer the Mexican market, but I'm convinced that it will be significantly altered in the process.

The plan for our trip was a simple one. We wanted to spend most of our time in one location on the belief that that was the only way to get into the heart and soul of the place. It takes time before people will trust you enough to tell you their best stories and share their innermost beliefs. And if we chose our primary spot well enough, we could use it as a base camp from which to explore other places as well. If we could find a place where Robyn could also take a few Spanish lessons and maybe some art courses, and where the rent was affordable, we'd be all set.

It didn't take long for us to discover that San Miguel de Allende, five hours northwest of Mexico City, was the most feasible choice. Its location, only a short distance from many of the most historically important towns in Mexico, meant that it would make an excellent hub from which we could set out on exploratory day trips. Its language and art schools were considered by many to be the best in all of Mexico. And there were a couple of other added bonuses as well: it had an excellent library of English-language books about

Mexico and it was renowned as a haven for eccentrics. It sounded perfect. We found an apartment on the Internet for $375 a month, sent the owner, known to us only as Isadora, two months' rent, and bought two tickets for Mexico City.

As our plane descended through the clouds in preparation for landing at the Benito Juárez International Airport, I got an unusually good view of the vast sprawling city.

For me Mexico City is a very troubling place. It serves as a warning to every other city on the planet. Like old Jacob Marley clanking around in his chains, it says to us all: take care or you too could end up like this.

Population estimates range between 10 million and 21 million depending on how you define the boundaries. As large cities everywhere in the world continue to grow out and amalgamate with their neighbours, the problem of boundary identification persists. Anyway, if you take the larger number, 21 million, and you consider that they live in a space which is only 571 square miles in area, and you compare that to Canada where you have 30 million people living in a space 3,560,238 square miles in area, then I think it's pretty clear that Mexico City is a wee bit overcrowded.

The pollution problems in Mexico City are therefore partly caused by the sheer numbers of people. But air pollution is also exacerbated by the fact that the city lies in a basin 7,347 feet above sea level that is surrounded by mountains. Ozone, one of the key villains in air pollution, just adores the high altitude and all that sunshine, and the mountains very effectively keep the miasma from drifting away. The dominant winds in the area come out of the north-east, which also just happens to be where all the heavy industry is located, so that doesn't help either since all that pollution gets blown *into* the city instead of away from it.

And pollution isn't even the worst part about Mexico City. Crime is.

Here are a few little snippets from a United States Consulate Advisory:

> TAXICAB CRIME: Robbery and assaults on passengers in taxis are frequent and violent, with passengers subjected to beatings, shootings, and sexual assault. U.S. citizens visiting

> Mexico City should avoid taking any taxi not summoned by telephone or contacted in advance at the airport. In December 1997, a U.S. citizen was murdered in a taxi robbery . . . Visitors should be aware of their surroundings at all times, especially when visiting bars or nightclubs. Some establishments may contaminate or drug the drinks to gain control over the patron . . . So-called "express" kidnappings have reportedly taken place on well travelled highways such as the Toluca Highway leading out of Mexico City. These kidnappings are an attempt to get quick cash in exchange for the release of any individual, and they often appear to target not only the wealthy, but also middle-class persons.

Now of course it might also be instructive to have a look at the Mexican Consulate Advisory on Los Angeles, but let us not digress.

Here's a clip from the *US News* from July, 1997, describing an incident in Mexico City:

> This month, while riding in a bullet-proof car with four bodyguards, the principal of an exclusive private school was the victim of a kidnap attempt involving five cars of assailants armed with AK-47s. Authorities said the gang was led by a police commander. Two ex-policemen were arrested – but then released for lack of evidence.

So what happened? How did it get this bad?

Well, for starters, you can blame population density. And that in turn can be blamed, at least partly, on the water. Not because it contains such an inordinate number of festive and frolicking amoebas in big hats, but because of its abundance. In the past, the water collected by the mountains encircling the city was trapped in the Mexico City Basin, thus creating an impressive natural reservoir. That water then functioned as a magnet to draw people into the city, and once they began arriving, the water then made it possible for the population to grow to staggeringly high levels. Around 200 B.C., the establishment of the fabulous city-state, Teotihuacán in the Valley of Mexico, started the whole ball of wax rolling. There were over a thousand years of population growth in this concentrated area before the Aztecs even stepped foot on it in 1325. Under the Aztecs, Tenochtitlán, in effect Mexico City, came to dominate all of Central America. All roads led, and still do, to Mexico City. Now, even though the lake beds have all dried up, people are still drawn in to Mexico City's greedy grasp, although now it's in the name of jobs.

In the aftermath of the Second World War, things got worse quite rapidly. With the encouragement of the International Monetary Fund, Mexico embarked on a policy of "import substitution" as a means of reducing its dependency on foreign goods. No doubt this was an excellent idea in economic terms, because it created a boom in manufacturing, but unfortunately, there was one very negative consequence. The poor people from the countryside poured into the capital in droves in order to escape their rural poverty, and living conditions in Mexico City deteriorated even further.

Various schemes have been tried over the years to solve some of these problems. One of the most interesting, tackling air pollution, is the "Hoy No Circula" or "Don't Drive Today" program. The idea here is that during periods of particularly lethal air pollution, the kind where even rich people start falling over dead in the streets, you can't drive your car on certain days of the week based on the last digit of your licence plate. Plates ending in 5 or 6 can't drive on Mondays; those ending in 7 or 8 can't drive on Tuesdays; those ending in 3 or 4 can't drive on Wednesdays; those ending in 1 or 2 can't drive on Thursdays; those ending in 9 or 0 can't drive on Fridays; and on the weekends it's everybody polka till they drop. (I have no idea why the numbers follow one another in such cryptic order, but I suspect it's the sort of thing that causes squeals of piggy-like laughter to erupt from the offices of bureaucrats the world over.) Well, it hasn't worked. People just bought additional cheap cars to get around the restrictions, further aggravating the problem since inevitably these cars were in poor condition and then driven illegally anyway. Following the implementation of this policy, pollution levels did not go down and gasoline consumption increased by one quarter.

So what's to be done? I don't know. I wish them the best of luck. And as for Mexico City, I like to pretend that it's not really part of Mexico at all. It's just a necessary evil, like flying in a 747 jumbo jet. It's just a section of the tunnel along which I must travel to get to where I want to be.

We were arriving at 5:30 p.m., which would mean travelling to San Miguel, a four-hour journey, in the dark. Here's another little quote from the U.S. Consulate Advisory:

> All bus travel should be during daylight hours and on first-class conveyances. Although there have been several reports of bus hijackings and robberies on toll roads, buses on toll roads have a remarkably lower rate of incidents than buses (second- and third-class) that travel the less secure free highways. While many of the assaults have occurred in daylight, the U.S. Embassy nevertheless recommends daytime travel to lower the chance of vehicle accidents. The Embassy also advises caution when travelling by bus in the area north of the border between the states of Oaxaca and Guerrero (south of Acapulco). Armed robberies of entire busloads of passengers have recently been reported to the Embassy.

The best compromise we could come up with was to risk an overnight stay in Mexico City and travel by daylight the next morning – in a first-class bus. We booked into a great little hotel we knew called the Maria Cristina. It was expensive for us, about $70, but hopefully the pleasantness of the hotel would help compensate for having to make a stop here at all, and as long as we could get to and away from it in one piece, it would be well worth it. Getting from the airport to the hotel is undoubtedly the most dangerous link in the chain, but the decision is a fairly simple one to make because the options are so few. You can either a) take one of the yellow airport taxis, or b) take an independent taxi and remember to leave a note telling your children you love them.

After a great night's sleep in comfy beds, we took the hotel limo to the Terminal Norte bus terminal, arriving there at 8:30 a.m., half an hour before our 9 o'clock departure time. We had chosen to travel on the premier bus line in Mexico called the ETN because their buses travelled to San Miguel non-stop. (Mind you Mexican buses rarely stop anyway. Oncoming traffic, stop signs, and intersections are merely things used by the drivers to inspire the elaborate choreography of their exquisite bus ballets.) Another plus to travelling with ETN was that their buses have excellent suspension which causes them to drift hypnotically up and down and side to side in a very relaxing manner during the ride thus helping passengers to cope with the various life-threatening experiences they are sure to encounter on their trip. And, of course, you never have to look at the terrifying near-misses occurring in front of you, because it is impossible to see out the front of the bus due to a wall and a door that very effectively block the driver's area off from the passenger area. This wall makes it more pleasant for the driver as well since he can't be disturbed by all the screaming gringos. You can, however, see out the sides of the bus, an unfortunate design feature from a passenger's point of view, which I'm sure the bus companies would correct if they thought they could get away with it.

You can usually measure the level of danger you're in by monitoring the behaviour of the Mexicans on your bus. You will very rarely hear them scream, but when they start crossing themselves continuously, you know things are not going well. Our bus driver was apparently participating in some sort of bus rally of which we hadn't been informed. He was clearly determined to beat all the other buses to the freeway and at one point our bus came so close to the bus next to us that we could see the sweat on the brows of the rigid, terrified faces of the passengers in the other bus. Our row of windows would be in the lead for a moment, then theirs would slowly glide ahead, then ours, then theirs. We oscillated back and forth like a couple of side-by-side horses on a merry-go-round. The gap between the buses was a couple of feet, then a couple of inches. The row of strange faces in the other bus's windows tipped away from us, and then lunged towards us, like a ship being tossed on a stormy sea. At one point the other bus disappeared entirely from my field of view and the row of passenger faces that had run down its length was replaced by a long row of skulls carved into the side of an old building. In my agitated condition, I jumbled up the two images and for a moment I glimpsed them as a busload of skeletons returning home after a wild night of partying at a nearby cemetery.

I began to carefully monitor the behaviour of the two teenage Mexican girls sitting in front of us, hoping to use them as a guide to when it would be okay to start screaming, and to my horror, they actually started to shriek. Very un-Mexican to shriek I thought – not a very good sign at all.

Robyn, who loves a good roller coaster ride anyway and who had discovered the wonderful world of Dramamine since our last visit to Mexico, was either happily oblivious to it all or just plain stoned, so I had to claw the arm rests enough for the two of us.

When we finally made it to the freeway everyone on the bus heaved a great big collective sigh of relief, fairly confident that from here to San Miguel, it would be smooth sailing. It felt as if our ship had at last burst through one of those big walls of surf that crash near the shores of South Pacific islands. With a gentler patch of sea now ahead of us, our captain opened up his engines to full throttle, and we roared off confidently, as if skimming lightly over the tips of waves.

Able to look around at my surroundings for the first time without swallowing my tongue, I was indeed impressed with the high calibre of our bus.

The seats were laid out so that there were only about ten rows of seats with one seat to the left of the aisle and two seats to the right. The seats were huge and their backs could be tipped so that they went down almost flat. Thankfully, there was enough room between rows that when the person in front of you tipped their seat back you didn't feel obligated to clean their teeth or pick out a few nits. There was no smoking, the usual TV screens were in place of course, there was a little coffee bar area at the back, and a toilet. Robyn and I were seated beside one another in seats 26 and 28. There was no seat 27 (I know because I looked for it) which made me think that for a people whose ancestors the Mayans and Aztecs were totally obsessed with numbers, Mexicans are surprisingly blasé about them. But personally I'm with the Mexicans on this one. We probably have too many numbers any way. I say just remove the ones people aren't using. Nobody will even miss them.

Comfortably ensconced in this rolling cruise ship of a bus and under no compulsion to watch *Cool Running*, a John Candy movie about the 1988 Jamaican Olympic bobsled team, which I had already seen anyway, I gazed out over the passing landscape.

We were just thirty hair-raising minutes away from the Mexico

City bus terminal, but it looked as if we were several hundred years away. People were out in the corn fields cutting the stalks down with machetes and carrying it by the armload to mule drawn carts. The vast expanses of land were divided up by the rust-coloured walls of stacked-stone enclosures that defined the boundaries of thousands of small homesteads. Spiky blue-green hedgerows of agave, the source of all tequila, further divided up the fields, closing in areas where a few sheep could graze on a bare smear of green grass. Corn stalks, collected into bails that looked like little golden tepees, were tied together at the top, and laid out geometrically on the red earth.

Undoubtedly, this must be *ejido* land: land owned communally by the local campesinos, and the source of much debate in Mexico on how best to solve the linked issues of land reform and rural poverty. The story of the peasant farmer in Mexico is one where over the centuries, probably over the millennia, he has lost and regained ownership of his land, time after time after time. And nothing has ever changed in his condition. When he doesn't own the land, he is poor, and when he owns the land he is poor. So they all want to move into Mexico City hoping to make a better life for themselves and their children, a very unfortunate thing, because inevitably, things just get worse for them there. I've seen the poverty in the country and I've seen the poverty in the city, and it looks to me as if the ones in the country are a hell of a lot better off.

Which brings me to bus bathrooms, another very unfortunate thing. Robyn once told me of one where the toilet seat was actually spring-loaded and whenever the bus went over a bump, she would go flying up several inches, and the seat would hang onto her butt for dear life and go flying up with her. Apparently it made her feel a little like a toilet-seat rodeo cowgirl. So be forewarned: if you hear cries of, "Yee-haw!" coming from a bus's bathroom, you may be in for a very long wait.

Needing to take a leak, I walked to the rear of our bus, opened the door, stepped inside, and closed its various latches behind me. This was a big mistake as it turned out. (Having once locked myself into the lady's lavatory in the very respectable Canadian Imperial Bank of Commerce at Berkeley Square in London, England, and spent thirty minutes screaming, "Help!" before they finally came and broke down the door, I should have known better.)

I cleaned the seat as thoroughly as possible, considering I was now being hurled back and forth from wall to wall like a pebble in a maraca, and then sat down. Alas, the seat was not spring-loaded and so I flew several inches above it every time the bus found a little rise in the road. This meant that my sphincter had to try to squeeze and then relax in rhythm to the bounces in the road in order to deposit most of my urine in the toilet bowl and not all over me and the walls and the mirror and the ceiling, which were already adequately splattered. It's the sort of skill one wishes one had practised at home to the rhythm of aerobic workout music before setting out on the trip, "Hold it everyone, hold it, hold it, can you feel the burn? Hold it, hold it . . and . . . RELEASE!" But who ever thinks of these things at the time?

Anyway, I failed miserably at transferring my bodily fluids to the toilet bowl and had to spend a few more exasperating minutes cleaning up my mess, while still being banged around like the bus driver's own personal piñata. This operation was made all the more challenging because the tiny sink wouldn't drain properly and air was being forced back up the hole somehow, so that it was erupting like a little mini-geyser, and spraying the clean-up water back into my face.

In no time at all I looked as if I'd been taking a shower with all my clothes on, so I just gave up trying to clean things up, and turned to open the door. Now admittedly I was a little punchy, but the innumerable latches and knobs that awaited my attention were suddenly completely unfathomable to me. I hadn't the faintest idea how I had slid, twisted, and pushed them all on entering. In fact, the whole entering process was now a distant memory. As I fiddled with one or two, memories of the lady's loo, although thirty years old, flashed back to me as if it were yesterday, and I started to panic. It was incredibly hot, I mean incredibly hot, in that washroom; hot enough that a guy could faint, fall over, and cause great bodily damage to a whole variety of very important body parts if he couldn't get out very, very quickly. And it was loud, and I mean tremendously loud, so that I don't think anyone would have heard me screaming for help. I was doomed; it was déjà vu all over again. Oh God, what a way to go, and I could hear my mother saying,

"You were where when I had my stroke!? Oh really, Stephen!"

I have actually learned a few things since that horrible afternoon in 1971. I've learned to breathe in times of great stress for one thing, so I stopped clawing hysterically at the door, and just took a few deep breaths. That's better. Now what would a Mexican do under these circumstances, I thought to myself. Well, he or she would probably just try a little bit of this (I fiddled a knob) and a little bit of that (I pushed and pulled one of the latches), and then they'd keep doing that for as long as it . . . There, I got it! It's open. God, that was close.

I walked back to my seat, still dripping.

Robyn broke her gaze away from the TV screen just for an instant, gave me a quick glance and said, "Ridding the world of malicious garden hoses again are we?"

"Very funny."

"Boy is your face ever red. You okay?" said Robyn.

"It's quite hot in there. I'm fine. I got out alive, that's all that counts."

"That's nice," she said absently. I noticed that her eyes were streaming with tears as she turned her head and went back to watching the movie. It was the final emotional scene of the film where they have to carry their sled across the finish line because they wiped out and wrecked it, and the crowd breaks out into applause as a sign of respect for their noble efforts. I reached into my pocket for a Kleenex and tore it in two. I used one half to mop up my own sweat-drenched forehead, and gave the other half to Robyn to dry her tears.

It must be the altitude.

Chapter 3

Something stirs in a bus when it's about to reach its destination. If I'm asleep, I invariably wake up; if I'm reading, I can't concentrate anymore. There's a rustling sound and a turning of heads towards windows, and suddenly every swerve of the bus is more noticeable. So when I sensed that the stirring had begun, I looked out into the distant hills to try and get a glimpse of what our new home would look like.

I'd heard that San Miguel was an old colonial town preserved as a National Treasure, so I expected to see a quaint little village nestled between a couple of hills with perhaps a tall elegant church spire in the centre that was surrounded by a smattering of castle-like buildings. Well, what I saw was a bit of a shock: there was just a sprawl of modern, nondescript buildings that splayed out across a wide plain and then came to an abrupt halt at the edge of a long, flat topped mountain range. From a distance, it looked decidedly unpromising. After scouring the disappointing vista for about a minute, I did finally manage to spot a couple of churches, but that was about it.

We hopped out of the bus, and immediately the warm, balmy air enveloped us, bringing out matching spontaneous smiles.

I looked at Robyn.

"This feels good," I said.

"Oh yeah," she said, exhaling a long, journey's-end sigh.

Making sure we had the correct change, we got into one of the cabs waiting out front of the little terminal. Having the right change just means we'll have one less unpleasant memory from our cab ride. Cabs in Mexico are never metered, so you have to ask what the fare is for your particular destination before you step into the cab. If you don't have the correct change when he drops you off at your destination, you will often end up paying more. Nobody ever has enough change in Mexico, so if you think you can give somebody a 50-peso note for something that costs 20, forget about it. Since merchants don't like having to make change because they are constantly running out, consumers end up hoarding their change so as not to be caught without the exact amount for their purchase. This of course makes matters worse, taking a lot of change out of circulation, and then the merchants never have enough, and around and around we go.

Here are a few suggestions for coping with this problem:

Hang out a lot with a certain type of little old grey-haired gringa (a female gringo), who can always be identified by the way she swings her very large, heavy purse full of change into the midriffs of those foolish enough to have wandered unknowingly into her path. These women have excellent technique. Watch them and learn.

Never tip your hand too soon by showing the merchant your small change right away. Learn to conceal your small bills behind the large ones in your wallet even though this is counterintuitive to the way we do it in the north. The element of surprise is essential if you are to have any success whatsoever. To this avail you must distract your opponent with whatever means you have at your disposal. (I favour the nonsensical question, as it seems to come quite naturally anyway, something like: "25 pesos, sure señor, and how twisted is your mango? I know I prefer the ones with feathers." Then quickly bring out the biggest bill you think you can get away with, and if they resist breaking it, try another question: "Do your hemorrhoids rattle a little when you cough? Don't you just hate that?" If they hesitate, that might be a good sign. They might be caving in under the pressure. Of course they might also be reaching for a baseball bat, so be alert and always scout out an escape route.

If that doesn't work, you can then miraculously discover one bill just a little smaller, and then a little smaller and so on and so on. It's basically a battle with both sides using the same tactics. The one who ends up with the smallest coins and bills at the end wins.

Forget about crying or whining or getting angry, it will not solve your problem. Although you can occasionally beat a Mexican at this game, be assured you will always be forced to play it. Robyn once tried unsuccessfully for an hour to get anybody in San Miguel to sell her a 6-peso can of pop using a 100-peso note (worth about 10 dollars) and arrived back at our apartment positively awash in tears. But it was a lesson well learned. She has developed into one of the world's truly great "change-hoarding masters," and now can always be easily picked out in a crowd because of all the clinking and jangling that accompanies her wherever she goes.

Oh, and by the way, there is one other nifty way of getting ahold of small change that very few people have ever managed to figure out. Get it from a bank.

The outskirts of most Mexican cities have an oily, broken-down, and depressing air about them. The people there generally look angrier and poorer than those you see in town. The outskirts are a kind of wasteland wedged in between the fresh and pretty countryside, and the old and elegant town centre. Of course some cities are all outskirts, places like Salamanca or Celaya or Leon. They are often completely ignored by travel guides because there is no reason to visit them. So, as we drove through San Miguel's outskirts, it appeared as though San Miguel would be no different in this regard from all the rest. Tire shops, car-repair shops, and welding shops spilled out onto the edges of the ramshackle, crumbling streets. Small buses known as *urbanos* roared unmuffled through this mess of confusion and spewed their black sooty exhaust fumes behind them as they went. Greasy men carrying car parts and stringy old women selling tamales lined the streets.

Fortunately though, San Miguel is small enough that its outskirts were gone in a flash, and before we knew it, we were smack dab in the heart of colonial Mexico surrounded by narrow cobbled streets, charming old buildings, and shady arcades. Our driver was compelled to drive slowly on account of the numerous little intersections we had to pass through and because of the knobbliness of the road surface, but we were in no hurry, so we sat back and watched the town bounce by.

The best way I can think to describe the view out your car window when you're driving through the streets of central San Miguel is that it looks as if you're driving up the aisle of an old French cathedral that has no pews and is only twenty feet wide. Everywhere you look there seem to be old stone walls, tall shapely pillars, graceful archways, mysterious alleys, and huge carved doors. Some of the doors are at street level, but many are not. The houses here have always been built to fulfil a logic all their own, and sometimes that logic relates more to the way the street looked three hundred years ago. So if a door ends up being several steps up or several steps down from the street level, then so be it.

The kind of shops we were passing was very encouraging. My fear had been that we would pass store after store selling nothing but tourist shlock – stuff like T-shirts of Bart Simpson in a sombrero or shot glasses with humongous breasts, not the sort of thing we were likely to be interested in. So, it was nice instead to see real Mexican shopkeepers running ordinary everyday businesses out of all these wonderful old buildings. There were lots of those ubiquitous stationery stores called *papelerías*. There were one or two small fabric stores, the kind that have legions of fabric bolts standing guard along every wall and more young women clerks than could ever possibly be needed to wait on the customers. There were toy stores, chicken stores, newspaper stores, and enough mop, broom, and bucket stores to clean up Mexico eight times over. Everything we saw out our windows was so drenched in the character of Mexico, we felt as if we could wallow in it.

We took the cab straight to Isadora's. We had arranged to meet her at the house at three o'clock, so we were only a little early when we knocked on her door at two-thirty. As I waited for the door to do something, I tried to imagine what Isadora would be like, since up to this point, we had only communicated by e-mail.

I saw her as a light-skinned, upper class Mexican woman, probably middle-aged, whose excellent English indicated she had spent a fair bit of time in the United States. She would be intelligent, sophisticated, and sensible, yet with a nice, casual sense of humour. She would dress stylishly, and be what some people would call – a handsome woman.

"Owwww, you're early! I was just on my way out. Didn't expect you until five," accused the American woman who opened the door. She was wearing a black turtleneck, black tights, a black fedora, and a bright red cape that hung theatrically off one shoulder. Her voice was a hoarse croak, with an accent that sounded like a New Yorker putting on airs.

"Owwww come i-in. I'm Isadora. Thalia shut up!" Isadora liked to sing her words whenever possible. For her, words like "five" and "in" were two syllable words, that started up high and finished way down low. On entering, we looked down at the floor and saw that Thalia was a furry little cream-coloured sausage of a dog who stood so low to the ground you couldn't see her feet.

Isadora was a short, round woman, about fifty-five years old, with reddish brown, permed hair, and a heavily made-up face. Circling both her eyes were thick black lines, and her plump, luxurious lips were painted a flashy, fire-engine red.

On first impressions Isadora came across as unpleasant, loud, and overbearing, and I was getting fully prepared to loathe this woman utterly. Then she turned and headed back down the hall, and I saw by the way she walked that she was in some sort of physical discomfort. Seeing her like that gave me pause, and my heart began to melt a little. I resolved to rein in my negative thoughts, and for the time being, I decided to give her the benefit of the doubt. It was just as well I did, because as it turned out, by the time our five months in Mexico were over, crazy Isadora had become one of our favourite San Miguel characters.

Here's a description of Isadora's place taken from an e-mail I wrote on December 28 to those of our cold, damp friends back home who had little more than the glow from their computer monitors to keep themselves warm. It's kind of out of sequence here, but what the heck. It'll give you a little voyeuristic peek past the bead curtain of that first day in San Miguel into the incense haze of our future in that most extraordinary Mexican town.

Hi everybody,

I was thinking maybe you'd like to know what things look like here. So here's a description of where we live.

We're on a narrow street just wide enough for one lane of traffic, and when people park beside their homes, the road is sometimes blocked entirely. Sidewalks that are both very narrow and very high run down both sides of the street. They use common rocks about the size of a fist for pavement and they are simply imbedded into the earth. It looks good, it's cheap, and it's easy to repair. It's also dusty, causes twisted ankles, and helps to obscure the ever-dangerous bomba, also known as the dog turd.

There are no spaces between these old colonial houses and they are built right up to the edge of the sidewalk, so they form one continuous concrete wall that borders the sidewalk and runs the whole length of the street. This means that you never see a garden or a yard, either in the front or the back of a house, the way you do back home. The interiors of San Miguel homes are only ever glimpsed in brief flirtatious flashes through partly opened doorways that are hastily flung shut before you can really be sure of what it was you saw. If you're quick though, you can catch sight of tiled courtyards, arched passageways, old leather and wooden furniture, pretty little fountains, and a plethora of flowering plants spilling out from handmade ceramic pots. The outsides of the buildings are painted in an assortment of oddly beautiful Mexican colours: dark brick-red terra cottas, vibrant grassy greens, magenta, and orangey-tan. We can't quite figure out why the colours never seem to clash. I used to think the Mexican government had a Ministry of Colour that simply controlled the whole thing by forbidding paint dealers to sell hideous colours, and indeed San Miguel's "National Treasure" status may restrict people's choices somewhat, but the government here operates in a such an atmosphere of complete anarchy that I really think colour co-ordination by the State is an unlikely reason why the colours are so beautiful. I just think that Mexicans, like children, have an innate sense of the joy of colour. They like it intense and they don't like grey.

Our place has two finely carved reddish brown doors that front onto the street and are always locked. As you swing the door shut and hear it lock behind you, you find yourself in a fairly dark hallway about forty-five feet long and about seven feet wide. Watch your step, the landlady actually greases the floor because she thinks it looks good that way, never mind that it's like trying to walk down a water slide. There are also occasional steps, too shallow to really notice until you've stumbled down them a few times, but San Miguel is located on a steep hill so you kind of get used to going up and down all the time, even inside the houses. As you walk along the hallway you are greeted on the side walls by huge paintings done by our landlady, Isadora, of herself; her maid; her Indian guru; a matador; and Albert Schweitzer. They all have big sad eyes and they all look like Isadora. She is obsessed with Albert Schweitzer; there are photos of him everywhere. I asked her why, half expecting that she'd had an affair with him in Greenwich Village when she was twenty and he was ninety, but she just said that she liked his face. Be sure not to miss the little tacky sculpture of King Kong atop the Empire State Building on the left side of the hall down by the floor.

Carrying on down the hall, there is a common kitchen on the right-hand side. It has a plastic bag of water swinging in the doorway which I am forever bashing my face on. Apparently the theory is that flies will stay away because they see themselves magnified in the bag and then run away in terror. The thing about theories like that is that it's practically impossible to disprove them because nobody has done the research. So until this tragic oversight in global research priorities has been corrected, it makes perfect sense to Isadora to just continue hanging up her plastic bags of water. Evidently, in her mind, she would rather bump into a dangling bag of water than risk the inundation of flies that removing that bag might lead to. As vindication, Isadora can point to all the dead flies found in the general vicinity and then declare that they must have all been frightened to death by their own overblown reflections. I must admit it's an elegant hypothesis. The death of the flies becomes so Shakespearean when you look at it that way.

The kitchen is a nightmare of dirty dishes, old chipped enamel pots and pans, food-encrusted place mats, trinkets, incense burners, and guru photographs. And yet, it's kind of a nice place to meet with the other renters and talk about where we're from, where we're going, and whether we enjoy detoxifying ourselves with cayenne enemas or not.

Carry on down the hall and you come to the first room. Its benefits are that it only costs $275 a month; it has a little fireplace, a little bathroom, and use of the kitchen; and you may get a free chakra adjustment from all the Hare Krishna chanting that goes on when Isadora has her friends over. Its drawbacks are that there is *no window; Isadora's tiny room is just down the hall so you have to listen to her complaining about George Bush all day; it has a glass door that stays partly open all the time; and – being quite proud of your chakras just the way they are – you may not want a free chakra adjustment from all the Hare Krishna chanting that goes on when Isadora has her friends over. The always-open door actually works quite well for the current tenant Marissa, a very sexually liberated nineteen-year-old from Pennsylvania: there's less door banging as the men come and go throughout the night. Go a little farther past the gold-painted plaster sculpture of Isadora and you come to our stairs. (If you reach the sculpture of Albert Schweitzer you've gone too far.) The treads are only big enough for the front half of your foot and Raoul, Isadora's young Mexican helper, greases each one of them with a particular gusto, no doubt his quiet revenge for gringo atrocities against Mexico, so watch your step. At the top, there is another unexpected hazard, namely, pools of dog urine and an occasional bomba. I know it sounds disgusting, but if we just move quickly past this rather unfortunate spot and turn right, we will pass through another doorway into a very nice little patio area across which lies the entrance to our room.*

The room is huge, and at $375 a month, the pièce de résistance of Isadora's house. It's twelve feet high, twenty feet wide, and twenty feet long, with white concrete walls, black wooden ceiling beams, a tile floor, and a beehive-shaped concrete fireplace moulded into one corner. One wall is covered in windows whose primary responsibility appears to be to keep the world's largest lethal plant from crawling inside and murdering us in our sleep. We have been assured by several people that it is indeed deadly, but no one can tell us its modus operandi, so we keep a big stick on hand just in case. The kitchen area is painted a rusty brown and is equipped with the kind of fixtures you would have found in a grungy basement flat in Toronto back in the Fifties: a dirty gas stove; a deep, chipped, enamel sink; and free-standing wooden shelves that fall over when you brush against them. The legs on our dining room table lean over at about a sixty-degree angle and we're waiting for the day the whole thing just collapses in a heap. The bathroom door only opens part way before it slams into the bathroom sink, but at least there is plenty of hot water. More paintings on the walls by Isa-

dora. One looks like Isadora as she might have looked had she been born a Cherokee Indian chief. I suppose it was her green period because the chief has a bright green face, or perhaps she just painted it that colour so it would match the cheap little bedside lamp that sits under it. On the opposite wall is a young, rather stoic-looking Isadora in rust and green that goes well with the refrigerator, which is also rust and green.

We've just begun using our very elegant corner fireplace. I resisted for a while because you pay about $12 for one burro load of mesquite, the equivalent of two armloads, but this cold spell has forced us to give it a try and so for the past few days we've been having nice cosy fires at night. Finding the wood is a battle in itself since the wood sellers are impossible to reach by phone and you pretty much have to just stumble across them. When they need a little extra money they pack up three or four burros and go out and flog the stuff for whatever they can get. My guys started off at 180 pesos, came down to 120 when I protested, and then came down even further to 100 when Isadora started working them over. As they were carrying in our wood, there were three young gringos in a pickup truck across the street unloading their hot-air balloon basket and a bunch of leaky propane tanks. One of them felt obliged to inform me that I shouldn't be burning wood: I was trading BTU's for environmental degradation. The gringos down here love to tell you how to live your life. Isadora had been telling us for weeks what fools we were for <u>*not*</u> *burning wood. I told the balloon man I was planning to cut down on my greenhouse emissions this month by avoiding frivolous hot-air balloon rides.*

The first time I tried to light a fire down here, I used the tried and true techniques of a Canadian backwoodsman. Marissa had asked me to light her fire for a dinner party she was having. There I was using newspaper and kindling and proudly showing off my expertise while the whole time Isadora kept insisting that she just drenches the stuff in gasoline and it starts right up. Well, it turned out that the mesquite firewood was decidedly unimpressed by all the tricks I pulled out of my red-plaid hunting cap, and it practically yawned with disinterest when I threatened it with my Swiss Army Knife. So I'm afraid I finally had to give up in despair on Marissa's fire. Now, just like Isadora said, I just drench the stuff in gasoline. Well actually, Robyn and I use white gas, also called naphtha, which is slightly less explosive, but it still gives you a pretty good flash. I soak newspaper in gas, pour it liberally over every piece of wood, we put on our sunglasses, and then sit ourselves down about six feet from the fireplace. I light a match, fling it towards the fireplace, and after a few tries we get the most wonderful – SWOOSH – and the whole room lights up. Wow! What an amazing sight! I think I'll be a white-gas man forever now. No more kindling for this guy. And yeah, there's not a lot to do here in the evenings without TV.

If you come back outside to the patio with me, I'll show you the spiral staircase that leads up to our roof deck. From there you can look out over the Parroquia, a Gaudiesque church which reminds me a lot of the Disney castle that Tinkerbell used to fly around on Sunday evenings back in the Sixties. Glance off to the left of the church and there, just beyond an assortment of storybook Mexican homes, you will see, off in the distance, a view of rolling cactus-covered scrubland ringed by the faded forms of old volcanic mountains. It looks a lot like the view you get sitting on the Helliwell bluffs at home on Hornby, looking south across the sea towards Vancouver, except there is cactus in the water and the ocean is green.

Hasta luego,
Stephen and Robyn

Now back to the afternoon of Nov. 4.

There were a few drawbacks to the room. The bathroom smelled funny, the bathtub didn't drain, the beds periodically rolled off their brick supports and came crashing to the floor and I suppose the furnishings in general at Isadora's looked a lot as if a giant baby had dismantled everything while Mummy was napping and no one could quite remember how to put it all back together again. But on our budget, we never really expected the Ritz, and it did feel a little like an artist's garret in Paris from around 1900.

We were blissfully happy just to finally be there. We chose our beds, flopped some of our stuff down around them, and went out to stock up on a few essentials. When we got back, it was around seven o'clock, and after fixing ourselves a cheese omelette and washing it down with a couple of beers, it was nine o'clock and we were ready for bed.

Our journey from Vancouver had taken about fifteen hours if you include everything. So we were exhausted. Unfortunately for us, Mexico doesn't go to sleep until about four a.m. Mexico is a very noisy place.

As I lay in my bed, eagerly anticipating a deep, motionless, slack-jawed and drooling, sleep of the dead, the rhythmic sound of crickets started up outside our open window. Sometimes a pleasant sound, this particular variety of cricket had learned everything it knew about rubbing its wings together from watching Alfred Hitchcock's classic movie *Psycho*. There is a repetitive violin shriek in that movie which is used just as Janet Leigh is about to be murdered in the famous "knife in the shower" scene, and these little guys had mastered it. Their greatest pleasure in life, it would seem, was to stretch out that horrifying moment of terror for as long as possible. They were like thousands of little sadistic concert pianists playing the crescendo of a concerto that keeps building but never reaches its climax until suddenly, they all just decide to stop playing, get up, and leave. No bow, no nothing, just suddenly they're gone. Seriously twisted crickets if you ask me.

And then right on cue, as soon as the crickets stopped, Monica Seles started playing tennis on the patio outside our door.

She has that grunt that goes *uh-UH . . . uh-UH . . . uh-UH.* There's a sort of urgent eroticism about it. I'd say it's about halfway between an anguished cry of pain and a difficult bowel movement. So either she was there in person launching balls and grunting at her feckless opponent, or there was a bird on our patio that sounded just like her. Getting to sleep was proving to be rather difficult, and little did we know, things were about to get worse.

Now I should explain that my bed was on the second story and shoved right up against the east wall of the house, fronting directly onto the street. This house was over two hundred years old and the walls of the room were quite thick, everywhere except where my ear was. The wall at that point was actually just a couple of loosely fitted doors that at one time had been used to access a tiny little balcony overlooking the street. So, just as the Monica Seles birds had finished their last set, and sleep seemed to be within my grasp, a couple of disco fiends parked their motorized rock concert directly under our balcony and cranked the music up to brain-damage level. How is it that no matter how poor people are in Mexico, they can always find enough money to buy the latest in eardrum-destruction technology? There was enough noise pounding through our room to provide for three Smashing Pumpkins concerts with enough left over to ice a sonic boom's birthday cake. You know, I do sometimes wonder if the euphoria gringos sometimes experience in Mexico is really just the result of sleep deprivation.

It's at times like this that you start to worry that your whole idea of coming to Mexico was a huge mid-life blunder. Then, as the thought of having to return home and face endless dinner conversations in which your friends gloat over the fact that your Once-in-a-Lifetime Trip was a total disaster, you rally. And then, at the sound of an engine starting and an impending departure, your spirits lift even higher, and you think about painting your face black and breaking into a rousing rendition of *Mammy*.

And then your spirits collapse utterly as you realize, they're not leaving, they're just recharging their car's battery. And then the exhaust fumes start filling your nostrils; you try closing the windows but that just seems to keep the fumes inside, so you open them again; you start envying all your friends back home because, even though the constant darkness has turned some of them into serial axe murderers, at least they can breathe, at least they can sleep, albeit, with one eye open; and then you start laughing and crying simultaneously because you realize that *they're* all busy envying *you*. So you settle down a little and resort to rocking in your bed like some psyche-ward inmate and you take some comfort in repeating over and over the words: "If I can just make it till morning, I'll be fine . . . If I can just make it till morning, I'll be fine . . ."

Sometime in the night, after they were certain I had been well and truly asphyxiated, they moved on to their next victim. The silence was eery. No crickets, no birds, no music. It must have been about three in the morning. Now sleep would come. Surely even Mexicans eventually have to succumb.

I was just beginning to drift off, just entering that foggy moor between awake and asleep, when I heard the distinctive *clop-clop* sound of horse's hooves echoing off the old eighteenth-century walls that lined the street. It was a sound that had probably changed even less than the buildings themselves over the past three hundred years, and it felt like a visitation from an apparition. It stopped just below my window, and I wanted to get up and have a look, but I was glued to my bed with fatigue.

In my mind's eye though, I saw a silhouette of a caped rider and a horse, with sword and spurs winking multiple silver flashes in the moonlight. The horse had wild eyes, flared nostrils, and a sheen of sweat on his coat from riding through the night. Then the *clop-clop* started up again, and little by little it slowly faded away into the night, leaving behind only mystery and a hollow silence.

And at that moment, as if to reassure any poor sleepless gringos that, in Mexico, they need never be afraid of the night, a church bell went *bong, bong, bong.*

Fifteen minutes later, it went *ding-dong, bong, bong, bong*. Fifteen after that, it went *ding-dong-ding-dong, bong, bong, bong.*

Can you imagine the reaction in Canada or the United States if you told people that you were going to place bells in every neighbourhood that would ring every fifteen minutes, right through the night, and ring so loud that no one could miss hearing them? In the Eighties in Ottawa, they passed a bylaw making it illegal for your budgie to sing after ten o'clock at night – I have no doubt bell ringing would have set off a popular insurrection. Does anyone really need public bells to tell them it's three-fifteen in the morning? Apparently in San Miguel they do.

As it happens, there are over eighty-seven bells just in churches alone in San Miguel. There are five more that live in clocks and many more that reside in public buildings. The Godzilla of all bells is the one hanging in the Parroquia, San Miguel's most famous church. The thing is six feet tall and its rim is eight and a half inches thick. You could probably hear "Miguel," as it is called, from ten miles away. We were two blocks away. At the other end of the bell spectrum there is also a little teeny weenie pest of a thing in a church called, San José de la Montana, that is only five inches tall and whose high-pitched scream is guaranteed to peel the wax off your ears, or at least keep dogs and the criminally insane informed of the correct time.

There are as many reasons for sounding bells in Mexico as there are excuses for the performance of the national soccer team. A visit from the vice-president of Coca-Cola; the arrival of a new fire truck; the feast day of the saint after which the bell is named; the creation of a new flavour of ice cream – all are good reasons to ring the bells. In the mornings the bells announce Mass, and another soft clanging signifies the moment of transubstantiation during the Mass (the instant when the bread and wine are considered to have changed into the blood and body of Christ). On certain days, all the bells are rung at once, making enough glorious noise to drown out a thousand mariachis; and on one day each year, the ringers take the day off.

On Good Friday, the bells of San Miguel go silent – silent out of respect for Christ on the Cross. It must be a very empty, eery feeling for the residents of San Miguel to wake up and find that their usually happy and vibrant hometown has been suddenly cloaked in a deathly silence and turned, for the moment, into a mournful ghost town. I think a Mexican's worst nightmare is to be alone – and I think they equate silence with loneliness. Babies here are smothered in affection and noise from the moment of their birth. The sounds of fiestas and parades and family contact are the stuff of a Mexican's life. Work's only function is to act as a filler for the spaces in between. They are frightened by silence; it's like a disease to them.

So, I figure the bells take on a more significant role than just telling the time or calling the people to Mass: they reassure people that all is well; they tie the society together; during the daytime, they effectively distract people from the drudgery of their work; and during the night, they offer a perfect substitute for the reassuring beat of a mother's heart.

I knew, of course, that one of the most ancient functions of a tolling bell was to announce a person's death, but what I didn't know was that they can also *cause* a person's death – death by clanging I suppose it would be called. That first night in San Miguel, I think I heard every one of those eighty-seven bells tolling, and I swear that each and every one of them was tolling just for me.

Chapter 4

I know it was eight-thirty when we woke up, because that's when school starts in San Miguel, and our room was directly across the street from one. Since the streets were only about twenty feet wide, it sounded a little as if our beds had been gently carried during the night right into the middle of the schoolyard. I half expected to see soccer balls with kids in hot pursuit flying across my bed. Even compared to the night before, the noise was impressive.

At my school when I was a kid, the noise used to lessen considerably as soon as school got started. Not here. Here the noise just gets a little more organized. This day (and every other school day as we were to discover) started with a rousing patriotic song played by someone belonging to The Association of the World's Worst Bugle Players. I have heard these bugle players all across Mexico and the sounds they make alone are enough to convince me that Mexicans live in a different cosmic reality from the rest of us.

Then the callisthenics began.

"Uno, dos! Uno, dos! Arriba, abajo! Arriba, abajo! Uno, dos! Uno, dos!"

Now you might think that all this noise would have been very annoying after all the racket from the night before, but it wasn't, not at all actually. When I first phoned Isadora from Hornby to enquire about renting a room, I had asked her if the room was noisy and she'd said, "No. Oh, except for that wonderful noise of children playing across the street in the schoolyard." Well, I certainly didn't share her opinion about the room not being noisy, the noise was in fact relentless, so I suppose I should have been angry with her for misleading us so blatantly about it. But I did share wholeheartedly her feelings about the sound of the children, about how delightful it was, so any anger towards her that was on the verge of manifesting inside me was quickly melted away by that cheerful chorus that came bouncing across our room that morning. It really was the nicest, freshest, and most joyful sound to wake up to. If I could program my alarm clock to have a ring like that, I would do so without hesitation, minus the bugle of course.

Robyn and I were planning to cook most of our own meals in our room, but so as not to feel too terribly hard done by, we conceded that breakfast out every morning was probably a good idea.

So we decided to head for the *jardín*, the central plaza, and look for a promising café. It was a beautiful, warm, bright morning when we stepped out the front door of Isadora's house and onto the cobbled street.

I live in the country. At home when I step outside my front door, I am confronted with trees and sky. That's all. Very nice, I'm not really complaining, but that's it, just trees and sky. When you step outside your front door in San Miguel, you walk into a living museum, a living three-dimensional art show, a time machine. You feel as if history has dropped pieces of itself all around you. The streets echo with tales of romance and revolution, tyranny and frivolity. You are just as likely to see burros piled high with mesquite firewood as you are medieval troubadours playing mandolins.

And you just don't get that from trees.

There are, however, a couple of bonus prizes that are included when you sign up for a five-month subscription to the streets of San Miguel, and I'm quite certain their absence would have caused no tears on our account, whatsoever.

Gringo traps and bombas.

Gringo traps are usually placed on the little raised sidewalks that run along the edges of most of the streets in town. I'm sure that studies have proven that their placement on the sidewalks increases their effectiveness considerably.

The traps are actually well-disguised holes in the cobbled sidewalks that operate on the principle that eventually a gringo will be distracted for a split second, and fall into one. There are usually sharp metal rods or bars at the bottom of them that assist in spearing the game and preventing its flight. It is best, therefore, for gringos to walk one behind the other and not two abreast so that there is a greater likelihood that one member of the party will survive and be able to rescue the victim or, if necessary, put the poor thing out of its misery.

The other undesirable bonus on the streets of San Miguel is the dreaded bomba. This is worse than the gringo trap really since it turns its victim into a social pariah, and neither screaming nor calling an ambulance will rid you of its deadly impact. I have concluded that there are three main reasons why gringos move to San Miguel: 1) the maids are cheap; 2) you can speak hopelessly bad Spanish and all your friends will be terribly, terribly impressed; and 3) you get no hassles from anyone when little Frou-Frou lays a big steamy turd, what we call a bomba, on the sidewalk.

Now, unfortunately, all those beautiful cobblestones act as excellent camouflage for both the bombas and the gringo traps so you really have to scan the zone in front of you with great care as you proceed. You must learn to walk with your head down using your eyes like mine sweepers to check out the area directly in front of your intended course of advance. Unfortunately, this means that you'll hardly ever get a chance to really see all the lovely street scenes of San Miguel that were the reason you came here in the first place, but then you really don't want to see the inside of a Mexican hospital while having a metal rod extracted from your butt either, now do you?

As we entered the jardín, we had our first chance to get a good look at the wonderful Parroquia, and we stopped walking to do so.

The original church was built in 1683, but it's the incredible façade built in 1880 that attracts all the attention. Many churches in Mexico blend nicely and politely into the general look of the city in which they reside. The Parroquia, on the other hand, commands your attention with the same kind of power that's exerted by a haunted castle perched high on a lonely hill. At the sight of the church, fear and magnetism seem to be operating in tandem, leaving you frozen where you stand. Take twenty or thirty candles of various heights and place them upright on a table; gather them into a circle with the tallest in the middle and allow them to burn for a while until the lower parts become one solid mass; carve out a few tall, narrow, arched openings, like eye sockets in a skull, and you have the Gaudí-Disney-Gothic look of the Parroquia.

One of the bold concepts of the design was that the church basically looks similar from any angle thanks to the conical layout of the spires. Walk around a tiered wedding cake and the profile is similar from wherever you are – it's like that with the Parroquia.

And one of the things I love best about the façade is that it was designed by an illiterate Indian brick-layer based on a picture he'd seen of a French cathedral on a postcard. Isn't that great! Apparently, he explained to his workers what he wanted them to do each day by drawing pictures in the dirt with a stick. His name was Ceferino Gutiérrez.

Ever since I started coming to Mexico, I've been impressed by their fearless and often bizarre approach to the world of artistic expression. Not only do they make art out of almost anything – boxes out of orange rinds, masks out of mysterious bits of curly space-alien vegetation, elaborately-carved Cinderella carriages out of gourds – but they also have a wonderful flair for creating quirky images. The colourful and frightening wooden monsters of Oaxaca, the fancily attired skeleton figurines in shop windows, and the horrific-looking cherubs in churches with their troubling, bleeding eyes, are just a few examples that come to mind. The lovely madness of the Parroquia seemed to me to be in keeping with all of this, and you have to wonder what it is that makes this Addams Family approach to art seem so normal here. What is it in the Mexican that causes all this wacky creativity? Maybe the answer lies with their forebears: the Indians and the Spanish.

Indians in the Americas have always given great spiritual significance to the dream state, and to the state of madness. We lock up our crazy people; they revere them. So when a Mexican is looking around for somebody to produce their religious art or design one of their cathedrals, the Indian side of their nature figures the best candidate would probably be somebody touched by the hand of God. And why not? Intensity and deep passion are inherent qualities in a Mexican's relationship with the spiritual. And wherever those two guys go, madness is usually dancing the tarantella not too far behind.

And as for the Spanish contribution to this deification of the bizarre, well God, I don't know, maybe it was something in the water, but the fact is that Spain has always produced more than its fair share of nutty artists. Salvador Dalí, Pablo Picasso, and Antonio Gaudí certainly all had a few screws loose. The fact that Gutiérrez was untrained, simply wasn't the issue for those folks charged with the building of the parish church in old San Miguel. *Was he inspired* was all that mattered to them.

The Parroquia takes up almost all of the south side of the jardín. We had been gazing rapturously up at that fairy-tale castle for several minutes, when the sweet ambrosial smell of freshly brewed coffee came wafting past our upraised olfactory receptors. We turned and, like a couple of cartoon sleepwalkers, began to walk in the direction of its source.

Before we reached the café however, we were once again forced to halt, this time in front of a piece of grand colonial architecture called Allende House, the beautiful home of the martyred hero of the War of Independence, Ignacio Allende.

Home perhaps is a little too comfy-cozy sounding for a building like the Allende House, but it was the place where he was born and raised. It is a very large, two-story, square colonial mansion in the neo-classic design with baroque decoration. It now houses San Miguel's best museum.

By any standards, the Mexican War of Independence was a very nasty piece of work. And like the French and American Revolutions that had partly inspired it, it was basically a conflict between two elite upper classes, the winning team being the slightly less elite of the two. The lower classes made up the necessary cannon fodder so that these two groups could play their little game on a vast and very grand scale. Probably one of the reasons that the Mexican war was such an out and out bloodfest and continued for eleven dreadful years was because there was such a very large pool of Indians willing to be led to the slaughter. Although the Indian population had been decimated by war and disease in the years following the Conquest, by the eighteenth century they had built their numbers back up almost threefold to five million. This compared to only about a million white people.

But the white population was divided into two major groups, and the spoils of the conquistadores were not being divvied up equally between the two. The insignificance of what divided them is almost impossible to believe, and yet it was that one small distinction that lay at the root of the independence movement.

In New Spain, if you were a white Catholic and had been born in Spain, you were called a *peninsular*. If you were a white Catholic born in Mexico – even though your parents were both white Catholics born in Spain – you were called a *criollo*. In other words, there was no difference culturally, ethnically, or denominationally, between the two groups. But criollos, those born in Mexico, were considered lesser beings.

Now you can call me "dickhead" if you like and as long as the laws of the land are the same for both of us, I don't really give a damn (you stupid git). But if our government, in its wisdom, makes the rules different for dickheads than for gits, then I suppose I might get a little ticked off. Well the Spanish government and the Church did, in fact, make the rules different for the peninsulares and the criollos. They restricted access to important positions of authority in New Spain to only a limited number of criollos, i.e. Mexican-born whites, and gave preference for the great majority of the positions to the peninsulares, i.e. Spanish-born whites. Out of the approximately one million whites born of Spanish ancestors who were living in New Spain, there were only 50,000 peninsulares, and the special privileges that they received ultimately led to the outbreak of war.

Captain Allende was a criollo. (The unfortunate pronunciation of this word is "cree-yo-yo.") He was the head of a literary circle in nearby Querétaro where they discussed the works of the great writers of the Enlightenment, people like Voltaire and Rousseau, whose ideas had already kindled several other revolutions. It was at these gatherings that he got to know the father of Mexican independence called, appropriately enough, Father Hidalgo. Allende appears to have been of the cool and steady military temperament, whereas Hidalgo was basically an impassioned fanatical Bolshevik type who was bent on mending the ills of Mexican society, particularly the problem of Indian slavery. These literary circles gradually evolved into secret meetings for the purpose of plotting political machinations. In a house owned by Allende's brother (located diagonally across the jardín from Allende's house) parties and dances were held in the front section, while clandestine meetings of the conspirators went on in the back. It must have been a time filled with high drama and intrigue rather like that scene from *Gone With The Wind* where Melanie, surrounded by a retinue of genteel Southern ladies, sits calmly knitting in her parlour, a concealed gun on her lap, while John, the suspicious Yankee Captain, tries unsuccessfully to discover where all the men have gone.

But unfortunately the fun was not to last.

The insurgency, which began in 1810, went well in the beginning with many towns just surrendering immediately rather than risking total annihilation at the hands of the Indian masses. But Hidalgo was no military genius and by the end of July 1811, ten and a half months after it all began, Hidalgo and Allende had both been executed. Their heads, along with those of two others, were hung in metal cages from the four corners of the Guanajuato granary, where they remained for another ten years until independence in 1821. (Throughout its entirety, Mexican history has been drenched in copious quantities of blood. It may have started with the Olmecs, the Toltecs, and the Aztecs, but the tradition continued right into the twentieth century. The recent election of Vicente Fox was the first time ever for a peaceful transition of power from one party to another in Mexico. The contrast of all this with Canadian history is more than a trifle unsettling. In the 1840s while the Mexican politicians were busy killing each other and fighting the Americans, Canadian politicians were sitting around in their smoking jackets puffing on pipes and considering the possible benefits of representational government. Being dull does have its advantages.)

The Allende House and Museum definitely looked worth a visit sometime, but not this morning. We had a much more pressing matter to deal with: coffee. After slipping our noses into each one of the cafés surrounding the jardín, we concluded that they were all just a bit pricey for us, and we decided to go back to a less expensive-looking place we'd walked past on our way to the jardín, called the Laughing Muffin. Being a place with a mostly American clientele, we thought it was also probably a good bet for decent coffee, a hard thing to find in the Mexican interior.

We walked into the muffin place and were greeted from behind the counter by an American male in his twenties, the owner as it turned out. He looked a little forlorn, as if he'd been moping around all morning over a postcard from his surfer-dude friends in Hawaii who'd written, "Surf's gnarly man wish you were here," and all he could think about was that here he was stuck in the middle of the desert, making muffins. Acting as if his ticket out of town might just depend on selling us two plates of bacon and eggs, he pounced:

"Hey there, friends. I'm Billy and you've come to the right place all right," he said with way too much bravado.

"Oh, then this would be the San Miguel Colonoscopy Clinic?" I replied.

"Well I wouldn't know about that," he said, a little confused. "But I could probably tune it up for you. What year's your car?"

Better just to drop this line of conversation entirely, I thought. I somehow didn't think Billy and I were going to have a real strong male-bonding experience with one another. "Do you have coffee?" I pleaded.

"We have the best breakfast deal in town. You get fresh fruit, a three-egg omelette with Gouda cheese, toast and bacon or sausage, hash browns, and uh . . . something else." He smiled lamely. "Uh, I can't remember the other thing, but I'm sure there's something else."

"Coffee?" I suggested.

He beamed, "That's it! Yeah, coffee, a bottomless cup, and the whole thing is just 22 pesos. You can't beat that, now can you?"

Normally this kind of cockiness puts me right off a place, and I'm out the door in a flash. But there was something about this guy's earnest, youthful attempt at old-fashioned Yankee hustle that kind of appealed to me. I turned to Robyn and she smiled her approval, so we sat down.

There were only six tables in Billy's place, two in the front and four in the back near the kitchen. The walls were nicely painted in rusts and golds, and there was some fairly interesting local art on the walls. The café shared a small alcove with a Mail Boxes R Us depot and the constant flow of Americans picking up their mail probably brought Billy in a little business. It quickly became clear to me that the Laughing Muffin was the real thing: an authentic old-hand hangout.

A heart-stoppingly gorgeous Mayan woman who was about four

feet tall brought us our breakfast and while we cheerfully munched our way from egg to bacon to toast and back again, we also unfurled our antennas to listen in on the conversation at a nearby table.

"Hey there, Marcy. How's it goin'?" This from a comfortably plump, twenty-something fake blonde as she and her Hell's Angel-sized, grey-bearded and much older boyfriend sat down at Marcy's table.

"Hi, Linda. Oh, notta lotta. How 'bout you?" There was a certain Louis XIV disdain-for-work tone in her voice.

"Ah my cat's sick," said Linda. "I took her to the vet. What a rip-off. He said she had lupus or something. Told me I had to buy these rip-off pills and keep giving them to her for the rest of her rip-off life. What a rip-off, huh?"

Marcy, about forty-five, had one of those gaunt, deeply furrowed faces made leathery from years of smoking, and yet she seemed to think she was still eighteen. Looking a little hung over, she kind of slurred her response between sucks on her cigarette. "Yeah, that's why I don't have a cat. I have a man, he's trouble enough." She turned towards Marcy's boyfriend, the Hell's Angel wannabe and said, "Hey Hank, you gonna play in the pool tournament over at Sancho's?"

"Oh yeah. Gotta pay the rent somehow you know. Have you seen John, Marcy?"

"Nah, I heard he was real sick and went back to the States for an operation."

"No, not that John, the other John," said Big Hank. "But what's he sick with anyway?"

Billy, the owner, saunters by and draws up a chair. "Oh he's real bad. He's gonna die. It's AIDS. He's gone home to die."

Eyes move back to Hank who says, "Jeez, that's too bad. We played a lot of pool, him and me. I still got four of his gold teeth somewhere that I won off him last year. Jeez, I wonder where those teeth are. Honey, have you seen them teeth?"

Linda shook her head.

"Jeez, do you think maybe I should send them back to him now that he's dyin' and all? Course, they may be worth somethin' too, and if he's gonna die anyway well . . . Hey Bert, how ya doin'?"

And in walked a balding but still-cool Bert, former owner of the café. The nice thing about old-hand cafés is that, like cocktail parties, there is always somebody coming along to interrupt the conversation before it gets too complicated. In environments like these you're actually praised for not going too deeply into messy moral issues like whether to return a dying man's teeth.

But old-hand cafés can also be great sources of useful information, so, sadly, I am compelled to seek them out.

As we were leaving, Billy shouted out from behind the counter, "Hey guys, you should try out our corned beef sandwiches for lunch. We managed to get ahold of this really incredible stuff made by a little butcher in Salamanca. The meat is so, so, so . . . "

"Delicious?" I offered.

"Yeah, but it's more than that, it's, it's, it's . . . "

"A religious experience?" still trying to help a man in way over his head.

"No, it's, it's . . . soft. Yeah, soft and . . . soft."

"Thanks, Billy. Bye now."

We spent the rest of the day scouting out the necessities of life without which we could not survive. We found a library for books; a grocery store for coffee, tequila, and chocolate donuts; and a pharmacy for Dr. Scholl's foot powder, the real secret to a successful marriage.

On Saturday, November 11, we spotted two big colourful rodeo advertisements in the jardín that were covered with pictures of elegantly dressed Mexican cowboys showing off their masterly horsemanship skills, and when we discovered that the event was set to take place the very next day, we immediately decided to go. It looked like a golden opportunity to combine two of our favourite things: drinking beer and sitting in the sunshine.

So Sunday morning we set out to walk the three miles or so to the grounds on the outskirts of town, partly for the exercise, partly because walking's the most interesting way to travel, and mostly because we were too cheap to take a cab.

Robyn always dresses very casually when she's on holiday and that particular morning she was wearing a smart pair of jeans and a T-shirt with the words "I'll Have a Lobotomy to Go Please" printed on it. I wondered a little if such a flippant remark would be thought of as appropriate for wearing in public in such a conservative society as Mexico's, but my worries were soon laid to rest. After walking only a couple of blocks, we watched in stunned fascination as a little four-year-old Mexican girl was led across the street by her very proper and sensible-looking, middle-aged mother who was wearing a T-shirt that said in big block letters: "THIS ISN'T A BEER BELLY . . . IT'S A FUEL TANK FOR A SEX MACHINE."

Oh dear, I thought, we have only five months to try and make some sense of this place.

Lightweight T-shirts seem to be the garment of choice for most people in the tropics, but I prefer to wear clothes that more closely resemble full-body, hazardous material, detoxification suits. I don't set out to look ridiculous, you understand, it just seems to always end up that way. You see, I'm cautious when it comes to the sun. I once offended every single bather on a beach in the Baja when I showed up dressed in long pants, a long-sleeved shirt, a wide-brimmed Tilley hat, sunglasses, shoes, a scarf, and a sun-reflecting plastic survival blanket. I thought they were going to ride me out of town on a thong, they all looked so angry. Evidently, I was a threat to their very way of life. I hadn't felt that embarrassed since I was a university student in Montreal in the Sixties standing on a street corner waiting for the light to change and a well-meaning guy leaned over and gave me two bucks to buy myself a little lunch. A thing like that really forces you to reassess your fashion sense.

So, with Robyn in her lobotomy T-shirt and me in my usual anti-ultraviolet protective gear, minus the reflective survival blanket, we headed out towards the rodeo grounds along Ancha de San Antonio.

Strolling along Ancha de San Antonio was completely out of the question – like trying to stroll through the streets of downtown Rome. Tiny and often-blocked sidewalks meant that it took every ounce of concentration to keep from getting smucked by all the darting and scooting traffic on that bustling little stretch of road. Between attempts to leap out of the way of screeching tires however, we did manage to catch quick glimpses of a whole host of charming little gift and antique shops that looked worthy of exploration some other time. A few stressful minutes later we reached the doors of the very impressive Instituto Allende, and came to an abrupt halt. It was here that Robyn had enrolled to take a four-week course in conversational Spanish.

The Instituto is a central part of San Miguel's identity. Ask anyone with a passing knowledge of the town to offer a brief summary of it, and they will invariably tell you that San Miguel is a pretty colonial town with a large artist community and an internationally renowned art school. The Instituto is that art school.

It was originally the country estate of the wealthiest family in San Miguel, the Canal family, and construction was started in 1735. Perhaps sensing that the natives were not only restless but getting extremely ticked off as well, the Canal family sold it to an order of nuns just one year before the onset of the War of Independence, in 1809.

We took a few steps inside its massive, fifteen-foot-high doors to take a little look. Responsible for drawing large numbers of gringos to the region since its rebirth as an art and language school in the 1950s, it now looked run-down and abandoned – truly showing its age. Hardly a thriving hub of artistic expression anymore, it seemed. Yet the connection between the arts and San Miguel is still intensely strong. It seems that almost everyone here is either a painter or lives with one, and the Instituto is one of the main reasons for that. Maybe it was the off season, or maybe now there were other art schools more in vogue; we didn't know. But there was a dark, decaying sadness about the Instituto that day – it seemed to me to be a place with all of its greatness firmly lodged in the past.

After walking for what seemed like hours, we had still not reached the rodeo grounds. Before setting out we had asked directions from a man in the street and had been led to believe it would only be a short walk.

And we believed him! Fools!! When venturing out on a journey to practically any destination in Mexico at all, if you enquire of a local Mexican if it is possible to walk there, he will invariably answer yes (and also tell you the salsa isn't hot). But you see, Mexicans figure you can walk anywhere, it just depends on your time horizon. Having got along just fine for centuries without draught animals or the wheel before the Europeans came, Mexicans have infinite patience and have become superior walkers. Henry David Thoreau would have loved it here.

So we got a cab. When we arrived at the gate, we bought our tickets, found our seats, and like the intrepid explorers we were, dove face-first into two never-before-tasted styles of unusually flavoured potato chips.

My idea of a horsy show, is thirty-two guys in wide-brimmed Stetsons and scarlet serge jackets carrying long skinny lances with cute little red and white pennants on the ends. Yes, that would be the Royal Canadian Mounted Police, who, although they also participated in untold acts of great heroism during the wild frontier days of the Canadian hinterland, are probably best known now for their Musical Ride.

And the rodeo started out looking as if it might be the same kind of thing, except with different hats and no lances. One at a time, the riders charged down the straight stretch coming to an abrupt hi-ho-silver-and-away, big-clouds-of-dust kind of stop, just in front of the gasping and applauding crowd. Now watching that, and eating copious quantities of junk food, I could have done all day. But when they started to compete to see which horseman could best drag a calf around by its tail, and slam it down onto the ground without ripping the thing right off, our mood began to change. I noticed that most of the calves still had open sores from the last time they were subjected to this unwarranted brutality, and I wasn't sure how much more of this I could watch. Finally when they managed to lasso one poor bedraggled calf around the neck causing it to foam at the mouth from strangulation, we decided to leave. According to the Mexicans seated around us, it was destined to get even better, but we didn't want to know by what form of torture that might be.

We headed home on a small local bus and all I could think about was the huge gulf that existed between me and the Mexicans sitting all around us. When we got home, I went up onto our patio to have a beer and a few quiet moments watching the sun go down.

I felt as if I didn't belong here any more. When we first came to Mexico years ago, people said be careful, Mexicans are dangerous. They will kill you for the ring on your finger; shedding blood means nothing to them; they don't respect human life the same way we do.

Over the years, as I've begun to feel more at home in Mexico, I've often told people that I feel much safer there than in California – safer even than in Vancouver. Just avoid dangerous situations, as you should do anywhere, and everything will be fine. They're a gentle people, I said, less violent than most.

Sitting on the roof under the reddening sky and gazing out over the distant valley and the surrounding hills, I began to think maybe I was wrong. Maybe I'd been in denial. I'd been searching for a heaven on earth and had convinced myself that Mexico was it. But the gap between their sensibilities and my own was beginning to seem insurmountably large. Maybe I'd been naïve. The Mexicans smiled and cheered as those calves were being hurled around and injured. Some of the animals looked as if this might be their last time in the ring.

But that night up on the terrace I realized I wasn't being fair. I was expecting the people of Mexico to encapsulate all my dreams, to be a shining example to all of what mankind could aspire to. Sheesh. You raise a kid that way and you end up creating a homicidal maniac. Simmer down boy. Get a grip. Have another drink.

The fact is, one of Mexico's most enjoyable qualities is that it still dwells very much in the past, and when it comes to things like family unity, food, music, and art, we praise Mexico for its old ways. But when its firm links to the past involve the continuation of what we in the laser-guided, smart-bomb north consider to be harsh and brutal traditions, we condemn them.

I figure maybe Mexico and I were just finished with the dating phase, that's all. Now we would find out if we could live together. Hopefully, we wouldn't have to abandon all the good stuff just because of a few little things that drove us up the friggin' wall.

While poking around town the next day, I spotted a small establishment with the unlikely name of Bici-Burro. Thinking they might sell burritos and bickies, and considering it my duty as a travel writer to eat whenever and wherever possible, I walked in.

Turned out to be a bicycle touring business and the only food in sight was a torta being wolfed down by an old guy at a desk. It quickly became clear that he spoke absolutely no English. It always amazes me the way gringos complain about the lack of English spoken in Mexico. Guess what folks? Mexico is a foreign country. They even use Mexican money. Go figure.

So I spoke my severely butchered form of Spanish at him and he was kind enough not to laugh, and even handed me a brochure in between chomps on his torta. I thanked him and went on my way and I was just about to toss the brochure in a trash can, when I thought it might be worth a read.

It said:

You're not to blame. Do you want to be happy? Well, let's go! Cross rivers, avoid bulls, donkeys, cows and goats, greet the country people, escape the dogs chasing you! Ride up and down like crazy; take in the most beautiful views in the countryside. We leave at 10:00 in the morning from Bici-Burro and 45 minutes later we will find ourselves in Pozos, a small 15th century mining town.

It's always nice to be absolved of all blame by a tourist brochure, don't you think? But that aside, this Pozos place did sound as if it might be a pretty interesting place to visit, although maybe not on a bicycle that's being chased by dogs (but, oh boy, that does sound like fun). No, I was thinking maybe on a bus, thanks just the same.

As I was heading along Correo on my way home, I passed by the Laughing Muffin and decided on a whim that a second opinion about Pozos from a local gringo might be a good idea. Old hands can often be very helpful; you just have to weed out all that painful attitude. A grey-haired lady with a small dog on a leash and an armload of packages and mail was on her way out of Billy's when I got there, and I thought she might be a good person to ask.

"Hi, excuse me for asking you a question right out of the blue like this, but my wife and I are thinking of taking a trip to Pozos and I wondered if you knew anything about the place."

Her right arm was pulled straight out in front of her by the leash as her dog did its best to drag her into the oncoming traffic, but she managed to hold the animal back for about a second as she blurted out, "Lovely place, worth a trip," and then proceeded to basically ski behind the dog as it yipped its way down the sidewalk. In the distance I saw her head turn briefly as she managed one last blurt, "I'm sorry, but I'm late. Watch out for the holes though, some go down for miles. Good luck!"

Thinking that sounded an awful lot like something the White Rabbit might have said just before he disappeared, I called out after her, "Thanks, uh, you too."

And you know, I never did see that lady again – now that I think of it.

Chapter 5

The next morning Robyn and I set out for Pozos. It was only forty-five minutes away by car but because the buses took a very indirect route, our trip was going to take about three hours. We felt no great hardship about this though because, for us, it just meant we'd get a chance to see a few new places along the way.

So, we hopped into a cab, arrived at the bus depot ten minutes later, and went up to the ticket counter to buy our tickets.

There are zillions of bus lines in Mexico and it can be extremely daunting to try and figure out which one to take. I think the government allows the industry to operate in a kind of loosely regulated, free-for-all environment because that way more people are provided with employment. It may also be because unregulated mayhem is just the Mexican way.

But it means that when you arrive at the counter in a bus terminal, sometimes you have two, three, or even four people yelling at you to take their bus to your destination. So which one do you choose? The answer is in fact quite simple: take Primera Plus – the highest-class ticket they will sell you. ETN is also good, but they're more expensive and don't go to as many places. That's it. That's all you need to know. Problem solved. Well, sort of.

We walked up to the Primera Plus counter and I asked the lady there how we could get to Pozos.

She looked vacant for several moments. I tried again. "Pozos?" She asked the other clerk what I was saying. He said, "Pozos." And she said, "Oh, Pozos."

Off to a roaring start.

She said we would have to go to Dolores, then San Luis de la Paz, and then Pozos.

I said fine. Then I said, "Now, can you tell me when all the buses leave, and how much the whole trip will cost?" I expected her to start jabbing away at her keyboard and then to bring up all the information on her snazzy little computer screen. Instead, she shook her head and stared back at me as if I'd asked her for fifty pounds of Gorgonzola cheese. She could get me to Dolores and after that we were on our own.

A big company like Primera Plus that runs buses all over the country, obviously has all this information about schedules and fares somewhere. Probably even on a computer, probably even on a computer that could easily connect with this lady's computer. But if you asked a Primera Plus executive why they don't do all that, he would probably say, "Why bother? Nobody else has ever asked for it."

And he'd be right, probably nobody has. Nobody expects customer service in Mexico; service just isn't on the menu.

And to what, you may well ask, can we attribute this sorry state of affairs? Well, I would suggest that one thing would be the long-standing tradition in Mexico of the company store.

Historically, in Mexico, there often was nowhere else to shop. In fact, for hundreds of years and right into this century, Mexicans were frequently totally dependent on the company store. If you were a lowly campesino, and you went to the company store and complained about the quality of service, on a good day you'd get thrown out the door; on a bad day you'd get thrown down a mine shaft. I suspect in the old days, the shopkeepers put up with the common riffraff as one of the unfortunate necessities of doing business. The campesinos and miners, for their part, simply got used to keeping their expectations very, very low.

So that's why when you get the blank look after you've asked for something that seemed perfectly reasonable to you, remember that from their point of view, you're being insolent. And raving will get you nowhere. I know this. I've raved enough for all of us.

In spite of its name, which means "sorrows," Dolores is absolutely delightful. It doesn't have the same fabulous colonial architecture as San Miguel, but it is the quintessential, small, friendly, sunny Mexican town, and on top of all that, it's extremely clean. It is best known for two things: its Talavera-style pottery and for being the cradle of Mexican independence.

It was here, in 1810, that the famed Grito de Dolores (Cry of Dolores) was exhorted by a diminutive priest, Father Miguel Hidalgo y Costilla. Speaking to the large assembly of Indians and mestizos on September 16, he said, "Will you be free? Will you make the effort to recover from the hated Spaniards the lands stolen from your forefathers three hundred years ago?" And then, "Mexicans! Long live Mexico! Death to gachupines!"

Now, gachupines were exactly the same thing as peninsulars (Spanish-born white folks) and it was understandable why Father Hidalgo, being one of the underprivileged criollos (Mexican-born whites) might say such a thing about the gachupines. However, it seems that the old padre was a little too good at working a crowd and he whipped up the masses into such a state of frenzy with his fiery speech that they rushed off and went on a murderous rampage killing anyone at all with white skin. This wasn't so much a problem for Hidalgo who had built up a large following of supporters from his years of fighting for the rights of Indians. But for folks like Allende and his other criollo friends, it was a big problem. Allende actually had to go around throwing all his friends in jail as quickly as possible to prevent them from being slaughtered by the rampaging hordes. Unfortunately, Hidalgo was an intellectual and his plans for a civilized and orderly insurrection didn't mesh well with those of the Indians. After a few hundred years of oppression, his philosophical subtleties were of very little importance to them. Hidalgo had even wanted to maintain Mexico's allegiance to the King of Spain, much in the same way that the Americans had with George III in the early going of their revolution, but unfortunately Hidalgo had unleashed a monster, and in the end he was unable to control it.

We turned left outside the bus terminal and walked towards the central jardín. About halfway to the jardín we came to a beautiful little market street, practically devoid of traffic, and decided to take a stroll along it.

The friendliest towns in Mexico are the ones where the women and young people laugh at you. I know that sounds weird, but it's true. If they send you furtive glances and snicker gleefully from behind a screen of upraised fingers as you stroll past, it usually means that they don't see very many tourists in this neck of the woods, and they see you as something rather exotic. (Of course, it could also mean you have your trousers on backwards, but let's try and be positive here.)

Well, we sure cracked them up at that market in Dolores Hidalgo. Commerce ground to a complete halt along the street as people paused for a quick look and a giggle at the two strange weirdos who had just landed on them out of the blue. The whole street seemed momentarily transformed from a place to sell merchandise into a sound stage to showcase our antics. If I'd burst into song with a stirring rendition of *Oklahoma*, I don't think we could have attracted any more attention. We were a big hit.

The camaraderie of the Mexican market is infectious. For everyone there, it's much more than just a business experience. D.H.Lawrence described a Oaxacan market in 1924 this way:

> It is fulfilled what they came to market for. They have sold and bought. But more than that they have had their moment of contact and centripetal flow. They have been part of a great stream of men flowing to a centre, to the vortex of the market place. And here they have felt life concentrate upon them; they have been jammed between the soft hot bodies of strange men come from afar. They have had the sound of strangers' voices in their ears; they have asked and been answered in unaccustomed ways.

For sure, Lawrence is a bit wordy on the subject, and I'm not sure at my age I want to know what exactly is involved with having a moment of centripetal flow, but I like the gist of what he says.

There were wonderful and colourful piled-fruit displays, leathery-smelling shoe shops, and festive and cheery wedding boutiques. And crammed in between those shops there were stacks of soft yellow chickens being carried off by flies, and heaps of gigantic, deep fried, golden pork rinds like topographical representations of a bubbling Sahara Desert. There were Indian women sitting with their backs against shop walls selling wet and glistening, emerald green, Ping-Pong-paddle vegetables called nopales; and bins, chock-full of the twisty, wrinkled, horn-like shapes of purple and green peppers. To me this was, figuratively and literally, the very stuff of life. I wanted nothing more from life than to be able to spend my mornings in this small Mexican town gathering jewels from this cornucopia of the earth's bounty; and then, after a leisurely lunch and a peaceful siesta, to spend an hour or two putting it all together into a sumptuous feast for a gathering of a few good friends. That was my idea of heaven on earth.

We eventually emerged from the market and went straight to the jardín. A jardín can often set the tone for an entire Mexican town and I loved Dolores's right away. For one thing, it was large and well kept, and because the trees were mostly tall and widely spaced, it was full of light. When we arrived, there were school children in uniforms scrambling about the place, enlivening it with their happy and boisterous energy. We made one complete circuit of the jardín looking for a restaurant where we could get a little lunch, and finally ended up right back where we started, outside the front of a place called El Carruaje (The Carriage).

We entered the restaurant and had our spirits immediately lifted even higher by the bright and festive look of the inside courtyard. The courtyard was surrounded on all four sides by old, arched colonnades; the chairs were all painted and carved beautifully in that chunky Mexican way; and the plates sat on hammered copper dishes on top of cheery, green, blue, and gold tablecloths. On the floor, in the centre, was a gigantic, colourful, pottery urn standing about five feet tall that was filled with huge silk poppies in shades of orange, yellow, and white. A large canvas canopy hung over the entire courtyard making it feel as if we were inside a circus tent, and there were hundreds of long, orange and black streamers radiated out like spokes from its centre. Hanging from the streamers were hundreds of paper cut-outs of pumpkins and witches. The Halloween theme seemed a little odd. Mexicans don't do Halloween; the Day of the Dead is quite different. But they do love decorating, so I suppose, for some, any excuse will do.

The waiter who arrived promptly at our table was a young guy in a simple uniform of white shirt and black pants who obviously didn't speak a word of English, and as he came to a full stop beside us, he smiled and then froze solid, as if he'd just caught sight of Medusa. I always suspect that people like him have been psychologically damaged from having been previously exposed to the rantings of a hysterical gringo tourist at some point in their impressionable youth, and that they now live in perpetual fear of a repeat performance.

"Dos tortas de jamón, por favor," I said, hoping to see a few signs of life: a breath, a twitch, anything.

There was a pause. I looked at Robyn, my face full of defeat. She raised her eyebrows at him expectantly.

He looked very cautiously at us, as if he thought one wrong move might detonate something. Suddenly, he turned his head towards the kitchen and with his hands cupped around his mouth for amplification, he screamed, "Hit the deck! I think they're gonna blow!!" Just kidding. Actually he replied very meekly, "Tortas?"

"Sí, tortas. Dos."

Huge look of relief on his face. Phew! Okay, now I'll just slip away before they have any more ideas.

"Oh and señor?" I said.

Hijo de la chingada, too late, he thought.

"Dos tés negros, por favor." (Two black teas, please.)

Okay, thought the waiter, so the gringo wants some iced tea as well. I think we can handle that.

I continued speaking, "Caliente, con leche separada, por favor."

Not cold, he wants it hot, and with milk on the side. At this point what the waiter wanted to say was, "Fine. And would His Highness like that shaken or stirred? With honey, molasses, demerara, cane or beet sugar? In a cup or a mug or just served up directly onto His lap?" But being a well-behaved Mexican, he just nodded and tried to slip away.

But I wasn't finished. "Puede darme, también, un recipiente de agua caliente para hacer un poco más té?" (Could you bring me also a container of hot water to make a little more tea?)

I'll bring him his tea, because that's my job. But afterwards, I'm going to kill him, slowly and painfully, and then chop him into little pieces and feed him to my chickens.

"Sí, señor."

And with that he ran from the room, unusually quickly for a Mexican, I thought.

The torta was marvellous, and so was the tea, actually. The torta was made with avocado, mayonnaise, lettuce, tomato, ranchero cheese, ham and beans, and served in a very tender, just-baked, fresh bun. We devoured them, and then sucked our tea back like a pair of fourteen-amp vacuum cleaners. I should say, also, that for these excellent tortas, in this very classy restaurant, we paid 12 pesos each. That's $1.20, after-dinner mints included. Incredible. There *are* still some cheap restaurants and hotels in Mexico. Sadly, you'll spend a fortune criss-crossing back and forth all over the country trying to find any of them.

After lunch, we took a quick swing around the jardín one more time just to soak up a little more of its invigorating energy before heading back to the bus terminal. There were pedlars selling homemade ice cream all around the perimeter of the jardín and we'd heard that they had some pretty exceptional flavours. With great difficulty I peeled Robyn away from one of these ice-cream carts. She was extremely determined – she was clinging to it the way our cat clings to the sofa with her claws when I'm about to put her outside – because apparently they had tequila flavour, a favourite of hers. I tried to convince her that getting sick from street food so early on in our trip could really mess things up, and she responded by glaring at me silently for a few moments.

If you took a small portion of that glare and you analyzed it inside a Cosmic Ray Isotope Spectrometer (CRIS), this is what the printout would say: "Okay buster, but you get me back here for a jumbo-sized tequila ice cream before we leave Mexico or it's curtains for you." You know those nice old married couples that look so content sitting around on park benches, supposedly enjoying their blissful state of silent harmony? They're actually glaring at each other with their peripheral vision.

We headed back towards the bus terminal, and, in an attempt to make amends, I kept my eyes peeled for a small store that might sell a packaged ice-cream snack of some kind. This entailed checking almost every single store along our route because in Mexico, shops frequently sell widely disparate types of merchandise. (I once came across a store that sold vegetables and children's coffins and nothing else. Regrettably, they were probably both good sellers.) I did finally have success, in a little clothing store that was so filled with dresses and slacks that you could hardly see the little freezer buried beneath all the other assorted debris. After a minute or two of rummaging around in its frigid depths like some vet trying to turn a breech calf, my hand emerged clutching a rather battered and bruised Nutty Cone-type thing which I immediately purchased trying to show as much enthusiasm for it as I could muster. Robyn, however, was unimpressed and bought nothing, shrugging with disdain. Ice-cream snobs, I thought. Humph. They're all the same.

The bus trip to San Luis de la Paz was pretty uneventful, although there was a very odd bang followed by a constant thump-thump sound that started mid-way through the trip. The driver was apparently unperturbed by the noise – or else he hadn't heard it over the blare of trumpets emanating from his boom box. In any event, the bus just kept on rolling merrily along. Looking out through the windows, we were kept mildly entertained by herds of sheep grazing on barren fields of dry dirt, as well as by several flocks of school kids in colourful uniforms. (I've often wished they had a field guide to Mexican school uniforms. Think of the tourism potential for a thing like that. Can't you just visualize groups of people in Tilley hats and Bermuda shorts with binoculars and cameras draped all over them saying things like, "Look, Audrey honey, over there by the Cypress tree. I think those ones are from the School of the Daughters of the Insurgency over in Michoacan. They're hardly ever seen this far north." I certainly can.)

At one point we stopped outside a school, and the bus was suddenly inundated with the noise and excitement of onloading kids. Then, just as suddenly, the whole group of them went quiet and giggly when they spotted us. I felt like the principal of a school who'd just walked in on a spitball fight. This tense silence persisted for several minutes until finally the tension was broken when the majority of them offloaded about eight miles down the road. Robyn and I watched, somewhat mystified, as they all headed out into a wasteland worthy of T.S. Eliot.

Cheerfully, they marched off towards a barren plain of nothingness. Can there really be houses out there? Can people actually live on land like this? Where on earth will all those kids find work? God help them, hopefully not in Mexico City.

We arrived at the little San Luis de la Paz bus terminal, had a quick Coke, and discovered that the bus to Pozos was leaving right away. We rushed over to it and climbed on board. It was a small urbano-style bus with room for about 40 people-chickens (30 people plus 10 chickens or 20 people plus 20 chickens etc.), and it was jam-packed. There appeared to be no seats left at all.

But after closer scrutiny of the situation, I discerned that the two seats right next to where I was standing had only one occupant – a lone woman who had carefully sprinkled all of her purchases over the empty adjacent seat. Not only that, she was defending the empty window seat by planting herself stubbornly in the aisle seat, thus thwarting anyone's attempt to find a weakness in her fortifications. I bent down to face her, eyeball to eyeball, and said politely but firmly in Spanish, "Move please, I want to sit down."

She pretended not to hear me and then not to understand me, but by firmly repeating my request several times more, she moved far enough over that I was able to slowly cream myself in alongside her.

Robyn was still standing, so I pointed to the seat beside her where a woman similar to the one I was sitting beside was occupying her territory by similar means. Robyn's woman also had a small child crawling amongst her debris, but, to me, the child looked small enough to hold on a lap. Well, due to the fact that Robyn is extremely respectful of the Mexican culture and always acts in a very humble manner towards all Mexicans because we are, after all, only visitors here, she refused to ask the woman to share her seat and remained standing.

The bus driver, however, took one look in his rear view mirror and threw up his hands in frustration. Practically all of his seat pairs had single occupants – people who were sprawled out over two seats where one seat would do. These little urbano buses are independently owned by the drivers and with fares this low and fuel costs this high they have to pack them as full as possible if they want to return home at the end of the day with any money at all. So, he got right ticked off, which, in public at least, is very unusual in Mexico, and came stomping down the aisle and demanded that the woman make space for Robyn and that Robyn damn well sit down whether she wanted to or not. Ever obedient to authority, and especially when it comes to furious Mexican bus drivers, Robyn did as she was told.

The town of Pozos appears suddenly out of the middle of nowhere. You can't help wondering if the place is just a figment of your imagination and if people in local towns will avert their eyes and deny its existence when questioned on the subject. The usual tire and auto repair shops that precede most Mexican towns are absent. The streets are mostly empty. Pozos is a ghost town, and it feels like one. As you gaze out over the town, you are reminded of war-zone rubble – most of the square, brick and stucco houses being roofless now, with only vestiges of their walls remaining intact.

Mining by Europeans was begun in Pozos back in the sixteenth century by the Jesuits. They mined silver, gold, lead, and mercury and you can still see the remnants of the three large ovens they used to bake the ore. But Pozos was always greatly affected by the tides of history, and in 1767 when the governments of France, Spain, and Portugal decided they had to limit papal authority in their colonies, the Jesuits were expelled from Mexico, and the mines were closed.

During the dictatorship of Porfirio Díaz (1872-1910), the Mexican economy was opened up to foreign investment and with the help of American money, the Pozos mines were put back into production. These were the boom days in Pozos and the population ballooned to 70,000 people. The wealth generated by the mines led to a flurry of construction of a whole host of beautiful structures including churches, haciendas, and mine buildings.

By 1940, the population had dropped to forty people. Today, the town looks like a salvage yard for the ruins of ancient Greece.

So what happened? The 1910 Mexican Revolution happened. All over Mexico you can still see the effects of that devastating civil war. In San Luis de la Paz there is a church whose two steeples are quite different from one another. The war halted construction on the church after only one of its steeples had been built and they only got around to building the other one in the last few years. By then, it had become too difficult and too expensive to find matching materials. But the war didn't only disrupt the day-to-day functioning of the mines, it also drove away foreign investment, the life blood of any large-scale mining enterprise.

An attempt was made to start them up again with the return of stability after the declaration of the Constitution of 1917, but conflict again swept through the region between 1926 and 1929, with the outbreak of the Cristero Rebellion. This was a kind of counter-revolution instigated by the Church which had been stripped of its lands and privileges after the Revolution. It happened that many of the Cristero rebels came from the vicinity of Pozos, and so when the government began its bloody retaliation against them, the town was once again demolished and the mines had to close. (The intense spirituality of the Mexican should not be misconstrued as a love for the Catholic Church as an institution. For at least a hundred and fifty years, the people and the Church have been engaged in conflicts of one sort or another.)

So, today the mines are flooded with water and people say it's just too expensive to pump them out, so they remain abandoned. A couple of artists, one a photographer and the other a sculptor, have moved to Pozos and there are a few fledgling bed and breakfasts, but mostly it's known in the area as a place where you keep your eyes open for holes, because some of them go down for miles.

We stepped off the bus in little Pozos, and the bus sped away leaving us alone on a completely deserted street with only each other and the settling dust to keep us company. I'm mildly asthmatic, so I'm pretty sensitive to air quality, so once the dust from the bus had settled, I noticed something about Pozos right away. The air here was crystal clear. That's what an absence of people will do, I guess. My airways opened wide to its freshness and immediately I was able to breathe better here than I had anywhere since we'd arrived in Mexico. And not only was the air clear, but so was the light. The blue in the sky was no longer just a soft baby blue – it had become a vibrant, energized, deep royal blue. The sandy tones of the tumbled rock walls and archways that littered the entire town were clean, golden, and rich. We slowly made our way up a very steep street to the top of one of several little hillocks in town and from there we were able to look out over much of the village and even to the mountains beyond. The visibility was incredible, effectively making distant details appear almost touchable. My eyes felt as if they'd been given super-vision and they darted from point to point with such ease that I almost felt as if my body might too if I just tried to take a little leap. We were completely entranced. Gods and spirits move into empty places like this, I thought – and they make them feel full.

Empty spaces have always thrilled me. I worked at a summer theatre festival back in 1972 and the part I loved the best was dropping in to the theatre two or three hours before the performance and just being there in the emptiness. Somehow the magic of the theatre seemed stronger to me when there were no people around to clutter things up. In the quiet, I felt a little like a piano string whose sound came not from the impact of the piano's own small wooden hammers, but instead from the resonance created by sympathetic harmony with other sounds from far away. It felt as if the universe were breathing in and out of its own accord without any input from me, and I found that a very soothing thought.

Darwin wrote of experiencing this peculiar state while travelling through Patagonia in his book, *The Voyage of the Beagle*, but he was unable to explain why those "arid wastes" had been so much more moving for him than any of the other places he'd visited.

W.H. Hudson, an author writing in the 1860s, devoted a whole chapter of his book, *Idle Days in Patagonia* to trying to give expression to this feeling, and his best answer was that "desert wanderers discover in themselves a primeval calmness (known also to the simplest savage), which is perhaps the same as the Peace of God."

We decided to walk, although waft might be a better way to describe it, towards a ruined church across a dip in one of the main streets. There were broken fragments of the original buildings on either side of us, and you could still see the general layout of most of the houses. It was eery because you were allowed to see into places that were never meant to be seen into, like you'd finally received that pair of x-ray glasses you'd ordered from the back page of a comic book forty years previously. Only they'd improved them since then – now they could see back in time as well.

We passed by an open door of a small shop and I decided to take a look inside. And what mystical sight greeted me? A half-dozen teenage boys playing Nintendo, firing their nifty little super mushrooms and doing awesome super-mini-boost slides. When they turned to look at me, and I didn't even bounce or slide or anything, I think they were a little stunned.

"Is there a restaurant in town?" I said to one of them.

"No," was the somewhat startled reply.

"Can you tell us where the mines are?"

"There are no mines here."

My turn to look startled. I thanked them, and stepped out of their cool, shady den back into the blinding sunshine of the street, leaving them to get back to their super-laser, battle-mode lives.

I have no idea why they told me that there were no mines, but this kind of divergent reality happens so often in Mexico, that it's really best to just chalk it up to two trains on different tracks: if occasionally the trains get close enough for the passengers to actually wave back and forth to one another, even if only briefly, consider it one of life's little miracles. As for the rest of the time, just sit back and enjoy the ride.

We continued on up towards the church ruins that lay at the top of the hill. As we approached them, the dignity and power that still radiated from the church's crumbling remains were impressive. With only a small portion of its original self still intact, the church bore itself with remarkable poise, and like the shattered visage of Ozymandias, it still loomed mightily over the town.

Ruins are like wise old souls. They're also often more beautiful than their younger selves. They are more complex visually, because the regularity of their original lines have been interrupted and rearranged; they are more complex emotionally because they require the viewer to participate in both the seen and the unseen.

The church's gate was locked, an odd gesture towards propriety considering that the gaping holes in the sides of the church provided easy entry to all. Robyn waited "outside" for a moment as I walked through the wall and into the church. You could tell it must have been a fine structure. The front wall behind the altar still stood tall and majestic, and the masonry work was exquisite. There was a fresh wind blowing through the place and bright green grass was growing up between the tiles where the pews had once been. The great blue dome of the sky had done such an outstanding job as understudy to the original vaulted-arch roof that it had been given the job indefinitely. You could see the hidden opening the priest used to unobtrusively access the pulpit – one of many little tricks that served to enhance the mystique of their position – and it wasn't hard to envisage pilgrims walking on their knees up to the altar. A bell tower high up and off to one side was empty now but had found a new role for itself by providing a frame within which the blue sky and fluffy white clouds could assume poses throughout the day, providing passers-by with an infinite series of surrealist paintings by Magritte. I began to wonder if God maybe even preferred the church in this condition, and had intentionally sculpted it slowly over the years to better suit His or Her own personal taste.

We left the church and walked back into the centre of town. It was three-thirty, so our expedition in search of the mines of Pozos would have to wait till another day. When we reached the little jardín next to where the bus had dumped us, there was what looked like a little restaurant.

"Tea?" I said, smiling at Robyn.

"Cake?" she said, smiling back.

"Let's go," we both chimed simultaneously.

We walked into the Casa Mexicana, and it was as if we had stepped through a magic doorway out of a dusty desert ghost town and come out into a chi-chi California art gallery.

On the white walls of the gallery there was a group of photographs by someone called Geoff Winningham. One particularly striking one depicted a trail of orange marigold petals scattered across a darkened patio of weathered tiles (a custom associated with the Day of the Dead), and there was a ghost-like half-image of an Indian woman's bare feet walking over the strewn flowers.

Adjacent to the photographs was a series of black raku pottery skulls, each one separated from its neighbour by a burning candle pinned to the wall. It was an extremely dramatic effect, but for whose benefit, it was difficult to tell. The gallery was completely empty and its location in a virtual ghost town would surely guarantee that it stayed that way. It made the presentation seem more like someone's own personal religious rite than a display for the purpose of selling art. We were creeping gingerly around and quietly looking at the work, feeling a little like infidel intruders, when all of a sudden there was a *phwack!!* and one of the candles went tumbling to the floor, sputtering momentarily before finally extinguishing itself.

Starting to feel a little freaked out by all this and under the general impression that tea and cake were probably not in the offing, we made our way briskly towards the exit. There I found a brochure describing a two week photography course taking place in Pozos in a few months and costing a mere $2400, not including airfare and film. As that was about half of what we intended to live on for our entire five-month stay in Mexico, we sensed we were a little out of our league here and, after saying thank you to the empty gallery, we headed straight over to a little food store where we bought four chocolate cupcakes and two 7-Ups for about $1.20. Relishing the thought that the $2400 we would save by not taking the photography course would finance an additional 8000 cupcakes and 4000 7-Ups, we sat down at the side of the road and munched away contentedly while awaiting the arrival of the next bus out.

Chapter 6

A few days later, Robyn and I were walking past the jardín in San Miguel, blissing out over the beautiful sunny weather, when a very tall and formidable woman in her sixties careened awkwardly in our direction, and swallowed up our entire field of vision with her beaming eyes and her jumbo-sized, toothy smile.

"Isn't it a gorgeous day!?" she blared out at us.

By her confident stride, I guessed she was a member San Miguel's expat community. There were deep laugh lines furrowing her well-tanned skin, and there was a nice, genuine, cheerful air about her. She would have made a perfect eccentric spinster aunt and her "in your face" high spirits would undoubtedly have caused members of her family to either love her or loathe her – there surely could be no in-between. Maggie Smith would have played her to a tee.

"It certainly is," I said as we passed by one another. I figured that would be the end to this brief but pleasant interlude and was just beginning to get my mind focussed back onto some other more pressing matter, like whether or not my nostril hairs needed clipping, when I sensed with those invisible feelers that one has at the back of one's neck, that she had stopped dead in her tracks. Robyn and I stopped too, and turned around to face her.

"Do you have a car?" the woman said, looking puzzled.

"No, I'm afraid I don't. Do you need some help moving something?" I said.

Clearly not the response she expected, her puzzled look suddenly changed into a slightly disarmed smile.

"No, I have a car. There's a pilgrimage tomorrow at a small town called San Martin, about an hour's drive from here. I'm told that there will be 10,000 men on horses attending it and I'm going with a friend, but we have space for two extra people in the back seat. Bring water, and a lunch, and meet us outside Independencia 35 at nine o'clock tomorrow morning if you want to come. If you're not there by nine sharp, we'll assume you're not coming. Okay? Now get on with enjoying this gorgeous day."

And with that she turned and marched off.

Robyn and I stood there stunned for a moment. This idea needed careful and serious consideration and every bit of grown-up reasoning the two of us could muster.

"How bad could it be?" I said.

"They could be a pair of psychopathic axe murderers paying for their retirement by rolling naïve, unsuspecting tourists."

"That's what I thought too. Let's go."

At nine a.m. sharp we were there, water and lunch in hand, and so were Florence and her friend Marge.

Red is the national colour of Canada. Florence was Canadian. And so, to make sure that there could be absolutely no doubt in anyone's mind about her nationality, she was wearing a red and white T-shirt with Canada printed on it, a red dress, red tear drop earrings, and a red Canadian flag pin. If Florence were flapping from the top of a flagpole, you'd swear it was the Canadian flag up there.

Now I know many Americans think we Canadians are very silly for all those red maple leaves we plaster all over ourselves when we travel about the world. But there actually are some very practical reasons why we do so.

Envisage this: You're a Canadian sitting in a Tokyo bar having a nice cold beer alongside a bunch of Japanese business men, enjoying a *Dallas* rerun, when they interrupt regular programming to announce that a U.S. destroyer has just accidentally launched a Patriot missile directly at Kyoto. Who wouldn't want to be wearing a silly little Canadian stickpin at a time like that? Or when you're eating fried banana chips at a poolside bar in Jamaica and CNN reports that Dan Quayle has just told a crowded hall full of people that he loves California because Phoenix is one of his favourite cities – I tell you, one little Canadian flag can make your whole day.

Florence's car was an ancient, pale blue Renault with no gas gauge, no seat belts in the back where we were sitting, and doors that could only open from the outside, meaning that if you were *inside* you had to reach *outside* through the window to open the door. As soon as Florence pulled away from the curb and into the street, the car stalled. Now, here in town, your car breaks down, it's no big deal. But out there in the boonies, well that's a whole nuther kettle of worms. One hopes that those stories about tourists in Mexico being dismembered while trying to hitchhike to the nearest auto-repair shop aren't true. But it would be a whole lot nicer if one never had to put their veracity to the test. Florence got it going again after three or four determined twists of her key, but let's just say it wasn't the beginning I'd hoped for.

Once we were out on the highway, it quickly became obvious that Florence had acquired her own very unique way of driving. She was capable of the amazing feat of pivoting her head almost a full 180 degrees (thus appearing to have her head on backwards), and she used this novel talent to carry on conversations with people in the back seat while lurching her way through traffic at the same time. It seems that Florence had been a schoolteacher for most of her life, and had never entirely divested herself of the habit of sharing her wealth of knowledge with the rest of the world. She behaved as if she felt it was her duty to see that we all made the most of the very limited amount of time we had left to live on Planet Earth, and for the four of us trapped in her car, that was probably sadly true. She had also been blessed with the talent of being able to steer cars with her knees, and she clearly intended to make good use of it. Her arms and head were constantly flinging out in unpredictable directions as the little Renault flew merrily along across the vast, ranging, grey-green, cactus-riddled landscape apparently of its own accord, and the whole time Florence never stopped talking; never stopped giddily describing everything to the side and back of us. She was, evidently, totally disinterested in anything that lay in front of us. At one point we were passing a dried-up river bed with sandy-coloured slopes that was deeply creased with parallel trenches that were left over from the rainy season, when she craned her neck out the window, veered into the oncoming traffic, and roared out like Leonardo DiCaprio on the prow of the Titanic:

"DON'T YOU JUST LOVE EROSION!!" She was practically licking her chops.

"Not as much as I love breathing," said Marge through clenched teeth. In a fruitless attempt to tame Florence's driving, Marge refused to take her eyes off the road in front of us for even a split second to look at anything Florence was pointing out.

"Did you know," said Florence with an evil glint in her eye, which was, as usual, facing towards us in the back seat, "that the only thing you need for a driver's licence in Mexico is a blood test?"

"No, Florence, I didn't know that. And uh," I fumbled for a polite way to phrase it, "did you get your licence here or in Canada?"

Evil glint changed to maniacal look.

"Hee, hee." And I'm afraid that was all she said on the subject.

Not that she remained silent for long, however. En route to San Martin, Florence spilled over with torrents of unrelated information, as if trying to compensate for the arid terrain whizzing by all around us.

"Those blue flowers over there are called Virgin's mantle . . . Look at the morning glory draping itself around all that gorgeous cactus . . . Toller Cranston, the great Canadian figure skater, lives in San Miguel . . . We are in our fifteenth year of drought . . . The state is trying to outlaw abortion . . . They found a pyramid over there near Cañada de la Virgen but the land was bought by a German woman who is refusing anyone access . . . There's a horrible little town over there full of pigs and drunks where they stoned a woman to death . . . Isn't it amazing to think that all of this land was once underneath the ocean? . . . Anyone have to pee?"

We counted only fifty-one pilgrims on horseback on the way to San Martin, which meant that, if Florence was right, we would see 9949 more before the day was out.

The San Martin (pronounced "san marteen") of this particular pilgrimage was San Martin de Tours, patron saint of horsemen, beggars, soldiers, tailors, vintners, innkeepers, alcoholics – and geese. I kid you not. Geese have their own patron saint. San Martin is usually shown sitting astride a horse while appearing to be about to skewer a poor beggar with his sword. I spent quite some time trying to figure out the logic behind this image the first time I saw it. It really looked to me as if the beggar was probably the better candidate of the two for sainthood.

Well, the story goes like this. San Martin was a Roman cavalry officer who lived in Amiens, France, during the fourth century. One day while travelling around the countryside on horseback, he encountered a beggar. Having nothing to give the beggar but the clothes off his back, he cut (thus the dagger) his heavy officer's cloak in half and gave one of the pieces to the beggar. Not exactly an earth-shattering moment in the history of mankind, but for a Roman, it was probably a big deal.

By the way, there is another San Martin with whom this one should not be confused: San Martin de Porres. He is an extremely popular saint in Mexico whose images can be found in churches throughout the country, but it's easy to tell the difference between the two – San Martin de Porres was black.

He was, in fact, the first black American saint. He was born in Lima in 1579, the illegitimate son of a Spanish nobleman, and after spending some years as a slave, was eventually freed, and then raised by a kindly surgeon-barber. One of his titles is Saint of the Broom, which although a little lacking in the cachet department, does perhaps express with a certain monkish simplicity one of his most important tenets: *Be devoted to your work, no matter how trivial.* (It alarms me just how easily I relate to that thought.) He became the patron saint of barbers, hairdressers, hair stylists, innkeepers, the poor, and television. Yes, that's right. Television. Don't ask me; it wasn't my idea.

Although the lives of these two guys may have lacked the glamour of martyrdom that spices up the stories of so many of the saints – they both died in their old age of natural causes – it has to be said that during their lives they were responsible for doing a lot of very good work and helping out a lot of desperately poor people and, for that, they do deserve more than a little respect.

Florence pulled off the main highway and continued to the tiny village along a windy, bumpy, and occasionally submerged dirt track. She was remarkably adventurous with her little blue car, and appeared to be completely without fear. But then, you see, Florence was a devout Anglican, and I figure you're probably safer being driven by Mike the Headless Chicken than by a religious zealot. I think they take the view that, since we're all in God's hands anyway, let's batten down the hatches, man the torpedoes, and let 'er rip.

San Martin is a very picturesque little village of probably about a hundred people consisting of a few houses and a beautiful church nestled into a small depression surrounded by low-lying, overlapping hills. But once a year it becomes overrun with people and takes on the look of a Mexican Woodstock. We parked a long way from the church to avoid having to drive through the large crowds, and began our trek in.

A pilgrimage of this size is not really one homogeneous entity, but more a series of concentric rings of activity, each one behaving quite differently from the others. Visualize a giant dartboard with the church in the bull's eye and I think you'll get the idea.

The first zone at the outer edge is the picnic zone, where clusters of people gather in nice family groups to eat and drink and cool off in whatever little bit of shade they can find, which isn't much. We passed through this zone quite quickly because the crowds were still quite thin out there.

If the year was 1955, and you were taking a department store elevator to the second zone of the pilgrimage, the attendant would have called out as he slid open the cage doors, "Zone Two. Junk food, toys, kitchenware, millinery, music, and baked goods. Watch your step, please, and keep moving. Thank you!"

This was the play zone, the carnival midway, the mecca for shoppers and kids. Everywhere there were pickup trucks fronted by makeshift booths where the owners went about their business of casually flogging their wares. There were black-haired, pony-tailed Indian women, dressed in skirts and pink aprons, who sat around glowing mesquite fires plopping flattened corn tortillas onto hot griddles improvised from discarded oil drum lids. There were large vats full of huge hunks of beef swimming around in an unknown brown substance. There were men standing under large orange tarps selling fancy, yellow-and-pink loaves of festival bread. Candy booths were crammed next to each other and packed top to bottom with plastic-wrapped pink chunks of homemade, chewy confection, and there wasn't a child in sight who wasn't munching some. Women were buying straw hats with flowers attached to their brims, and men were strutting about proudly, showing off their brand-new, white cowboy hats.

As the four of us got closer to the church, inevitably, we became separated from one another, forced to give in to the whims of the swirling crowd. So I happened to be by myself when I came upon a wonderful piece of theatre.

A man stood all alone on a raised platform under a huge expansive tarpaulin, and he had a microphone harnessed to his head as if he were a Mexican male version of Britney Spears – that's easy to visualize, right? Nine hundred million trillion decibels of sound were coming from two speakers to either side of him in the form of a kind of Spanish-rap sales pitch he was giving. The purpose of all this noise was to draw our attention to the sculptures he was creating out of a variety of galvanized buckets and tubs on the platform in front of him. I put my earplugs in and found myself an out-of-the-way spot from which to enjoy the show.

In the early stages of construction, his stacks of buckets invariably looked like exactly that, a stack of buckets. But part way through the process, there would be a moment of transformation. Suddenly, with the addition of just one more element, his stack would change into a shiny new silver robot recently arrived in town to promote its latest *Star Wars* movie. Some of his stacks had a more molecular look to them, as if they were meant to serve as models in a chemistry lecture, and still others were just geometrically wonderful to gaze upon. I imagined them in New York art galleries, in the lobbies of ritzy hotels, on the plush green lawns of the rich and famous. And then he made one that positively dazzled me. I wanted to blurt out, "Stop! Don't change a thing! I must have that one for underneath the Japanese maple!" But thankfully I was saved from myself by his having just sold it to a very nice-looking Mexican family off to my right. He tossed it (with great insensitivity I thought) piece by piece to his assistant and then started all over again on a new one. People were buying that fellow's bucket sets just as fast as his assistant could collect the money.

Now in case you think this feeding frenzy was actually because the locals had suddenly all simultaneously worn out their buckets and tubs, think again. There was another guy selling exactly the same stuff under exactly the same roof, with exactly the same number of decibels coming out of his speakers, who couldn't sell a tub if his life depended on it. Why? Because he didn't have any talent. His stacks didn't look like anything. They looked like stacks. No, it was the show and the artistic flair that the audience loved, and they were craving to participate. Of course, it probably helped that buckets were the one thing in the entire universe that the whole family could agree upon – you can never have too many buckets, right? But more than that, it was like going to the circus, except that the performers allowed you to take the props home with you after the show. Hell, those folks were probably going to take those tubs home, crank up the old ghetto-blasters, and while away the rest of the day just stacking tubs for the sheer fun of it.

I didn't so much walk to the church, the bull's eye zone of the pilgrimage, as I was swallowed and digested by a giant serpent with an incredibly slow-moving metabolism. This feeling of being drawn along while embedded in a mass of people was exactly the same feeling I had had in the Taxco market a couple of years earlier. It's an odd and slightly scary feeling being pressed together like a pack of dates in a crowd like this – the idea of being trampled invariably comes to mind. But eventually, the serpent expelled what was left of me safely behind a wall of horses' asses in the church courtyard. There, after a great deal of squeezing and polite nudging, I was able to obtain a slightly less anal view of the proceedings. With the noise level considerably lower here at the church, thanks to the absence of merchants and their throbbing sound systems, I could at last remove my trusty earplugs.

The mood here was totally different from the one outside the church gate. There was a profound sense of holiness here. When I turned to speak to the person next to me, I realized right away that I was intruding on a silent conversation. Everyone here was lost in a dialogue with an invisible presence. And when several thousand people are united in a silent dialogue with the same invisible presence, they come very close to manifesting it – right there before your very eyes.

Basically, two great walls of horsemen, about a hundred yards long and four horses deep on each side, defined a straight pathway that led from the church's front gate through a pretty courtyard to the main doors of the sanctuary. Down the centre of the pathway moved groups of pilgrims carrying gilded pennants decorated with masses of multi-coloured balloons. (For the purposes of a celebration, a Mexican's love of balloons is only surpassed by his love of loud noises, and no occasion is too small or too pious to render a balloon inappropriate. Indeed, if you need a balloon in a hurry, Mexico is the place to be. Most corner stores sell singles.)

Many of the village groups were accompanied by their very own little local brass band which processed right through into the church along with everybody else. These local bands can be heard in the plazas throughout Mexico screeching out a terrible racket of discordant music that often sounds like a German oom-pah-pah band made up of drunken high school students still attempting to play their instruments after a debauched night of revelry. But on sacred occasions like this, they dig into their chest of ancestral memories and pull out a lovely, soft, melodic, and mournful sound, that is totally bewitching to the listener. I couldn't get inside the church because I was stuck in a stationary section of the crowd, an eddy in the flow, you might say, but I could hear the wailing coming from within as the impassioned pilgrims on their knees became overwhelmed by the spirit of San Martin, and it was deeply moving. A profoundly devotional aura hung thick in the air. At one point there was a great commotion as a young teenage girl, who had fainted from the emotional intensity of it all, was rushed away to be administered first-aid, and you could feel the extra surge of electricity that ran through the crowd as she was carried through it. That deep Mexican religious passion was in full bloom that day, rising up from its very deep and ancient well. It would seem that throughout their history, a history filled with cruelty and oppression, that that passion has been the one thing that has never been fully wrenched from their tight-fisted grasp.

As impressive as this display of Mexican spirituality was, the thing that was even more impressive was that I managed to experience all of this intense emotion while the force of the crowd was mashing my face up against the biggest horse's ass I'd ever seen.

I eventually headed back to our pre-arranged rendezvous by taking a back road around the perimeter of the crowd. It was eerily quiet and empty of people on that hot, dusty lane, but there was one lovely otherworldly moment when I passed by a lone pedlar going in the opposite direction playing a miniature violin and dangling dozens more about his body. He ignored me entirely, and it had the effect of making me feel as if I weren't really there – as if *I* were the one drifting along like a ghost, not him.

Later, I met up with the others and we gushed back and forth at one another about all the interesting things we'd seen. Florence, miraculously and most definitely through the grace of God, got us all back to San Miguel in one piece. We thanked Florence and Marge for their wonderful hospitality and then walked home along a steep cobbled street back to Isadora's place. That night, I lay in bed and got to thinking just how different the world we visited that day was from our own world back in Canada.

It can be very easy to ridicule and make light of the foibles and ideas of the religious establishment. But when it comes to a beautiful gathering like this one, only a box of rocks could have returned from it emotionally untouched. Mexicans have taken their mysticism and made it into a living, functional aspect of their real world, just as real as breathing in and breathing out, and as I drifted off to sleep, I thought about how much I envied them their easy access to their magical world. It sure would be nice to tap in to some of that someday.

Again, through my window, I heard the echoing sound of horse's hooves clop, clop, clopping from somewhere outside in the street. The sound was like a messenger from the past, whose quest was to scour the moonlit streets of San Miguel in search of a true believer. It was a sound that was exactly the same at that moment as it would have been three centuries earlier. I lay there in my half-sleep wishing that somehow I could jump onto that sound and let it carry me back into the past with it.

I'm the one you want, I thought. Take me . . . take me.

One evening, a few days later, we were in our room. I was tapping away at my laptop and Robyn was lying on her bed doing a crossword puzzle. Then suddenly, the power failed. Lights went out, my computer died – Robyn and I were reduced to being just two voices adrift in the dark. A few seconds later Isadora's voice came wailing up through the stairwell, "Steve!!?" Short pause. "Stee-eeve!!?"

"Yes, Isadora," I replied.

"Do you know anything about fuses?"

In answering Isadora's questions, my good sense was often overridden by my pathetically old-fashioned inclination to rescue a fellow creature in distress.

"I know a little," I said reluctantly. "I'll be right down."

I grabbed a flashlight and started down the stairs to the main floor hallway. I arrived quite quickly at the bottom of the stairs thanks in large part to Raoul's very diligent greasing job. The fuse box was near the front door and when I got there I found Isadora poking at it, the way a little kid will poke at a snake.

I peered into the open fuse box with my flashlight and its insides didn't look anything like the kind of consumer-friendly things we had at home. This one looked more like a nineteenth-century electric chair for mice – not a single insulated wire or plastic fuse in the entire box.

"You have to reach in there and pull out that big glass cylinder," said Isadora, like some old witch from a fairy-tale trying to murder the handsome young Prince.

"And why don't *you* just pull it out Isadora?"

She smiled demurely, understanding immediately the gist of my remark, and said, "Oh, no, my fingers aren't strong enough. Oh, I would if I could, but I can't."

I tipped the flashlight down to look at her hands. She had butcher's hands, tough as nails. I decided not to fall into her wicked little trap. Making it onto the front page of the National Enquirer as the "Moron Fried to a Crisp for the Sake of His Landlady" was not how I wanted to make my mark on the world.

Fortunately, Margaret, the massage therapist from Ladysmith, British Columbia, arrived to rescue both of us, otherwise I suspect Isadora and I would still be there hissing suspiciously at one another and poking at the box with the end of a broomstick. Margaret just reached fearlessly into the box and yanked out the old fuse, replacing it with a new one, and marched out the front door to spend the rest of evening out on the town.

Well, yeah, sure. But she wasn't Isadora's intended victim.

When we decided on making San Miguel our base camp for exploring the colonial interior of Mexico, we were afraid that the worst thing about it would be that it would be crammed full of weirdos wanting to spend time with us. Well, sometimes that *was* the worst thing. And sometimes, it was the best.

As difficult as it was to live with Isadora, after a while we actually found ourselves starting to like her. Her personality was composed of an intriguing blend of vulnerability and chutzpah, both of which she fearlessly displayed for the whole world to see. I don't pretend to fully understand it, but she did begin to grow on us. Perhaps in a world of guarded emotions, it was just plain refreshing to be around a person with such an unbridled spirit.

Another housemate of ours with lots of personality was Marissa. One night, the nineteen-year-old from Pennsylvania invited Robyn and me to join her, Isadora, and three friends for dinner. Getting a little tired of chicken stew and looking forward to meeting some new people, we leapt at the chance.

Now I should clarify that, as far as I know, Marissa was not a prostitute. But she *was* extremely enthusiastic. And no part of the house was neglected by Marissa; she enjoyed having her little trysts in every imaginable part of it. When word got out about her, men started to arrive regularly, like roaming dogs. There were so many of them and they came by so often that we eventually had to stop answering the door. Even Isadora was flabbergasted, and she didn't flabbergast easily. And the thing was, superficially, Marissa was everybody's idea of a nice, well-mannered, pretty young girl on her first little adventure.

At first glance she came across as sheer innocence itself. When she talked to her parents on the phone, she made her voice all perky-like and tried to sound as if she were about ten years old. She reassured them that she was eating well, getting lots of exercise (well I suppose that part was true), and that everything at the kindergarten where she worked was just tickity-boo. If you have a teenage daughter who talks to you like that on the phone, believe me, you're in big trouble. After she hangs up, she's probably getting ready to push her tongue down the throat of the guy standing next to her. ("Oh you worry too much Henry, our little darling's just spreading her wings.") Uh-huh, sure. Cling to that thought.

There were six of us when we finally sat down to Marissa's feast of spaghetti and meatballs. Apart from Isadora, Marissa, Robyn and me, there were Marissa's date, Mateo, who was a good-looking young Mexican; Alfredo from Miami; and Christel from East Germany.

The common links between the young people at the table were the local youth hostel and Mama Mia's, a bar, where Mateo worked and the others partied. The sexually charged energy between the young people was so strong at the table, you could practically smell it.

The young people focussed most of their conversation on subjects like who had been dancing with whom the night before at Mama Mia's and what impressively large amounts of alcohol they had all consumed. Christel, who really was a stunningly attractive eighteen-year-old, explained in detail how she had wanted to bug one particular girl whom she didn't like very much and so had walked up to the girl's boyfriend on the dance floor and given him the deepest, wettest French kiss in her repertoire. Unfortunately, her karmic repayment for this devious little ploy was several hours of vomiting followed by an admission to the local hospital with a perilously high fever, presumably all a consequence of the germs the boy had given her in return for her generous gift.

On account of her fever, Alfredo, who was her dinner date at Marissa's party, was earnestly trying to dissuade her from going dancing again tonight.

"When I am dead," she said defiantly, "there will be plenty of time to rest." A hush in respect of such a lofty, if a bit arrogant, piece of wisdom ensued and poor Alfredo's radar blip disappeared entirely off the screen for a while. Finally, our sweet hostess, Marissa, broke the silence:

"Isadora tells me you have a serious back problem, Stephen," she said, plunking my plate of spaghetti in front of me, and trying desperately not to flirt with an old guy whose wife was sitting right next to him.

"Yeah. Earlier this year I had about four months when I had to lie flat on my back, almost completely immobilized, and in quite a lot of pain most of the time. Not a nice experience – pretty hard on everybody around me too," I said, looking over at Robyn.

"Oh," croaked Isadora, "you know, when I was having my first child, Jasmine, it was the Sixties, and we all had to give birth surrounded by crowds of people." A handful of chuckles rippled around the table. "Oh yeah, there was my husband and a couple of friends and a midwife and a coach. Oh, it was like I was a prize fighter about to climb into the ring or something, which I suppose I was a little." More chuckles from the audience. "Anyway, this woman who was coaching me through the contractions – and oh my God, you think you had pain, Steve, oh, it was nothing compared to mine – well, she would say to me," at this point Isadora changed the tone of her voice into that of a spaced-out hippie on LSD, " 'Like, just think of a wave and you're floating like, up and down with that wave, and when you get to the top, just like say – groooooovy.' " And then a long, slow, husky-toned, hah-hah laugh rumbled from the depths of Isadora's throat.

"The first time they took me to the hospital," she continued, "I was so disgusted by the whole birthing thing that I just hopped in a cab and went home. To hell with this, I said. I'm not going through with it." And then another round of hearty hah-hahs issued forth from Isadora.

At this point, shy, quiet, unimposing, cute-as-a-button Robyn chimed in, "The mother of a friend of mine once likened giving birth to shitting a watermelon."

Dead silence. All the blood drained from Marissa's face. Isadora sat stunned and speechless. Mateo and Alfredo and Christel smiled briefly, then quickly reeled their smiles back in, sensing danger.

"Oh my God," said Isadora, "what an awful analogy." In hopes of finding a brighter and cheerier observation concerning the birthing process, Isadora asked me, "Steve, what was your daughter's birth like?"

I paused, took a deep breath, and then said, "My wife screamed non-stop for twenty-six hours in the hospital. You could hear the screaming three floors away. As for the birth, there was blood everywhere, they had to cut her open to make enough room for the baby to get out. It was probably the most horrible thing I've ever experienced in my entire life."

Marissa slumped down at the table, all the sexually charged energy now completely washed away.

She said, "I am SO not ready to have children."

You are SO right, I thought.

"Anyway," I said, "this is great tomato sauce, Marissa."
"Uh, yeah, thanks," she replied rather weakly.

The next day I was roundly chastised by Isadora for what I had said.

"You should never ever tell a young, impressionable girl things like that," she said. "Screaming! Oh dear, dear, never."

"You mean she didn't know childbirth was painful?" I said. "If she didn't know that, it was about time somebody told her, don't you think?"

Isadora turned and walked back to her room muttering as she went, "Oh no, you can't tell them that, you just can't tell them that, oh no . . no . . no . . ."

Chapter 7

A travel tale doesn't describe reality at all, you know. It describes a fantasy, as experienced by the traveller.

I have sometimes extolled the wonders of a particular landscape or culture to such an extent that, on occasion, a friend or two have actually been inspired enough to visit one of these places. Then on their return, after experiencing the most wretched holiday of their entire lives in a place they considered to be an excellent representation of hell on earth, I couldn't help but feel somewhat responsible.

So, for any of you who might find yourselves overwhelmed with giddiness at the thought of taking the next plane out to one of the destinations described in this book, I have this to say:

It's your holiday; you make it up as you go along; and what you read on these pages is only what it felt like to me.

Without trying to sound too wifty, I guess what I'm trying to say here is that you get what it's in you to get. The people who always expressed the most love for the pottery I used to make were the people who were already overflowing with love before they even stepped in the door. I think they were leaking love and just needed someplace to put it, that's all. I think people leak on their holiday destinations as well.

I tell you all this now, because of a little side trip Robyn and I took to a place called Guanajuato, another colonial town about eighty kilometers from San Miguel, and we loved it. But if you don't like it, don't come whining to me, okay?

Today Guanajuato is a spirited university town whose cozy medieval lanes and alleys echo constantly with the sounds of a talented array of street musicians and choirs. Nowadays, the city is world-renowned for its performing arts festival, the Cervantino. Once upon a time, however, it was the centre of a brutal mining industry, and the location of one of the bloodiest episodes in the Mexican War of Independence.

The initial stages of the War of Independence went quite well for Hidalgo and his followers, with many small towns capitulating right, left, and centre to the fearsome onslaught of his very dishevelled army.

But in Guanajuato, they met a slightly more prepared and combative opposition of loyalists that had taken measures to stock up on provisions and barricade themselves inside the fortress-like Alhóndiga granary. The conflict turned into a horrific blood bath for both sides, and in the end, the loyalists were unable to hold out against the endless rampaging of the insurgents, and the trapped gachupines were eventually defeated. The loyalist cause was badly shaken by this debacle, but when they managed to temporarily turn the tide in the summer of 1811 with the capture of the ringleaders of the revolt – Hidalgo, Allende, Jimenez, and Aldama – the loyalists took their revenge by placing the four severed heads of their captives in cages and hanging one cage on each of the four corners of the granary, a not too subtle reminder to the people to be better behaved in the future. The heads remained there until independence was finally achieved in 1821.

From the very first, mining, particularly for silver and gold, was the economic engine of Mexico. Spain didn't want them to do anything else. The Spanish crown forbade Mexico from making or growing anything that would compete with producers from the motherland. Mexico was expected to provide the gold and silver that propped up Spain's failing economy, as well as serve as a market to which Spain could sell its limited assortment of goods. Ludicrously, it was forbidden to grow olives or grapes in Mexico, in spite of the fact that it had a climate quite favourable to their cultivation. Instead, wine and olives had to be shipped all the way across the Atlantic Ocean. (One of the ways Father Hidalgo infuriated the gachupine establishment in Mexico was by aiding his Indian and mestizo parishioners in their attempts to cultivate grapevines in direct contravention of the laws of the land.) This economic scheme backfired badly against Spain in the long run, since most of the gold they acquired eventually ended up in other countries anyway. The English had discovered the benefits of manufacturing products for a global marketplace, and the Spanish sent much of their gold to England in order to buy those products from them. Manufacturing remained stunted in Spain, and when the gold supplies finally started to dwindle, there was no manufacturing sector in place to take up the economic slack.

The largest mine owners of Mexico were some of the richest plutocrats in the Spanish Empire. The great divisions between rich and poor in Mexico probably came about, at least partially, as a result of the fact that mining was the fundamental source of wealth. It could take years to establish a mine, and the large capital investments that were required to sink the shafts and build the elaborate water-pumping systems meant that only the very rich had the wherewithal to succeed. (This contrasts sharply with the early conditions in New England where a strong middle class was able to thrive thanks to the suitability of the land for small-scale agriculture.)

I can't imagine that mining has ever been much fun, anywhere or at any time, but it must have been a very miserable existence indeed for the Mexican people following the Conquest.

At first, the mines were simple surface affairs with the ore being carried to the refineries by a work force composed of Indian slaves housed in prison-like conditions. (The slaves were expected to regularly transport 200 to 300 lb. bags of ore on their backs.) Refinery work began with grinding the ore into a fine powder with a device called an *arrastre*, which used humans or horses to drag heavy stones over a stone floor. Then the powder was either smelted in a blast furnace or mixed into a slurry with mercury which would then bind with the silver to facilitate its separation from the ore. The mercury was later burned away leaving the silver, and quite a few poisoned miners, behind. (Spain retained rigid control of mercury supplies in the colony as a way of keeping a firm grip on the industry.)

But very rapidly, all the easy pickin's were used up. Then it became necessary to follow the seams underground and the mine owners started to need more highly-skilled people to do the pick work, people called *barreteros*. At this point it became uneconomical to continue using untrained Indian slaves. Competition between the mine owners for the best workers actually started to force an improvement in working conditions, and by the 1700s, Mexico's 45,000 miners had become the best paid workers in the country, the bulk of their pay coming from the one bag of ore they were allowed to carry out each day for themselves.

But saying that the miners of Mexico made the best money in the country may not be saying much. The following is a fictional piece from a book by Vicki Baum called *Headless Angel*, which I think probably gives the flavour of the thing quite nicely. The year is about 1800, and the place is Guanajuato:

> He was a wise, lovable old braggart and I settled myself in the patio to fill another empty hour with his patter. "Have you a family, Tío Lalo? Sons? Children?"
>
> "God gave me twelve and God took nine," he said, crossing himself. "Ah, Your Grace, what a man I was! Not many miners can make as many children as I did. Mining is man's work and the mine sucks a man's strength worse than a sick whore. I have noticed how many miners die without any progeny and I have thought much about it. Mining is hard work, perhaps a little harder work than God planned for men to do; not enough food, not enough sleep, and then the heat down there! Your Grace, it is so hot in the pit that I sometimes thought: Lalo, my son, if your blast goes just one inch deeper, the bottom of the pit will drop out, and you will fall directly into hell; I swear that's how hot it feels down there. As if a man were boiling in a cauldron, with nothing between the fires of hell and the pit but a few handfuls of rock. Then you come up, all in a sweat, and it is so cold up there that your own sweat freezes to ice and you cough and cough as though you wanted to spit out your lungs. What do you do then? You go to the next cantina and drink until you get warm again. You thank the Virgen that another day has passed with you still alive, and you are happy and you are with friends and you drink and you want music and you drink some more; you don't want to eat, but you must

> drink to replace all the liquid you were sweating out in the pit. Then your friends carry you home and throw you on your mat and your wife screams at you and you kiss her and you try to lie with her and it does not work because you left too much of the stuff in the pit and you are sorry for yourself and you cry or you beat your wife for anger that she can't make you feel like a man. And the next morning you buy flowers to bring to the Virgen or to our Señor Jesucristo; you pray that you may not die that day either and you go down again."

The bus dropped us off just outside the pretty colonial part of the town in a busy commercial section of cheap, run-down hotels and sad-looking restaurants. We marched quickly along the crowded sidewalks heading as fast as possible for a highly recommended budget establishment called Casa Kloster. The guide book said something like, "Simple, popular with cheapskates, sometimes clean, patience a virtue if you insist on water, you'll have a view of a brick wall, but we've never picked up any horrible diseases there either." In other words, our kind of place.

The guidebook also said to get there early because it was popular, but it was one o'clock in the afternoon by the time we got there and indeed, the book was right this time – they were all full up. Nice place though, definitely energized with that European youth hostel feeling; a good choice for next time.

So we loped our way back out to the grungy, commercial hotel strip where the bus had originally dumped us, and had a second look.

Places that we'd passed the first time saying things like "What a disgusting, putrefied, pit of reeking dental waste" we now found ourselves reassessing with comments like "It's kind of quaint, don't you think? Sort of artist's garretty. And look what a pretty door-knob. Don't you just love the look of paint peeling off walls? Oh yeah, this will do fine."

We walked into the Central Hotel and Robyn noticed right away that it was really half a hotel, the hotel next door having served as the other half at some point in the past. And it wasn't as if the design of the original hotel had made this a particularly simple operation either. The original, tiny lobby was split down the middle by a makeshift wall; the upstairs gallery used for access to second-floor rooms was partially barricaded; improvised staircases were scattered about the place as if by a builder gone berserk. Frankly, it looked as if some poor demented soul had used Solomon's proposed solution to a child custody battle (splitting the child in two) for his main inspiration.

Normally hotel rooms are easy to find in Mexico, but there is one very important caveat to that: beware of holidays – national, regional, local, and religious. Since one of these seems to occur every five minutes, you have to be very careful. We arrived in Guanajuato two days before one very biggy – the anniversary of the Mexican Revolution – and we should have known better. The narrow passageway that now existed between the centre partition and the front desk was jammed with people trying to get rooms.

We piled in behind the others vying for rooms and watched as two foursomes in front of us were each turned away. When it was our turn, I sensed my Spanish had better be good today because the lady at the desk had a no nonsense, school-marmy brusqueness to her that said if you waste my time buddy, I'm going to pull on this cord here and you and your sweetie will become alligator food.

In Spanish I said as politely as possible, "Would you have a room for two?"

Her reply was too fast for me and her face gave nothing away. Oh dear.

"You do?" I said nodding hopefully.

"Sí."

A stroke victim taking first-year Spanish could have formulated his sentences faster than I did. "How . . . much . . . is . . . it?"

A sigh of exasperation from the lady, "350 pesos."

Twice the amount stated in the guidebook. I hesitated.

Meanwhile there was a Mexican lady behind me, who had started to speak over my shoulder impatiently to the hotel lady. I sensed I was about to be outmanoeuvred.

"Can . . I . . see . . the . . room?" I sputtered.

Now the lady behind me was starting to rant in earnest.

"He's wasting your time," she said in Spanish. "I'll take the room right now, no more of this nonsense!"

I expected the hotel lady to just pull the rope and have done with us, but instead she said to the disagreeable woman who was now trying to push me out of the way, "The señor speaks English, so give him a minute to understand, please."

The woman behind me now blurted out furiously, "I speak English too, so give me the room!"

The hotel lady turned back to me, willing to give me one last chance, and this time I fired back my Spanish reply muy pronto, "We will take it, thank you."

Wow, was that close. That was the last room in the hotel and probably the last room in Mexico. The irate woman and her entourage stomped out of the lobby and stormed onto the street, no doubt duly pumped for their next venomous assault.

As I was signing in, I caught the eye of the hotel lady and she smiled just a tiny little bit and in slow, easily understood Spanish she said, "I didn't like that woman, she was rude. People who are rude can go to hell. Here's your key."

Our room was certainly a bare-bones affair, but somehow, knowing it was probably the last one in town, we found it to be utterly delightful. We lay down on our beds – it was about two o'clock – and we didn't surface again until five-thirty.

When we emerged from the hotel in search of food, nighttime had just begun to settle on the city and halos of light from multitudes of small kerosene lamps were scattered about the darkness as if they'd been sprayed from a paint can by a delinquent elf. Food stalls that had looked unappetizing and mundane earlier on had now become like moody, romantic paintings, and the fragrant wafts from their tasty offerings lured us hypnotically towards them. But since we'd previously picked out a promising little place recommended in our guide book called Truco 7, in the old part of town, we kept on moving.

As we walked along, there was a dark, mysterious edge to everything, and I was reminded of a friend back home who had said that they found Guanajuato to be a place with a discomforting, even threatening air. We didn't find it to be that way at all, but there are a couple of things about Guanajuato that certainly qualify as peculiar.

It seems that at the local cemetery, they used to clear out all the non-paying customers once every five years to make room for new arrivals. When the keepers of the cemetery could no longer afford to cremate the exhumed bodies, they simply propped them up against a wall and left them standing there, hoping, I suppose, that they might just take a hike. Well apparently the cadavers found the view rather to their liking after so many years underground, and after a few years taking in all that marvellous dry mountain air, they effectively became mummified. (The mineral content of the soil may also have contributed to this.) Since Mexicans are very good at leaving well enough alone, this went on for some time, until one day the mummies' enthusiasm for their newfound freedom reached unacceptable levels. They got a little overly rambunctious and started misbehaving by falling on top of visiting relatives, freaking them out of their friggin' gourds.

So, the townsfolk decided to restrain them by placing them in glass cases in a museum called the Museum of the Mummies, and now holidaying Mexicans line up for blocks and blocks to take delight in their hideous, emaciated appearance. It seems a little bizarre perhaps, but really it's no more ghoulish than your average B-grade horror movie, and frankly, I've seen worse-looking bodies lying on Miami beaches.

Another bit of quirkiness about Guanajuato is that there are underground streets that honeycomb beneath the entire town.

The nearby Rio Guanajuato was prone to severe flooding in the past and would deposit huge volumes of mud onto the town, effectively submerging entire buildings. Instead of attempting to dig away the mud, the residents simply rebuilt over top of the old buildings, a typically utilitarian Mexican approach. This meant that in some places people had layers upon layers of homes piled up underneath their own, a situation that lent itself perfectly to the development over time of some deliciously spooky legends. There's one about an old musician who can still sometimes be heard playing the piano in an old elegant subterranean room, and another that claims you can still hear monks chanting and walking through the halls of the old San Diego monastery. To me these are just entertaining ghost stories, but to a Mexican, a person accustomed to dining with his ancestors on the Day of the Dead every year, perhaps they ring with a modicum of truth.

In recent years, some of the underground streets have been made accessible, either by the washing away of old mud by further flooding, or by the digging away of the mud by city workers in an effort to create tunnels for new roadways. We found them to be an interesting novelty, but I know for others, they cast a dark and sinister shadow over the atmosphere of the town.

We were about to turn the corner onto Truco street, when we practically walked straight into a giant sculpted brass head affixed to the side of a building. The thing was about four feet by three feet, with an angry, furrowed brow, and looked as if it were about to bellow, "Come forward! I am Oz, the Great and Powerful. Who are you?"

What is it about Mexicans and heads anyway? You see heads all over the place. They seem to collect them like stamps. There are those fierce and gigantic Olmec statues of heads from Veracruz dating from around 1200 B.C.; the Aztecs liked to collect heads, especially from the losing teams at sporting events; Churrigueresque church interiors are crammed with seemingly dismembered heads floating in oceans of gold leaf; there are the insurgents' heads that were hung from the four corners of the Alhóndiga granary; there's a park in Guadalajara filled with shrunken brass heads; and now this one, leering at us from the side of this building. I think it's very weird.

We arrived at Truco 7 and stepped inside. There was a queue for tables, which I always figure is a good sign, so we decided to wait until one became available.

Guanajuato is a university town and Truco 7 had a wonderful bohemian-intellectual quality to it. There was a small bar and espresso machine in the centre; the walls were tastefully decorated with an eclectic collection of appropriately ambiguous artwork and photos; and it was full of young students engaged in active dialogue and flirtation with one another. Truco 7 was a real, bona fide hangout.

We finally got seated at a table and shortly afterwards our waiter arrived. He was a very large scary guy who last smiled in 1967 after beating up a hippie. I ordered pan-fried chicken and Robyn ordered a burger and then we had a Mexican Moment.

"Para tomar?" said the waiter. (Something to drink?)

"Sí. Puede darme una jarra de agua natural, por favor?"(Can you bring me a jug of water, please?)

Nothing moved on his fearsome face except for two little dark eyes that just blinked at me as if from behind a gorilla mask. He turned and left without saying a word.

Welcome to service in the colonial heart of Mexico. He never did bring me any water. I'm sure he felt that I was being impertinent. And I don't for one minute believe that this guy was just having a bad day.

I've already had my say about the company store and what influence I think it had in bringing about the loss of the service gene in the Mexican genome. But a landmark piece of journalism about Mexico was written in 1984 by Alan Riding called *Distant Neighbors*, and in the interest of fair play (I'm sure he would do the same for me), I offer you his take on the subject.

First of all, he claims that, of all the countries in Central and South America, Mexico alone is truly mestizo, a blend of Indian and European blood, and that it is the oriental side of the Indian that still dominates the Mexican psyche. In countries like Peru and Argentina the Indians and the whites maintained an almost hermetically sealed separation from one another, and so there was almost no mixing of the blood. In the Caribbean a mestizo population never got established because the black slave population there became predominant. Only Mexico, according to Riding, is truly mestizo.

There is a strong focus on the emotional and the spiritual in the Mexican, and Riding believes this is accounted for by the Indian side of the mestizo, a side he considers to be distinctly oriental. To the average Mexican, the efficiency and punctuality of the Western mind seems to be only a preoccupation with the trivial. In the case of our waiter, my desire for water was of little consequence compared to the importance of preserving our traditional roles as dignified waiter and well-behaved customer.

Rider also thinks that Mexicans don't complain about things like bad service, because they are fatalists. You get what you get. Riding suggests that this fatalism is at least partly a result of the fact that although the Aztecs and other pre-Columbian cultures of Mexico were interested in the future, they basically felt that it was useless to try and influence its course.

As it turned out, our meal was first rate and Truco 7 was destined to become our restaurant of choice in Guanajuato. We did, in future however, avoid that particular waiter. Cultural differences be damned, we do like water with our meals. So, feeling well rested and well fed, we bounced our happy tummies out onto the street and prepared to take on the night.

Now it occurs to me that with all this talk about things Mexican, you may not have a very clear picture of Guanajuato itself. So I shall rectify that now, and try to paint you a picture into which you can insert yourself, if you so wish.

First of all, it's night and the old streets are dimly lit by those Spanish-style, curly, black metal lamps that throw long dark spooky shadows and give the place a certain Sherlock Holmesian flavour. The absence of cars in the downtown colonial core leaves the streets strangely quiet, and conversations are hushed, as if the children are napping and no one wants to waken them. There are pockets of people sauntering casually in and out of the dark murky shadows and you are flowing along with them. The narrow little labyrinthine streets of Guanajuato turn suddenly and randomly in unexpected ways so you quickly become disoriented and lost, but it doesn't really matter since you don't have to be anywhere important anyway and there are plenty of friendly Mexicans around to help you out. Old domed churches with busy baroque facades pop up around corners; little black wrought-iron balconies line the upper stories of buildings; tall stately pillars hold up large, gabled porticoes reminiscent of mini Parthenons; brightly lit antique stores and elegant hotel lobbies occupy the huge, weathered, archways built as carriage entrances for the great homes of the old mining barons, and if you stop for just a moment and squint a little, it's easy to imagine Benjamin Franklin and Voltaire stepping out of their carriages there in 1760 to attend an elegant ball. Walking again, you see in the half-light ahead of you that the flow of people in the street is splitting apart like a river round a rock, and as you get closer to that place, you see that the thing that is splitting them is an old man turning an even older barrel-organ. There, now hold onto that.

We reached the main jardín with its square-cut Indian laurel trees, and it was crammed with chattering, cheerful people, but the overall mood of the place was gentle and relaxing.

One of Guanajuato's most charming features is its tradition of the singing estudiantinas, and the jardín was full of them at this hour, warming up their voices and tuning up their instruments for the evening's performances. These are groups of musicians, usually men, often as many as ten or twelve, who sing old sentimental love ballads from Spain, and accompany themselves with mandolins and a whole assortment of other stringed instruments. They look very Elizabethan in their velvet jackets and capes covered in rosettes and dangling ribbons, and if the architecture of Guanajuato doesn't whisk you back to the seventeenth century, I guarantee the estudiantinas will.

There seemed to be some kind of outdoor theatre happening near the Teatro Juárez on the edge of the jardín, so we headed over in that direction.

There were broad palatial rows of steps leading up to the entrance of the very opulent theatre, but on this night (and on most nights as we later learned), the steps had been commandeered by the general public for use as bleachers for the sole purpose of watching an entertainment just as medieval as the estudiantinas: street clowns. It seemed fitting somehow that the common people had turned their backs on the ostentatious grandeur of the Teatro Juárez, and were making their own amusements outside in the streets, the true home of the Mexican culture.

Street theatre is such a delightfully simple form of entertainment. Dressed like traditional French mimes in whiteface and black and white striped T-shirts, the clowns took turns carrying the crowd away with them to their imaginary settings. The crowd and the clowns worked together to create their illusions and as an outsider I was again amazed at the ability of Mexicans to manifest things that were not really there. In one skit a clown had us watching him dance with his sweetheart around a glorious dance hall, and he raised or lowered our spirits in harmony with his own as we witnessed his poignant romance flourish, and then fail. The clown wasn't so much performing as he was leading a group improv. The clown spurred on the audience and the audience inspired the clown. We were like a single organism whose only purpose was to laugh or cry.

At the end of his skit, the lovelorn clown called for some young lady from the audience to come up and console him, causing chuckles to break out in the crowd. Finally one brave soul was goaded into doing it by her friends and she reluctantly walked up beside him. The poor sad clown turned his head sideways to her and shyly offered her his cheek for kissing. Then the crowd began to chant:

"Beso! Beso! Beso! Beso!" (Kiss! Kiss! Kiss! Kiss!)

She moved a bit closer, in order to give him a little peck, and then he suddenly turned his face towards her, depositing a quick surprise kiss straight onto her lips. The crowd shrieked gleefully in unison at his devilish trick, and as the girl was turning bright red, the people took up their chant once more, "Beso! Beso! Beso! Beso!" The young girl being both flattered and embarrassed at the same time decided to retreat as gracefully as possible back to the safety of her friends, and the clown, only momentarily defeated by her departure, began searching for new victims elsewhere in the crowd.

This was a show that, even though its punch line hadn't changed for six hundred years, was still getting laughs. Robyn and I felt as if we were a part of it, even though we were a couple of gringos who had basically gate-crashed another country's party, and we felt the same kind of stolen delight that a couple of kids feel when they have crept downstairs and been allowed by their indulgent parents to spend a few more moments with the family before bed.

It turns out that Guanajuato's chaotically arranged streets have effectively created dozens of little cul-de-sacs and squares which, because of the absence of automobiles, offer perfect little venues for small groups of musicians and actors, as well as for a variety of impromptu open-air markets. You can spend a little time listening to a thirty-person choir of estudiantinas in a setting straight out of the eighteenth century, and then take off down a mysteriously twisting lane and end up right next to a little modern jazz trio.

Robyn and I stumbled onto one very captivating square, about the size of Shakespeare's Globe Theatre, which was comprised of a fountain surrounded by pretty colonial homes. It looked as if a travelling carnival had moved in. Remember, it was nighttime, and every little scene we came across seemed to spring up out of the darkness. There were large vats bubbling with oil that were cooking hand-cut potato chips; tables selling three hotdogs for ten pesos; clowns selling balloons; an adjacent alley lined with cleverly improvised midway games; and lots more. But strangely, it was quite quiet, almost hushed really, perhaps a concession to the people living in homes around the edge of the square, and it made it feel a little dream-like, as if it might disappear suddenly if we were to turn away and then quickly look back.

Around nine o'clock we decided to return to the hotel, and after passing several pockets of performing estudiantinas, we were forced to battle against a tide of university students who were heading down to the jardín. Most of them were merrily transporting little pottery carafes filled with rum, considered standard equipment for a night with the minstrels. There we were, ready for bed, and they were only just getting started on their night of unabashed revelry. Oh dear. Our ages were showing. Christel's anthem-of-the-young danced seductively through my head, *"When I am dead, there will be plenty of time to rest."* But not in Guanajuato, I thought to myself. In this old town even the dead have a zest for living.

We awoke the next morning totally sleep-deprived, thanks in part to the loud explosive fireworks which sounded as if they went off right outside our door at six o'clock in the morning, and thanks also to the incessant door-knocking by a locked-out, spurned lover from the adjoining room. Friends spent many painful hours trying to calm and console the poor fellow and the guy's neurotic finger snapping kept us on the verge of screaming out at him all night long. As always under these circumstances my biggest fear was Robyn. Not what might happen to *her*, but what she might do to someone *else*. I kept visualizing her marching out and walloping the guy with our table lamp. Then I imagined the guy recovering from the blow and staggering into our room all bloody and determined to kill somebody; and I knew it would be *me* he would want to kill, and that not even my standing on the bed buck-naked and pleading for my life in bad Spanish would make any difference to him. It might even make matters worse. Robyn refrained, for which I shall be eternally grateful.

There were four things we wanted to see in town: the Diego Rivera Museum, the statue of Pípila, the Cervantes Museum, and the

Museum of the Mummies, but as time was short, we could only visit the first two.

The Diego Rivera Museum was actually the painter's home until he was six years old, and although not exactly a mansion, it shows that the painter's family was not without means. As you enter on the ground floor, there is a tiny courtyard and fountain in front of you, and if you look up, you can see that the second and third floors have galleries open to the courtyard that are neatly rimmed by iron balustrades. The whole thing is lopsided and out of square and the floors have so many dips and rises in them that walking on them makes you feel like an ant riding a sombrero across the Sea of Cortés. The ground floor has been nicely furnished with period pieces that give you a good sense of the place as a home, and they serve wonderfully to draw the viewer out of the present day and cast him back into the world of Rivera's childhood in the 1880s. The upper two floors are filled with remarkable works drawn from every stage of Rivera's career, and they show the dramatic changes in style that he progressed through until his death in 1957.

We were admiring the technical proficiency of one of his oils called *Classical Head* when Robyn commented, "Look, they've made a mistake here. The tag says he was twelve when he painted this."

Turned out there was no mistake. By the age of nine, Diego Rivera had become obsessed with art, and by the time he was twelve, he had mastered the basic techniques.

But although Rivera was one of the greatest Mexican muralists of all time, in some ways, his greatest creation of all was his own imaginary life.

Nothing ordinary, at least as recorded by Rivera, ever seemed to have happened to him. But for some mysterious reason, none of his fantastic assertions could ever be backed up by anybody else.

He wasn't just born, like the rest of us. No, he was thrown into a dung pail and then retrieved by his great aunt who saved his life by wrapping him in pigeon entrails. His twin brother didn't just die at the age of eighteen months from one of the common childhood illnesses of the day. Oh no, he was poisoned by the bile-riddled milk of his wet nurse after she had argued with Diego's wet nurse over a man they both loved.

There were plenty more stories – Rivera was nothing if not prolific – and he clearly had a penchant for tales with a Shakespearean or biblical bent.

According to him, at the age of two, Rivera was sent out to live in the wilderness around Guanajuato with his wet-nurse Antonia, a Taruscan Indian magician, where he roamed the forest in the company of snakes and jaguars.

In 1907, Rivera claimed, while awaiting a bursary that would enable him to study in Europe, he got to know a bunch of medical students who introduced him to the joys of cannibalism. Never had he felt so good, he declared in reference to the first time he'd feasted on the breaded ribs of a young female. In speaking to Gladys March, his biographer, he said, "I discovered that I liked to eat the legs and breasts of women . . . best of all, however, I relished women's brains in vinaigrette." The likely truth is that Gladys March, a young female herself, may simply have been the object of one of the most original pick-up conversations of all time.

When he returned to Mexico City in 1910, it was well documented that he was met at the railway station by his family and some reporters. But great painters don't just arrive at a railway station after being away for three years, said Diego to himself. Oh no, they arrive home and have mystical, out of body experiences.

According to Rivera, he arrived unannounced at the family home in Mexico City, walked inside, and was just about to embrace his mother (whom he despised for having sent him off to live with the jaguars when he was two) when his old Indian wet-nurse, Antonia, whom he loved as his true mother, magically materialized before their eyes. He was so moved by the sight of her that he turned away from his mother and went instead to embrace Antonia. (Definitely Shakespearean, I'd say.) She had apparently had a dream foretelling of his arrival and had walked for eight days in order to be with him again. Then he went upstairs for a nap. Wait for it, there's more.

Apparently then Rivera went up to his old room where his faithful old dog crept onto his lap and summarily died, presumably having waited for Rivera's return before doing so. Then Rivera, who quite honestly resembled a 300-pound frog, fainted Hollywood-style, and the two of them lay there in an exquisite tableau, perfectly posed, should some lucky artist just happen to drop by.

Don't get me wrong though. I think Rivera had the right idea. Why the hell shouldn't we have a little fun with our own biographies? Give those tired old historians a bit of a thrill, that's what I say. Did I tell you I was born in a hot-air balloon basket that ran aground in a hay field on the outskirts of Toronto, the product of a torrid affair between Princess Christina of Liechtenstein and her father's hot-air balloon navigator?

The odd thing, though, is that Rivera even bothered to make stuff up at all because his actual life was surreal enough anyway.

On one occasion Rivera was having lunch at his little local café, when a dozen gunmen crashed through the doors of the place and, in a haze of gunfire, blew away the guy in the table next to him. Another time, Rivera and a fellow muralist, Siqueiros, attended the same political rally supporting opposite factions, and the two of them pulled out their pistols and proceeded to shoot up the joint until the plaster from the ceiling started to fall off in clumps onto the participants below.

But the most intriguing episode in Rivera's life occurred when he became entangled with a Russian gentleman called Leon Trotsky. Rivera had become a passionate supporter of Leon Trotsky's anti-Stalinist form of Communism called the Fourth International, and it was Rivera who, in 1936, managed to convince the president of Mexico to give Trotsky asylum in hopes of protecting him against Stalin's assassins.

Rivera put up Trotsky in his own home, the Casa Azul, which he fortified for the purpose, and at first things went well and everybody got along. But Rivera's wife Frida Kahlo, a great painter, partier, and lover in her own right, couldn't resist having a little fling with the smitten Trotsky, and unfortunately, Diego didn't take it well and things went downhill very quickly after that. Diego kicked Trotsky out of the house, and poor old Leon ended up with an ice axe in his skull thanks to the persistence of a fellow called Ramon Mercader, a friend of Stalin's, and, suspiciously, also a friend of Frida's.

Who needs to make up stories with a bio like that?

Leaving the museum, we consulted our maps and started out in the direction of the gigantic statue of Pípila. (Pípila was an Indian who strapped a slab of stone to his back during the siege of the Alhóndiga granary in Guanajuato to protect him from the gunfire as he set fire to the front doors of the structure.) This was going to be a long, steep walk up to the top of a ridge above the city, so we fortified ourselves for our daunting ordeal by scarfing down any pizza slices and Pepsis that got in our way along the route.

The Pípila statue itself turned out to be quite a disappointment. It was a big chunky thing that looked like something Stalin would have enjoyed. But the long, twisty flight of stairs that led up to it was a definite treasure. It took about twenty-five minutes to climb them all the way to the top, and they were as asymmetrical a flight of stairs as you'll ever find anywhere. Imagine you've borrowed an architect's neat cardboard model of a long staircase for half an hour. Then imagine stuffing it into the toe of your shoe. Then take it out and back over it a few times with your car. Crumple it up into a ball and kick it once around the block. Now give it back to the architect (who may be just a trifle cranky, so be careful), and ask him to put it back into his model and to shove the buildings in around it so they fit better. That's what the Pípila staircase looked like. It was a real trip.

As we passed by a park full of brass frog sculptures on the way out of town, I mused about the similarities and differences between this city and San Miguel. I eventually came to the conclusion that Guanajuato was basically less focussed. It lacked something like the Parroquia to serve as an anchor to its ambling, unruly streets. And yes there *was* a dark mysterious quality to it, but there was also a silly, playful side – like those frogs. Guanajuato was basically San Miguel's twisted sister, and I liked it – I liked it a lot. But that's just *my* opinion, you understand.

Chapter 8

Back in San Miguel, Tuesday, November 23, and life seemed more and more reminiscent of Toulouse-Lautrec's Paris of the 1890s.

I was on the second floor, on the patio outside our room, washing out some clothes in a leaky outdoor porcelain sink, when Isadora's voice started speaking from a small square window near my feet. Evidently, Isadora was in the downstairs kitchen.

"Oh Steve, have you heard the latest about the election? Oh, it's a real mess. Oh, they're going to steal the election from Gore. Oh, it's terrible. Oh, America is doomed. Oh, I can't pull myself away from the TV. Oh, it's terrible."

The expat Americans in San Miguel are an odd lot if you ask me. They appear to have no use for the culture they've left behind. It's corrupt, it's pampered, it's bellicose, they say. But if as a non-American you try to express those same points of view, they tear your face off.

"I'll tell you how it all turns out," said the window.

I rolled my eyes, sighed, and said, "Oh good, thanks."

Gringos don't walk in San Miguel, they take cabs. The cab drivers and the gringos have formed a kind of mutual antagonization society, each group loathing its dependence on the other. But for the most part, we were able to opt out of the conflict because Robyn and I, being Canadians of a somewhat British background, walked everywhere in San Miguel. Consequently, people thought we were crazy. That we often went walking for the sheer pleasure of it was even more of a mystery to them. They reacted as if we'd told them that sometimes we got a kick out of slashing each other with knives.

One of my favourite walks was up to the top of the town to a cross where you could look out over a fabulous view of San Miguel and the distant hills. There were usually no people up there, and the air was much fresher than the rest of San Miguel, which unfortunately was plagued by the sooty black fumes of the beat-up, run-down, old city buses called urbanos.

On Wednesday, around noon, I was sitting up there by the cross reading my book, and a person appeared out of the corner of my eye. It was a woman, fairly attractive, about twenty-eight years old, and since she looked a little frightened at finding herself alone with a stranger in an isolated place like this, I turned back to my book and tried to look non-threatening. She took a few pictures of the city below and then tentatively approached me. At that moment, a great big, brown, bristly boar came snorting out of the bushes about twenty feet away and stopped to look at us. It was huge, and looked neither friendly nor intelligent. Now let's see: huge, unfriendly, and dumb. That can't be good.

Then suddenly, hurtling towards me like a freight train out of control came, not the boar, but the young lady. Attractive young women have not done this often to me in my life. I have to say – I quite liked it. A person could get used to a thing like that. When she got to within about three feet, I presumed she would stop and we would have a pleasant conversation about wild boars or something. But she didn't stop at three feet. In fact, she didn't stop at three inches. She ran right into me like a five-year-old running from the boogie man and just stuck there like an errant pancake from a pancake-flipping contest. If I'd known about the effect of wild boars on women when I was younger, I think I would have kept one around. ("Now be a good little piggy and go hide in those bushes over there until I call you, okay?")

"Hi there," I said nonchalantly, her head wedged under my chin. "Uh, my name's Stephen. What's yours?"

"Rachel. Do you think those things are dangerous?"

"Well, I did see some little baby boars around earlier on."

"Oh no! Oh my God! I'm from New York. We don't have wild

boars there."

Starting to feel a little frisky I said, "No? Well, it's okay. I'm from Canada. We have lots of wild things up there." I was about to ask her if she realized that far more people were killed every year by strangers on hilltops than by wild boars – but I thought better of it.

Meanwhile, after a few more brief moments of snorting and sniffling at the bushes nearby, the boar slipped off into the bushes from which it had come. It was probably nap time after a busy morning of rooting around.

So, Rachel and I, after getting off to a fairly heady start, disentangled from one another and started to chat. She told me she had flown down from New York to attend a girlfriend's wedding here in San Miguel, and that she was spending a few hours taking in the sights. I told her a few things about me, and before very long, we were talking about life and living and personal challenges and aspirations and lessons and God only knows what else. We talked for about twenty minutes altogether and then we parted, agreeing that we'd probably see one another around town sometime. But we never met again. That was all there was between Rachel and me. We embraced, we talked, and we parted. I suppose if I were Diego Rivera, I would be telling you that we made passionate love with unrestrained abandon in the highlands above San Miguel in the company of a wild boar who afterwards allowed us to suckle at its teats. Well, I'm not, and we didn't. It was just one of those odd and delightful little interludes that occasionally come along and break through the crust of our everyday public anonymity. It's amazing the way a chance encounter with a stranger in an unusual setting can bring individuals into a state of intimacy so quickly. People dispense with the usual small talk, and speak from their hearts, right from the start. It's very nice. When it happens, it's one of the best things about travel.

Margaret, the tall blond massage therapist from Ladysmith, was our chief source of up-to-date information in San Miguel, and she informed us one day that she was volunteering as an usher at the Teatro Angela Peralta for a performance by a jazz group from San Francisco called The Hot Club, whom she had heard were quite good and thought we might enjoy. Isadora was intending to go, so we decided to go too and arranged to meet them both after the show for a drink at the Agave Azul, a bar next door to the theatre.

The theatre was originally built as an opera house and was one of a whole raft of theatres built in Mexico during the late nineteenth century when large infusions of foreign capital were creating an impressive economic boom (at least for the wealthy). By the 1960s, however, the theatre had fallen on rough times and was only being used to show cheap, low quality B-movies. It has been somewhat refurbished since then, although from our cheap seats it was pretty difficult to tell. As befitted our position on the social ladder of San Miguel, we ended up on benches high up in the second balcony, our view consisting almost entirely of bald heads nestled like eggs in a basket full of big hair. Isadora planned to sit beside us only long enough to scout out one of the more comfortable and expensive seats down on the main floor by the stage, and true to her word, soon after our arrival, she slipped down a back stairwell. I pitied any poor usher who dared to challenge her.

Robyn and I, being a couple of inveterate people-watchers, soon became aware that the Angela Peralta Theatre provided the perfect vantage point from which to view the English-speaking society of San Miguel. And what we had begun to suspect while wandering about the streets and plazas of town was now strongly confirmed by the people we saw all around us: a very high percentage of the people in San Miguel were old women who liked to wear silly clothes. One elderly thing a few seats along from us was clinking her bangles and groovin' to the music in a bright red dress, a gold-lamé scarf, and something on her head that looked like a red fisherman's storm hat with a clown-sized silk flower plastered to it. And the scary thing was, she blended right in.

The band played nice, breezy, good-times music and the positive energy in the place was great. It was a bit hot though, way up where we were, and people kept coming in and squeezing us all together on our benches, a little tighter and tighter as the evening wore on. Robyn was on my right, and on my left were two very nice and extremely large Mexicans, evidently gay. Finally, two more women tried to squeeze in next to Robyn and they effectively mashed me up against these two friendly guys. They didn't seem to mind, but I think I got a little past my own particular comfort zone when our ears started rubbing together. Just then, a pungent and clearly identifiable methanous odour wafted past my nose. Oh great. Apparently, these two gentlemen were under the impression that breaking wind was some sort of recreational sport, and they were out for a little evening target practice. I looked at Robyn, certain that this would mean a most inauspicious ending to our evening, but she seemed quite oblivious to the whole thing, still definitely having a good time, so I decided to just stop breathing and enjoy the show. From time to time the large Mexican guy next to me, with whom I was beginning to merge, would turn and grin proudly at me as his latest triumph crept slowly along the aisle like some deadly fog from outer space. Not wanting to give him the pleasure of a reaction, I pretended not to notice, a smile pasted over my wince. In these kinds of contests, it's all about who blinks first.

The two ladies sitting next to Robyn, who had caused us all to be squished up against each other, finally couldn't take the stench anymore and got up and left.

As Robyn and I spread out into the extra space, I saw Robyn's beaming expression and cupped my hand to her ear, "I guess we should thank these two guys, eh?"

Robyn looked me straight in the eye, smiled, and then remained conspicuously silent. There was a little devil in that smile, I thought.

"You mean, it wasn't them?" I said.

Smile got bigger – prouder.

"You really are brilliant," I said, "and nobody would ever suspect a pretty little thing like you, now would they?"

Smile very smug now, taking a few well-deserved bows.

The band from San Francisco was actually just the warm-up band for the evening, getting us primed for a Cuban group whose lead musician, the organizers kept assuring us, was on a bus somewhere between Mexico City and San Miguel. So after the Americans finished off their gig with a nice long rambling Stephane Grappelli-type thing, we were left with two very ticked-off Cuban guys on the stage – one a drummer and the other playing the electric base – who sounded like a kindergarten music class run amuck, only louder. Margaret, Robyn, and I decided we'd heard enough. Without letting Isadora know, we went next door to the Agave Azul Bar.

Once we got ourselves seated, a constant stream of men stopped by our table to say hi to Margaret, who had clearly been making good use of her time and her looks while she'd been in town. Robyn and I tried not to seem like the two biggest losers in the world when she introduced us to them all. Since they were mostly very drunk and boring, and the music was extremely loud, it wasn't too hard to fool them into thinking we hung out in cool places like this all the time.

The three of us were sitting at a very small, intimate table, almost knocking heads as we leaned on our seats towards one another, and our six hands and three drinks had to jockey for position on the cramped surface. Margaret politely brushed off her suitors one after another and then turned her infectious, vivacious smile towards Robyn and me. Suddenly, the room seemed to shrink down to about the size of a small bed, and it was as if we were just three kids, under the covers late at night, having a heart to heart.

Margaret began carefully, "I have a bit of a problem, you guys. Well, not really a problem exactly. I mean, it's kind of a nice problem in a way I guess, but, uh . . . I'd like to know what you think. You see, I've met this man," and at this point Margaret kind of rolled her eyes and cranked her sexy smile up a couple of notches.

"Well, he's very nice and . . . well yes very rich also, and . . . well actually he's asked me to marry him."

I guess I never really explained all of Margaret's circumstances, and I suppose now would be a good time to do that.

Do you remember the movie *Roxanne* with Steve Martin and Daryl Hannah? The one where he has a huge nose, but a heart of gold? The producers of that film wanted a clean, pretty, healthy-looking, ideal sort of small town for the backdrop, and they chose Nelson, British Columbia. Well, Ladysmith, British Columbia, would have done just as well, and that's where Margaret came from. And in fact, Margaret was clean, pretty, healthy-looking and ideal as well. She was forty-nine years old, attractive, had a nice figure, bubbly blond hair, and always appeared keen to head off for another party or a new adventure. Forty-nine may not sound all that young to some people, but in San Miguel, it gave her a good thirty years on the next-youngest available woman.

Having recently gone through a divorce, she had sold her house and moved into in an apartment with her fifteen-year-old son. Feeling the need to give the next stage of her life a little jump-start, she then decided to let her son spend some quality time with Dad, while she went off to Mexico to have a little fling.

So you see, probably for the first time ever in her life, she had a good-sized wad of cash in her bank account, and even more importantly, she had the opportunity to take some time for herself. She was experiencing an unexpected rebirth and freedom, and was clearly pleased by the fact that she was a very hot commodity in San Miguel. Back in conservative little Ladysmith, as a well-behaved wife and mother, she had reached the point where she just blended into the background. But in San Miguel, men wanted to take her out, wanted to wine her and dine her, and she was starting to feel like an empowered twenty-year-old again; better in fact, because this time round she knew how to wield her power.

Not sure whether to uncork the champagne and congratulate Margaret on reeling in her very own sugar daddy, or whether to be slightly less crass, I said, "And how do you feel about that exactly? Do you like this guy?"

"Oh yeah, he's very nice, and he says he doesn't need me to be passionately in love with him or anything. He's just looking for a companion, someone to share his last few years with."

There was a pause. Then I asked, "Few years? Is there something wrong with him? Is he dying or something?"

Margaret had lost her sexy look by now and was beginning to look a little guilty, like someone caught with their hand in the cookie jar.

"Well no, but he's a good deal older than me."

"Oh God, Margaret," I sighed, "there's almost nine years difference between Robyn and me and it doesn't matter. What matters is whether you get along or not."

"Oh, he's very nice, and I think we get along just great, but you see, well there's a little more than nine years between us."

Robyn scoffed, "Even nineteen, it really doesn't matter, Margaret."

"More like twenty-nine actually," she said sheepishly.

"Oh," I said, "that would still only make him . . ."

"Seventy-eight," said Margaret.

"Well, now," I began, "that is getting along a wee bit, but you know the older you get, the less noticeable the difference seems. When you're say, seventy-eight for example, he'll be, uh . . ."

"A hundred and seven. All right let's cut the crap here guys, he's old, really old, and in exchange for companionship and, God help me, a little sex from time to time, I could live on easy street here in San Miguel like all these other old broads, and you know, I'm going to give it some real serious consideration."

I could see her point. Sometimes we just assume that life is supposed to be hard, and therefore marrying for money is evil, unacceptable, and way too easy. But really, what's the problem? If a person with money uses that money as a little extra incentive to win over a companion for his or her last few years, as long as he or she is up front about it, things might work out very nicely for both of them. I'm sure the heirs would be royally ticked off, but it's not really up to them now is it?

Margaret continued, "You know I've always lived a very straight life, and apart from my kid, who has been a joy, I'm not sure I had as much fun as I should have. And you know I'm getting real tired of all those cold winters in Canada. This just might be my last and best chance to do something about it. So what do you think, am I crazy?"

Robyn and I looked at one another, each waiting for the other to commit.

Robyn said, "Makes sense to me," and then they both turned their eyes on me, like guns locking on the target's co-ordinates.

I paused, fearing Margaret's question was one of those traps set to lure a guy into saying something sexist.

"It gets awful cold in Ladysmith," I said cautiously.

"Awful cold," agreed Margaret.

And we left it at that.

Journal, November 26

Ran into Giles today. Hadn't seen him for a while. Robyn says he gives her the creeps. He's a blobby middle-aged man with wispy strawberry-blond hair and a flaccid, jowly face. He has latched onto us a little because we are the only people in town who haven't told him to drop dead. He has a flair for extremely boring conversation, never looks you in the eye, and still lives at home with his father. Sounds like pervert material to me.

He told us he was just recovering from an abscessed tooth. He said they'd given him some very powerful drugs to combat the infection, which he said could get much worse down here because of being in the tropics and all. His tooth was just fine now, but the rest of him felt like hell. He figured whatever killed the bacteria was busy killing the rest of him as well.

Which reminds me. Don't ever tell anyone you're sick in San Miguel, and especially not in a crowded room. If you do, I guarantee you'll end up spending at least an hour and a half listening to the myriad of wacko remedies that circulate around town like little staphylococcal infections. Apparently, San Miguel is a town where shamans can cure the majority of your ailments, and the rest of them can be fixed by adjusting some mysterious little bone in your neck. Got a hip problem? It's your neck. Got pneumonia? It's your neck. Got two severed feet? It's all in your neck. And one more thing: beware of the word "healer."

Robyn and I and a sixtyish lady called Katherine were having a good laugh one morning about a cartoon we'd seen portraying George Dubya Bush as a simple-minded little weasel asking his advisors to explain to him one more time how he'd won the election, when suddenly the conversation began to transmogrify in a most unexpected way.

"I'm not feeling very well today," said Katherine.

"Oh dear," I said, "what do you think it is, a cold or something?"

"Oh yeah, or something, I don't know. But it's all right, I've got a healer."

"A healer you say? Robyn, Katherine has a *healer*. My, my, my, that does sound interesting. Now what exactly does your healer do for you, Katherine?"

Normally the word "healer" works like the foot pedal on the kitchen trash can of my mind, and gales of snarky comments start spewing forth like coiled-spring snakes from my mouth. But this time, I'm proud to say, I successfully managed to sit on my tongue.

Katherine continued.

"Well, he heals me. He's really quite incredible. And he doesn't even have to see me in person, that's the part I like. He just does it all over the phone. He used to design aircraft engines and now he does healing full time. Yeah, it's amazing. He doesn't even have to know what's wrong with you, and still he can heal you. My kids don't believe in any of this stuff, they think their mom's gone bonkers. It's caused quite a split between us, my two son-in-laws won't talk to me any more. But I don't care. I'm going to go on healing them whether they want me to or not. I asked John, that's my healer's name, to heal my grandchild, Cynthia, and she got better in a few weeks, and that was after all the conventional stuff they'd been trying had failed. So, now I just send John money on a regular basis, and he does the healing automatically. Hell, it's cheaper than medical insurance."

Thankfully for my tongue, which was getting very sore after being sat upon for so long, we soon got back to Bush-bashing, and she seemed like a perfectly normal raving socialist again.

I spent the morning of November 30th carefully wrapping a parcel of Christmas gifts to send back home. I used to ship my pottery to some fairly exotic, faraway places, and I never ever had anything broken from bad packing – I presume the horrendous amount of breakage was the shipper's fault.

So I was feeling quite smug when I took my parcel to the San Miguel post office and plopped it proudly down onto the counter.

The man on the other side was not quite so impressed. He shook his head and explained to me that the plastic packing tape, with which I had so merrily wrapped the entire parcel, was unacceptable.

"And why would that be?" I asked through my teeth.

"Because the address gets smeared if the parcel gets wet," he said. (I sort of thought that keeping the mail dry was one of the services offered by the post office in exchange for your money. Silly me.)

In an effort to demonstrate the problems involved with using packing tape, the man wet his finger with drool and smeared it all over my package. I was about to do the same all over something of his to see how *he* liked it, when I noticed that his slobber had had no effect whatsoever on the ink on my package. I had used a good quality, permanent marker and it wasn't going to smear for him even if he drooled on it all day.

"No hay una problema, señor," I said, trying not to gloat too much.

But I had misunderstood. This was not a negotiation. He had the power and the backing of the entire Mexican bureaucracy behind him, and it mattered not a whit, not a tittle, whether his rule made any sense. Clearly losing patience with me, he explained that if I wanted him to mail my package, I would have to wrap my parcel in sturdy brown paper, and then tie it up with string. As far as I could tell, brown paper was far less likely to stand up to the persistent slobbering of Mexican postal officials than my plastic wrapping tape was, but I could tell by his icy stare that he wasn't really interested in continuing a dialogue on the subject.

So, I traipsed off to a nearby papelería and purchased a sheet of the right sort of paper and the right sort of string and went home to repack my parcel.

An hour later, I arrived at the post office counter with my parcel properly wrapped, and again I plopped it down for his assessment. This time he was very pleased. He didn't smile – Mexican officials don't smile – but I could tell by the way he drew the parcel lovingly towards him, that he was positively tickled at the fine job I'd done. Absolutely giddy with delight, I'd say, although a less discerning eye might have missed it.

Then he asked me if I wanted to register it.

How the hell do I know!? If I don't register it, does that mean you just put it in the "Please Steal From Here" pile and that's it, gone forever?

I raised my eyebrows as high as they would go, tilted my head a little sideways, and gave the post office guy a little questioning smile, hoping to get a silent signal from him as to whether registration was a wise idea or not. I thought I saw an almost imperceptible nod. Yes, yes, I'm sure that's what that was, or was it just a twitch? Oh God, I don't know. Sure, I'll register the damn thing.

"Sí, señor," I replied.

He sent me to the lady next to him who was in charge of registration. And she looked even scarier than he did.

"Which type of registration do you want," she said bluntly in Spanish.

Oh no, please no. What did I do to deserve options?

"What types are there?" I replied.

Her answer was in such rapid-fire Spanish that I couldn't understand a word of it, but I did detect that one type of registration was more expensive than the other. Figuring by this time that my parcel was probably a lost cause anyway, I said, "The cheap kind please."

She looked at me as if to say she'd expect as much from a slob like me, then filled out a line in her very large book, took my money, and abruptly dismissed me.

I lost no time in getting back to the relative safety of Isadora's, and resolved not to venture out again for at least a week.

Journal, December 2

Went to an opening of new work by Tabuena this evening. The "art opening" is one of San Miguel's truly quintessential events. For anyone who likes free food and silly people, these things are a must.

They come in three styles. There's the dreadful amateur show, usually attended by the painter's friends and no one else. There's the very artsy show of entirely unmarketable, overpriced and pretentious shlock – things like glass display cases full of nails, and floor sculptures consisting of alarm clocks glued together into giant blobs. And lastly, there's the art show of real art by a real artist who all the other artists claim has sold out to the establishment and is just pumping out product. Tabuena fell into this last category. Being a trifle on the shallow side, I liked his stuff. But then I've got a whole galleryful of nails and alarm clocks I can browse through whenever I want. I call it – La Shed.

The show was starting at eight, so when I set out walking at seven-thirty, the streets were dark. Walking through the nighttime streets of San Miguel, with their mysterious, creepy-Gothic-horror ambience, is one of the greatest warm-up acts for an art show one could ever imagine. And the drama of the event would be heightened even further by the fact that it was being staged at the Bellas Artes art school, a grand eighteenth-century convent of dark stone pillars set around an enormous central patio.

The wealthy families of Mexico used to send their unmarried daughters and superfluous widows to mansions like these in exchange for substantial "donations," and they were really more like hotels than cloisters. Cells were purchased like condominiums, pets were permitted, and in many cases, (although reportedly not in this convent) servants were present in large numbers. It was a place just like this that Chaucer had so much fun ridiculing in *Canterbury Tales*, a book written a whole four centuries before this place even existed. Shows how effective ridicule is at changing things.

David Alfaro Siqueiros, the renowned muralist whom I mentioned earlier with regards to a public meeting in Mexico City where he and Rivera pulled out their guns and started shooting up the place, also had a brief connection with the Bellas Artes. There is an unfinished mural in the refectory on the west side of the patio that was painted by Siqueiros during a workshop he was conducting with the school's art students. Siqueiros' violent and theatrical style was a classic case of art imitating life. Apparently during one of his classes there, Siqueiros threw a student down one whole flight of stairs.

I passed through the large entranceway and quickly found myself surrounded by little groups of shmoozing high-society types, all of whom looked very pleased with themselves. Of course many of those smiles had probably been permanently etched into their faces by their cosmetic surgeons, and weren't connected to their states of mind at all. One poor old relic, who must have been very beautiful at one time judging by her excellent bone structure, had had her face pulled back and tucked behind her head with such force that she ended up looking as if she had three mouths, all of which were grinning simultaneously. I shuddered and walked on by.

While a small band was playing nondescript jazz just loud enough to render intelligent conversation useless, a small army of waiters in neat white jackets circulated through the crowd with trays of wine and went about setting up tables in the centre of the patio in preparation for the food.

Not recognizing anyone in the crowd right away, I snatched a glass of white wine for company and began perusing a collection of non-Tabuena paintings on the walls bordering the patio. (Tabuena's pictures were in a side section that had been closed off temporarily until after the speeches of pompous town notables and the formal cutting of a ribbon to herald the official opening of the show.) I soon realized that I was the only person in the whole place who was looking at any of the paintings. Everyone else had their backs turned to the paintings and was deeply involved in discussions about their clothing and the general decline of the quality of hors d'oeuvres at San Miguel art openings.

"Oh my God, dahling, you wouldn't believe it. Little cardboard sandwiches about the size of postage stamps with ham and cheese or some such thing. Highway robbery, that's what I call it."

And it was like this at every art show I ever attended in San Miguel. I went to one in a smaller gallery that had some very original stuff by a guy who painted Indian cave designs on pieces of carved and textured plaster in a whole range of exquisite colours, and in my ignorance I attempted a little conversation about them.

"Don't you just love the complexity of his work?" I had offered to the elderly woman standing beside me with her nose in the air and her back to the paintings.

She turned slightly, glanced at the picture indifferently, and said, "Have you put your name in for the door prize yet dear? No? Well now you better hurry." Then, smiling in a very contrived way she said, " Excuse me, I hear they're running out of smoked salmon." And off she went.

Back at the Bellas Artes, I was beginning to despair of the whole scene, and the food had not yet made an appearance, when I spotted Margaret in a little group and went over to see her.

"Oh, Stephen," Margaret beamed, "isn't this fun? Let me introduce you to Helen, she's from England, and these are two friends of hers, Jim and Bill."

We all smiled at each other mutely for a few moments and then the group suddenly disintegrated leaving Helen and me alone. She looked to be about thirty-five and fairly hip compared to me. We had to shout at each other to be heard above the noise of the band.

"So, have you been in Mexico a while?" I bellowed.

"Well, no, only about a week, but it feels much longer. You see I'm here by mistake."

"Really? How so?"

"Well, about two weeks ago this friend of mine, we're not exactly friends you understand, but we're, well I don't know what we are actually, but anyway, he called me up and said hey, Helen, lets take a crazy spontaneous trip somewhere. I thought that sounded good, and I'm a little like that anyway, so I said sure, where to? He said he'd always wanted to go to Mexico so why don't we go there, and I said fine, when do we leave. He said it would be too complicated to try and get cheap last-minute seats on the same flight so why don't we just each arrange our own tickets and then meet in the Mexico City airport on a certain day at a certain time. I said fine, we agreed on the day, and I was going to call him back after I'd bought my ticket to arrange the time of our meeting. I proceeded to buy my ticket, and when I tried to call him back, I couldn't reach him. In fact he basically disappeared off the face of the earth. I think, he stood me up, the loser. But I decided to say to hell with him and come anyway to a country I know absolutely nothing about. And to tell you the truth, I've been having one hell of a good time ever since I got here. I don't know what day it is and I don't care. Party-on, baby, that's what I say. Whoo-hoo!!"

Not being very good at the small-talk thing I then asked, "So what do you think of the art?"

She looked at me with total disgust, as if I'd just asked her if she'd like to sniff between my toes.

"Oh look," she said peering off over my shoulder, "there's Ricardo!" And with that she quickly scurried away.

After everybody was good and sozzled, Tabuena appeared. He was a wizened little Philippino gentleman who played the part of the great master very well. The dignitaries had their speeches and cut their ribbons, and when they were done, the rest of us were herded in to see the new work.

The paintings were large hotel-lobby-size paintings mostly of romanticized Mexican peasants in everyday street settings, and in spite of their obviously commercial style, I couldn't help but like them. He was clearly rooted in cubism, shaded areas were broken up into large angular blocks of a single colour, but the mouths and eyes were shaded more conventionally and he used that shading to portray the people of Mexico as kindly and noble, a sentiment I concurred with completely. There was a rough texture to the surface giving the whole thing the look of colourful pieces of crêpe paper that had been cut and applied to the canvas. I liked them all.

Suddenly, there was a mass exodus of people from the show as word got around that the food was finally being served out in the courtyard. Trying not to get trampled in the rush, I squeezed my way towards the food tables on the patio and was greatly impressed with what I saw. There were huge trays of piping-hot egg rolls, dry won ton, and pork dumplings, and people were madly piling up their little paper plates to overflowing with all the delectable treats. Wine was being poured with abandon, and there were many, many happy face-lifts in the crowd. Oh yes, there could be no doubt old Tabuena was a true master – a master of marketing that is. I spent another half-hour stuffing my face with all that delicious food and wine, and then just as I was leaving, I caught sight of the artist, nodding and smiling and playing his game so well. Things couldn't have gone better for him. He knew that when the reviews came out in the papers the next morning, the show would be hailed as a triumph, and when people gathered in the jardín to gossip about it, all the reports would be slight variations on the same profitable theme: "Wasn't the food marvellous!"

Chapter 9

The reason Canadians are so well suited to life in Mexico is probably because immediately after we come popping out of the womb, we are caught by our fathers and taken camping. ("Come on now little buddy, and for God's sake stop dragging your umbilical cord!") You see, in Mexico you can't just move in to an apartment, you really have to know how to camp in one. If you go to the landlord asking for something to be repaired:

"Excuse me but there is a cloud of poisonous gas in our room that has just killed my wife."

All you get is a perplexed look and a response like:

"Well no one has ever complained about the gas BEFORE."

And somehow that doesn't really address the problem.

So in San Miguel, rather than waste our breath, Robyn and I tended to fix most things ourselves.

By December 1st, it was getting extremely cold in San Miguel with temperatures heading down towards freezing at night. Day-time temperatures outside were quite warm and pleasant but unfortunately a foot or two of stone-cold concrete lay between all that warmth and the inside of our room. Rather than complain to Isadora about it, we decided to handle the problem ourselves. We bought Robyn a fleecy blanket, we stuffed newspaper into the gaps around the windows, we got the ancient propane heater going, and we ran our propane stove non-stop with the door wide open. As long as we slept in our clothes, all of them, all three layers of them, we kept moderately warm.

And then just when our little experiment in indoor camping

seemed to be going quite well, our refrigerator stopped working. Now I know I've made it sound as if we didn't really need one, but in fact the room wasn't cold enough to kill micro-organisms – humans, yes; micro-organisms, no. It eventually got so warm inside the refrigerator that we briefly considered leaving *its* door open to help heat the room, but that still wouldn't solve the food spoilage thing. So, there was no more avoiding it. I would have to complain to Isadora about the refrigerator.

I stood outside Isadora's door, sniffing the incense that leaked from all around its edges, and felt myself filling with dread.

Knock, knock. "Isadora? Isa-dor-a? It's Stephen."

"Whaddya want?" came a subterranean voice that sounded as if it had buried itself beneath two feet of blankets in an attempt to keep warm.

"Isadora, I need to speak to you!"

There was a thud. Probably Isadora rolling off her bed onto the floor. The door opened a few inches letting out a barrage of incense.

"Yeah, what?" she muttered, staring blearily into my chest.

"Isadora, our refrigerator has stopped working."

Her eyes lifted up towards mine with a look of pure frustration, and then she blared out, "So? What do you expect me to do about it!!? I don't know anything about refrigerators! I certainly don't have any money to fix one."

I wanted to just slug her and be done with it. But the thing about Isadora was that if you got combative with her, she just got worse. If you took a more supportive tone, your chances of making some progress were greatly enhanced.

"How about I look around for somebody to fix it for you, maybe I can find somebody cheap," I said.

She paused to try and clear her brain of all the cobwebs. "Well, all right, but I'm really broke. For the time being you can have a shelf in my fridge down the hall there."

"Great. Thanks Isadora."

"Sure."

I was beginning to catch on. You could fight things here and drive yourself crazy, or you could back off a little and start enjoying the ride.

Journal, December 2

Isadora just asked us whether we minded the sound of chanting because she and a friend wanted to do some. I told her I was not overly fond of it and I'd rather they did it while we were out. She said, well it was good for our inner selves to hear it anyway, even if we didn't like it, so they were just going to go ahead and chant.

Journal, December 3

Isadora was busy crashing and banging around in the room opposite ours this afternoon when the doorbell rang and she came running into our room with a spray can of Lysol saying, "Oh Jesus, Steve, could you do me a huge favour and spray this around in the empty room over there – it smells of cat piss everywhere. I've got somebody coming to look at the room. And for God's sake don't tell her about the car fumes and the noise. I'll close your door so she won't want to speak with you."

While Isadora let the person in and conducted a brief tour of the downstairs, I reluctantly sprayed some of the Lysol around the vacant room and then retreated back into ours, just catching sight of the two of them as they reached the top of the stairs. For the next twenty minutes I could hear Isadora talking with the prospective tenant, and although I couldn't hear her exact words, it sounded as if Isadora was trying very hard to come across as a well-organized, sensible person. From the brief glimpse I'd had of the woman, she appeared to be somewhere in her fifties and very straight-looking. Part of me wanted to go over and tell the poor thing to run for the hills and save herself now before it was too late. But part of me thought it would also be wise not to drive too big a wedge between Isadora and myself. And besides, who am I to deny someone from having a potentially life-altering experience?

When Isadora finished showing the woman the room, she gave me a wink and a thumbs-up before heading back down the stairs. I cringed momentarily at the thought of having become this woman's co-conspirator. Could it be that the wicked sorceress was drawing me into her web of evil? *At first it was just a little Lysol, but then, gradually over time, she had me doing other, more depraved things . . .*

A few days later, I decided to head out for a little trip to a small place called Xichú – sort of a scouting expedition to see whether it was worthwhile for Robyn and me to spend a little time there. A friend on Hornby had recommended it to us, describing it as very beautiful and like a piece of old-time Mexico. So I consulted my map and concluded that I would first have to go to a town called San Luis de la Paz, spend the night there, and then head out for Xichú the next morning.

I arrived in San Luis on a Monday afternoon, pretty tired after about three hours on a couple of pretty old buses. They are attempting to reduce bus accidents these days by attaching a special wire to the bus's wheels that is connected to a red light and a beeper inside the bus to let the passengers know when the driver is speeding. If the driver exceeds the 95-km/h speed limit, the theory is that the passengers will complain. Well, of course the people of Mexico – and the Olmecs and Toltecs and Aztecs before them – have learned very well what complaining accomplishes: absolutely nothing. (Except that you annoy a lot of people and maybe get sacrificed for your trouble.) So Mexicans have developed into a very polite people far too respectful of authority to complain about things, and the red light keeps flashing and the beeper keeps beeping and the sleep-deprived driver pulls out to pass in the middle of a bridge, and gringos like me are better off closing their eyes and being thankful that at least the driver isn't drunk. Well, probably isn't drunk.

When I got to San Luis I started looking for a hotel. The first one I walked into was in pretty rough shape – the front door almost fell off when I opened it and they were demolishing one whole section of the place. But it wasn't any worse than that Pay N Save that we stayed at in Vancouver the night before our flight to Mexico City, and at sixteen dollars, it was almost one third the price. For the sake of comparison, I went next door to another place where for fourteen dollars I could have a dirty room, questionable water, and a mattress so flimsy it swallowed me up to the waist and tried to steal one of my shoes. The first place was called Las Parras (The Grapevines), and that was where I decided to stay.

For reasons that never really became clear to me, San Luis de la

Paz was a very happy little town.

After dumping my bag in my room, I stepped back out onto the street and headed to the centre of town in search of a restaurant. Along the way, I stopped to gaze inside a cowboy-hat store whose entire front wall was open to the street, the way they usually are in Mexico. Practically every hat in the store was the same colour and the same style: white, and curvy-Mexican-cowboy. I wondered how on earth anyone could make a living in a small town selling nothing but white cowboy hats.

I hadn't stopped long before a handsome young guy with a great big smile came out to introduce himself. Carlo was his name, and while he casually brushed out a smudge on one of his hats with a toothbrush, we talked.

Carlo, who spoke perfect English, asked me where I was from. When I said Canada, he got quite excited and told me he'd lived in Minnesota, as if he thought maybe we might share a few mutual acquaintances. I just smiled and asked him how he liked it there. His momentary hesitation suggested he was trying to find words that wouldn't offend.

"Oh, it's okay. But I like it a lot better here!"

He said the weather was better here, there were more jobs, and he didn't have to work as hard. Made sense to me. I took a look around as we talked and noticed that the air in this bright, sunny little town was crystal clear and that everybody who passed by us on the sidewalk had a cheerful smile on his or her face, just like Carlo's. Then I noticed that every single male person between the ages of eighteen and eighty out there on that street was wearing a brand-spanking-new, white cowboy hat, just like the kind Carlo sold. Carlo had truly found his perfect niche. For Carlo, going away had helped him see more clearly just how good things really were back home.

Carlo and I parted with smiles and a handshake, and I continued on my search for a restaurant. I walked for several blocks and then suddenly remembered that, with the exception of tourist areas, small towns in Mexico don't really do restaurants. They go in more for street food like tacos and hamburguesas. Not in the mood for either of those, I ended up munching on some bread, some ham, and a chocolate doughnut, and then went back to my room for a nap.

About seven o'clock that evening, I woke up to a ferocious drumming sound that was coming from the street in front of the hotel. I threw on my shoes, grabbed my camera, and went out to see what was up. It was dark now but the street was lit here and there by store fronts and the occasional street lamp. There was a huge parade marching down the little main street of town, and what a delightfully incongruous bunch of marchers they were.

At the head of the parade was a pickup truck carrying a replica of the town's very ornate, twin-spired cathedral. Also in the pickup were half a dozen children and hundreds of (well, what else) coloured balloons. Following this came a very solemn procession consisting of a priest and about twenty members of his congregation. So far, it seemed like a fairly run-of-the-mill kind of religious pilgrimage thing. And then, I noticed the gorillas.

Some years ago, I figure a guy called Pedro says to his priest, "Padre, would you mind if we put a little something extra into the parade this year, you know, to keep it interesting, so people will want to come again next year?"

"Of course my son, if you and José can think of something that's not too expensive, I'm sure our blessed Virgin would approve, especially if it appeals to the children. I will leave it in your hands."

All right, so gorillas aren't quite what the padre has in mind. But José has all these old gorilla suits in his warehouse that aren't selling as well as they did last year, and so he decides to donate them all to the parish for use in the parade. So then, when the priest and his gloomy entourage are marching solemnly along the street, suddenly people in black gorilla costumes start leaping into the crowd and making everybody laugh. The gorillas are a huge hit. Everyone thanks the padre for a such a nice parade, and every year since then, the padre has been hoping those old gorilla suits would wear out; and every year the parishioners happily repair them because it would spoil it for the kids if there weren't any gorillas in the parade any more.

Anyway, that's *my* best shot as to why there would be gorillas in a religious procession. Feel free to come up with something else of your own.

Next came the mandatory military drum band. I think it says

somewhere in the Mexican Constitution that all parades must have a drum band. I think deep inside every calm, good-natured Mexican there's a madly flailing drummer just waiting to get out. And I must admit there's nothing quite stirs the soul as much as a bunch of people all neatly decked out in spiffy new uniforms pounding away as if headed out for a day of glorious slaughter. My ancestors, the Scots, could think of no better way of spending a day. The Aztecs always banged on their drums for hours before a battle. I've read that they loved it so much, in fact, that if their opponents didn't have any drums, they'd lend them some of theirs. No point in going to all that trouble of organizing a war, and missing out on the best part.

So after the drummers moved out of our field of view and took their noise and excitement along with them, the next group to come along was a solemn one (in the interest of keeping things balanced I suppose), namely, the pushcart battalion. One-person pushcarts are used by pedlars throughout Mexico to transport and market all the vast array of Mexican street merchandise. I think they look a little like a cross between a rickshaw and a wheelbarrow. Well, the owners of these particular carts had dolled up each of them with a large portrait of the Virgin of Guadalupe, masses of shimmering gold and silver sequins, and as many balloons as they could tie onto them. The five images of the Virgin, sitting in their five matching pushcarts, looked to me like elderly and infirm Dionne Quintuplets riding around in ice-cream wagons surrounded by balloons. At first I wanted to chuckle. But the owners were so dignified about it that I soon found myself just as caught up in the mysticism of it all as everyone else.

The Virgin of Guadalupe, for whom the parade was being held, was purported to have been a dark-skinned Virgin Mary who first arrived on the scene in 1531 in a vision to an otherwise ordinary Indian called Juan Diego. He saw the Virgin three times and it was on the third occasion that she told him to gather roses and present them to the local bishop with a request that a church be built in her honour. As Juan Diego unfolded his rose-filled cloak for the bishop, an image of the dark-skinned Virgin appeared on the garment and it was deemed a miracle.

At the risk of being crucified myself if the Mexicans ever even let me back into their country after I say this, I should let the reader know that there are some cynical people out there who doubt that Juan Diego ever existed at all. They say that the whole thing was a ploy by the Catholic Church to drum up more conversions; that maybe the Church was just trying to win over the Indian people by giving them a Catholic saint that parallelled their own earth goddess, Tonantzin, who just happened to have had a shrine at Tepeyac, where the miracle was said to have occurred. And then they say that having a version of the Virgin Mary that had dark skin and spoke the local Indian dialect didn't hurt matters either – since after the story broke, conversions were way up.

But that's just what the cynics think, not nice folks like you and me.

In keeping with the pattern of alternating a quiet group with a noisy one, the next group to come along was noisy – to put it mildly. Drums again, but this time they were Aztec. To the fierce pounding of a single, huge and explosive bass drum, a long line of magnificently feathered and masked Aztec warriors shook their shields and jabbed their spears. There is nothing even mildly amusing about a display like this. You just stand back and be thankful as hell that it isn't you these guys are mad at. I'd certainly pay up whatever tribute they requested. ("You want half my corn crop? No problem, do ya like squash, here take it all. Have a nice day and you won't be back until next year, right?") As in the case of the gorillas, I'm not too sure why the Aztecs get to march along with the Catholics in a parade for the Virgin. The only Aztec connection with virgins that I can think of is that they liked to sacrifice them. Their presence in the parade was probably just another case of the Church looking for a way to appease the indigenous people. But I tell you, these guys sure liven up a parade, I'll give them that. And I, for one, would not like to be the person chosen to tell them they couldn't march in it.

The festivities continued for quite a while as it seemed there were more people marching in the parade than there were watching it. So, I left the gorillas, the Aztecs, and the Catholics and went back to my room, where I watched a bad Anthony Hopkins movie about a corrupt South American dictatorial regime that threw foreign tourists into horrible prisons where, after they had been forced to fulfil the sick sexual fantasies of the other inmates, they were killed.

Got up at six the next morning to catch the seven o'clock bus to Xichú. It was dark and the streets were practically empty, except for a few food vendors who were setting up their simple stalls for the gradually emerging breakfast crowd. It was icy cold in the streets – a consequence of the high altitude, the time of year, and the cold air funnelling down from the mountains – and the bus station was just as bad. I walked over to buy my ticket from a plainly dressed guy standing on the platform. His change drawer consisted of a few stacks of coins and a fan of bills he created by gripping an assortment of denominations tightly between each of the knuckles of his left hand. He looked downright trigger-happy to turn anyone away who didn't have the correct change. True to his looks, he turned away both of the individuals in front of me – they were Mexican and should have known better – and he was no doubt salivating at the prospect of rejecting me as well, when I suddenly drew out a bulging handful of coins from my pocket like some gunslinging cowboy from the Wild West and forced him to sell me a ticket, which he did, grudgingly. I rewarded myself for this small but significant coup by going and getting myself a cup of the only hot drink available, black instant coffee, and then took a look around for my bus.

I have a few general rules for myself regarding bus travel in Mexico: try to stick to reputable bus lines; always take first class, if possible; never travel at night; never travel in bad weather; and avoid the treacherous mountain roads. Mexicans use a simpler rule: cross yourself and leave the rest up to God – when your time's up, your time's up. It probably works as well as my method, but I can't help thinking maybe, just maybe, I can improve the odds that God has to work with.

Judging by the excellent buses I saw in front of me, things were getting off to a very encouraging start. And the weather yesterday had been absolutely perfect with classic, clear blue Mexican skies, so that augured well too. I started reading the names on the buses: Guanajuato, Dolores, Mexico City . . . but no Xichú. Well that was normal, the buses usually arrive just before they're scheduled to depart and it wasn't seven o'clock yet, the time when mine was supposed to leave. No matter what else you may have heard of Mexican efficiency, I have found that their buses are pretty punctual. So when seven came around and there was still no Xichú bus, I got a little concerned. Before I could get myself too worked up about it, however, I looked through a gap between two of those fine new buses in front of me, and saw a not-so-new one with *Xichú* crayoned across its windshield, turning to pull alongside the rest.

When I got a little closer, I saw just how much of a wreck this bus really was. Its engine shuddered to a stop, practically sneezing a "Xichú!" as it did so. Every single window was broken. No, I'm exaggerating. There were two that just had bullet holes in them. It looked about sixty-five years old, and its headlights were both completely destroyed. Their absence gave the bus that sad, dark, sunken look that some blind people develop over time. All right, so the rule about always taking a first-class bus would have to be broken just this once. But maybe Xichú wasn't too far away; maybe the length of time I would be exposed to this slightly higher level of risk would be very short. As I stepped on the bus, I asked the driver sitting there in the cold, gloomy darkness how far it was to Xichú.

"Three hours . . . more or less."

Oh dear.

As our bus rose slowly into the mountains around San Luis de la Paz, I became entranced by the beautiful undulating hills of cactus and mesquite, occasionally punctuated by small herds of cattle, goats, and sheep. School children began to board the bus, and, as usual, I had as much fun watching them as they had watching me. These were not the spotlessly clean and perfectly tailored young people in their neat and tidy uniforms that are commonly seen in the cities and towns all over Mexico. These were country kids, a little grubbier, the boys in cowboy hats and the girls in jeans, but considering their simple dwellings and their lack of what we would call basic necessities, they looked pretty good. And anyway, they were a cheerful lot and a pleasant distraction. After about twenty minutes of mutual fascination, they got off and I took to gazing out the window once again.

We were now winding our way through a steep mountain pass on a very narrow road that was entirely without shoulders. There were absolutely no barriers at all to prevent us from slipping over its crumbling edges and doing a reverse two and a half pike with half twist into the valley below. And either the fog was descending onto us or we were ascending into the fog. Any way you look at it, our driver's visibility was getting severely reduced. With some apprehension, I peered out the front window of the bus to see what the driver's view was like. I was relieved to see that it was really pretty good, sort of, and maybe we were just in a little localized pocket of fog anyway.

Wrong. Fog got worse, then it started to rain. I had been clinging to the thought that at least the road was dry so that when we sped around blind corners on the wrong side of the road, at least we wouldn't skid. Well, with my nose pressed up against the rain-streaked glass to see how wet the road surface was getting, I had to admit that although body-surfing would be difficult, it probably wasn't out of the question. Still trying to resist the urge to start begging for just one more day to live, I started going over my rules again to see if there was anything to be optimistic about.

IT WAS STILL DAYTIME!!!YAYYY!!!

Daytime is of no use, you twit, if the fog becomes so thick the driver can't see anything.

Well then, how about this. The driver has probably driven this road many times before and in similar conditions. Right? So I asked the person next to me if the weather was often like this.

"Hardly ever." Of course.

Trust the driver, trust the driver, trust the . . .

Loud, crazy, Mexican oom-pah-pah music comes blasting and crackling from the improvised sound system up front, and I take a look to see if the two bus guys up there are going to break open a bottle of tequila and start dancing. No, but I did catch a glimpse of the bus driver, and he looked like a seventeen-year-old with a great big smile on his face who was more into the music than driving the bus.

I tried to look calm on the outside, but inside it was, "We're all gonna die! We're all gonna die!"

Did I mention that there was no heat on the bus and that they drove with the front door wide open, the driver's assistant dangling one foot out the door?

Some of you are probably getting fed up with my whining by this point. But hang in just a little while longer, okay? I suffered a lot for this little tale.

By this time I was seriously considering getting off the bus, but since I would be dropped in the middle of nowhere, with no return bus coming back for another five hours, I decided to hang in for a while longer. Then we passed a sign saying, “END OF PAVED ROAD,” and stopped at the edge of what can only be called a precipice. Looking through the front window, I saw a line of cars and one large bulldozer. It was then that I realized that this road wasn’t even finished yet. They were in the process of hacking into the cliff and had only just barely hacked in far enough for vehicles to get through. I decided to get out while the bus was stopped and have a look at things. I should have looked before I stepped out the door though because, as it happened, there was only a distance of about six inches between the bus and the edge of the road, and I think I would have fallen about a thousand feet before what was left of me reached Xichú. I looked down the road and saw one car after another very slowly trying to navigate a new and very narrow section and decided, cold or not, in the middle of nowhere or not, five hours to wait or not, I was not getting back onto that bus.

To a whole chorus of strange looks from the road workers, I headed off into the fog, back the way we came.

After a few minutes I realized I was not warming up the way I had expected to, and I wasn’t sure what kind of shape I’d be in after five more hours in this bitter-cold air. I trudged about two more miles along the twisting road and then spotted in the distance a group of three road workers standing under a shed roof by the side of the road. As I approached, I wondered about the possibility that there might be a little heat on in their shed and whether I might be able to wait there for the bus to return from Xichú. I decided it was worth a try.

“Is it a problem if I wait here for the bus?”

Two of them responded with smiles and glassy stares. The other said, “No.”

I thought if I asked for a place to sit down, they might tell me about a back room where they kept a little heat on.

“Got any place to sit?”

The chatty one went to the back of the shed and rolled over an old can, motioning me to have a seat. There was nothing at all warm or enticing about it. I declined politely.

So there I stood, chilled to the bone, in a wide-open shed surrounded by a frigid fog, with three very contented Mexicans who were apparently quite comfortable, and with about four and a half hours to wait until the bus came. One of them motioned to me to follow him to the back of the shed.

There he proceeded to open up a locked door, and again I prayed that this was the entrance to some magnificently warm room complete with hot chocolate and a crackling fire. Nope. It was a little storeroom, and he kindly offered me small packages of crackers and some pop. I said yes to the crackers and no to the pop. Then he pulled out the real secret to how these guys survived in this brutally cold environment. He had a war chest of little plastic bottles of tequila, probably provided by the highways department because it was cheaper than providing heat. And actually, these guys seemed quite content with the arrangement. When he offered me a handful of them, I was tempted, believe me. Images of Saint Bernards coming to the rescue of frozen trappers entered my head, but I also remembered reading somewhere that alcohol actually cools the body by dilating the blood vessels, so reluctantly, I declined. As he was locking up the room, I noticed a pickup truck behind the shed and a very dim light bulb in my hypothermic brain clicked on.

Not quite begging, but pretty close, I said, "I would gladly pay you something if you would take me back to San Luis in your truck."

He was clearly uncertain about the idea and said, "I would need 100 pesos for the gas, señor."

I wasted no time, and nodded my head emphatically, "That would be fine."

So, I introduced myself with an icy handshake and he told me his name was Rico, and Rico retrieved the key from the shed, and with much excitement, we got into the truck. The door had to be held shut with a rope and there was no seat belt, but I'd driven in worse cars back home on Hornby, so I was feelin' pretty good. Until he turned the key. *Ruh-ruh-ruh . . . ruh-ruh . . . ruh . . . click . . . click.* That, I said astutely to myself, would be the death rattle of a very cold, very dead battery. I knew this was too easy.

But Rico showed remarkable determination and, unwilling to give up, got his two bleary friends to come help. We all pushed the car back and forth and back and forth until I, for one, was finally getting warm. But it wouldn't start. Then Rico suddenly looked off towards the highway and indicated that a vehicle was coming. We couldn't see it at first because of the fog, but it had lost its muffler, probably many years ago, and so it was easy to hear. My heart sank when it finally did come into view because it was travelling at about ten miles an hour and looked even worse than the truck. Rico raced off to intercept it, which wasn't really very difficult considering its condition, and the beat-up old wreck of a car pulled off the road.

The two guys driving it looked like the parking attendants from *Ferris Bueller's Day Off* – very sleazy, very pool hall – and I was beginning to think that maybe I should have stayed on that bus after all. Turned out the plan was for them to give our battery a jump. Rico was handed a set of jumper cables by the scary-looking dude at the wheel of the old clunker, and he clamped them onto the terminals of both cars. The truck's battery terminals were both red, instead of one red and one black, so I was expecting to see a flash and a puff of smoke when he turned the key, but instead, the truck just started right up and I got ready to hop in. Cables were removed, what was left of the hoods was closed, and the rescue wreck with its two unsavoury occupants proceeded to back out onto the road. At which point it stalled. Since our vehicle was still going, we went through the same procedure all over again, except this time *we* jumped *their* battery. I suspect this was how people used to keep their fires going back in ancient times. Hopefully, there was always somebody with a few glowing embers to spare. (Maybe that was what caused the mysterious end of the Mayan civilization. One day everybody's fires just went out at the same time. Rather than going to the trouble of starting a new one from scratch, everybody just up and left, in search of a jump-start from some neighbouring civilization.)

Anyway, my nightmarish fear of being in a symbiotic relationship of perpetual battery-jumping with these five guys for the rest of my life was soon put to rest when our noble little truck lurched out onto the road with Rico and me clinging to it for dear life. In a desperate effort to keep the thing from falling apart beneath us, I spent the whole hour-long journey with my teeth and fists clenched. I guess it worked because that clattering wreck of a truck didn't stall and it didn't run out of gas, and after a few stops to wipe the rain off the windshield because of non-functioning wipers, we got to San Luis in one piece. You know those TV ads that show Mexico as a place of blue sky, hot beaches, and grandiose resorts? This was not like that. This was more like being in the mountains of Uzbekistan, in the middle of a slush storm, on a dying horse.

The rest of that day is mostly missing from my memory bank. I'm pretty sure I went to a bakery and ate thirty or forty cheesecake tarts, and I must have spent the night at the Parras Hotel again because I certainly woke up there the next morning, but apart from that, who knows? Maybe I won and lost several fortunes playing baccarat with Empress Carlota's mad grandnephew in his secluded mountain villa built on the site of an old Aztec sacrificial altar. But all I can remember for sure is that I got up briefly in the night to have a hot shower on account of how cold the room was, and that the water ran out almost immediately, and that there was only a thin little hand towel to dry myself off with, and that I ended up having to get back into bed still half wet and even colder than before, when all was said and done.

The next morning, I had no difficulty getting up. I was desperate to find a coffee and some place warm to drink it. I decided the bus depot was my best bet, so I quickly gathered my stuff together, shoved some leftover ham and a bun into my face, and scurried off.

Like the day before, it was almost as cold inside the bus depot as out, but after a couple of hot cups of very bad – but all the same greatly appreciated – coffee, I decided to try and salvage something useful from this rather absurd little adventure. I decided to go to Pozos again, that all-but-deserted mining town of ruins and rubble, and spend a few hours slowly wandering its eery streets, trying to see if I could harvest some half-decent pictures with my camera.

I stepped off the bus at the edge of the odd little town and started to cut directly across an area of ground strewn with crumbled walls and lonely, free-standing archways. For the most part, the remnants of the old buildings in this area were so scant and scattered that it was difficult to imagine them as buildings at all. They were mostly like what a deep-sea diver might see in the waters off the coast of Greece – lots of short, uneven walls, a sprinkling of debris all around, and here and there a toppled pillar lying at an odd angle. I shamelessly snapped pictures of anything and everything that held even the vaguest promise of being any good, and I'm sure I must have seemed an utter fool to all the goats and chickens that called all that stuff home. The light in Pozos was crystal clear as usual, and the golden colour of the old structures was beautifully balanced by the brilliant blue sky. I was in photographer's heaven; my camera and I devoured it.

Finally, about two hours later and pretty much satiated, I got myself back to the main street of town and started heading towards the little central jardín. There are brass door knockers found throughout this part of Mexico that are both beautiful and slightly bizarre. They look like a woman's severed hand gracefully dangling in mid-air with an apple in its grip. I never did find anyone who could explain their significance to me – my own suspicion is that they have none. They simply project a powerful, mystical image that somehow seems totally appropriate mounted on a door. While walking along Pozos' narrow little main street, I spotted a wonderful old example of one of these on a badly weathered door and stopped to take a picture. Eyes and hands glued to my camera, I moved to within about eighteen inches of the knocker and very carefully started to focus my lens. Just as I was about to take the picture, a giant skeleton key (and I mean giant, this thing was about ten inches long) slid slowly through the left of my camera frame and into the keyhole of the door. I stood back abruptly, and immediately started to apologize to the small elderly woman who was smiling at me and holding the key. I felt as if I'd been caught doing something naughty and was about to withdraw, babbling my usual collection of obsequious Spanish disclaimers, when the woman motioned as if to invite me in. She had a companion beside her, probably her maid, who responded to my perplexed look by nodding with encouragement. The door was opened, and the three of us stepped inside.

From the outside, the house just looked like one segment of the long, bashed and battered wall that lined the main street of Pozos.

But inside, it sprang to life like a pop-up book of a miniature hacienda. We passed through the little darkened hallway and then came out into a classic Mexican courtyard. It had a little fountain, lots of cheery potted plants, and a half-dozen inviting doorways leading to other parts of the house. She led me through one of these doorways and we emerged into what can only be described as a museum exhibit designed to extol the richness and splendour of the nineteenth century. The furniture looked like something Sarah Bernhardt would have draped herself across – all ornately detailed and upholstered in deep crimson plush velvet. Old family photos were everywhere, crowding the tops of tables and fighting for space on the walls. There were silver candelabras, a baby grand piano, gilded mirrors, a wonderful old wind-up gramophone, and several large family portraits painted in oils. The room must have been twenty-five feet long, huge for a Mexican home. Clearly, the room was never used anymore. And yet it was also clear by the way the señora escorted me around it that it wasn't just for show, either. It was a place where an old lady could stash away her memories; a way perhaps of keeping near to her the loved ones she had lost.

She asked me if I would stay for a cup of coffee, and I eagerly agreed. I felt as honoured as if the invitation had come directly from a queen.

After they gave me a quick tour of a couple of small but elegantly furnished downstairs bedrooms, she and her maid led me into a tiny kitchen and sat me down at a table that almost took up the entire room. There were hundreds of small, colourful, hand-decorated mugs and vases perched on specially made arched ledges on every wall. I was being treated as a privileged guest and I relished every moment of it.

A slightly uncomfortable silence settled on the three of us but I craved to find out more about this woman's life so I began to erupt with little Spanish phrases that burst into the quiet space like perky little belches, and the old woman began to look extremely confused. If I'd been barking, she couldn't have looked more surprised. On the other hand, her maid nodded and smiled and seemed to understand every word I said. So she translated for the old woman. The odd thing was that, I swear, the maid said exactly what I had just said, and in precisely the same way.

Imagine sitting at a table with two women. You look straight at one of the women and say, "My name is Stephen," and then she frowns and turns to her friend who says back to her, "He says his name is Stephen," and then the first woman nods and turns her head back towards you and gives you a big smile. Then the whole process begins again.

"I live in Canada," you say.

Old woman turns to her friend.

"He lives in Canada," the maid says.

Old woman turns back to you and smiles, awaiting your next piece of wisdom.

This is a phenomenon I have experienced elsewhere in Mexico, and it has always intrigued me. As you might expect by now, I have a theory about it.

I've heard that it's very dangerous to be a pedestrian in Denmark. You see, Denmark is an orderly society where people don't do things they're not supposed to, so if there is a pedestrian crossing the road where he shouldn't be crossing the road, well then he can't really be there at all, can he, because no one would do such a thing in Denmark. So the drivers feel free to just plow on right through the poor fellow because, you see, he isn't really there. Or something like that. Anyway, it's my belief that there are many Mexicans who believe that whatever a foreigner says must be unfathomable, because foreigners are supposed to be unfathomable. The fact that they may be speaking simple straightforward phrases in very plain Spanish is beside the point. Like with the Danes, a Mexican's fundamental belief about a situation carries far more weight than the reality of it. Anyway, that's my theory and I'm stickin' to it.

Eventually, I gleaned that the old woman was presently a resident of Mexico City, and that this had been the original family home. From time to time, she liked to get away from all the crime and pollution of the capital and touch base again with the gentler side of rural Mexico. Her visits also gave her a chance to make sure things were okay in the house and maybe to spend a little time at one of the lovely local churches. But while I listened to her talk, I realized how accustomed I had become to seeing Mexicans in large family groups. It made her seem very small and lonely sitting there beside her maid. I wondered if she had only this house full of memories to help her round out her life and comfort her in her later years.

At one point just before I left, when the old lady was out of the room for a moment, I asked the maid whether the señora had any children. Her response resonated with a pathos that seemed particularly poignant coming from the lips of a Mexican:

"No. Ella es sola." No. She is alone.

Chapter 10

Our visit to Querétaro was a little rough. But not nearly as rough as it was for Emperor Maximilian. They *executed* him.

For those of you not familiar with the emperor's tragi-comical Mexican vacation, here's a little taste.

The French had a bit of a last-minute panic in 1862 when they realized that everybody else had managed to acquire lots of scrumptious colonies, and somehow *their* colonial cupboard was looking horribly bare. Particularly irksome was North America where they had at one time had a significant presence, but where, by the mid-1800s, everything had been pretty much gobbled up by Britain, America, and Mexico. So while Mexico was going through one of its many fits of political chaos (this one induced by General Santa Ana's abysmal reign of stupidity which gave away much of the country to the Americans and left Mexico with a lovely monument to his amputated leg), the French invaded. They took Mexico City without much difficulty and then proceeded to ask around Europe if anyone would be interested in becoming emperor of this quiet and sunny little backwater of the New World – aristocrats only, please.

One gets the impression that Ferdinand Maximilian, a Habsburg from Austria, was feeling a little bored with the lifestyle of the rich and famous back at home, and that perhaps while sitting around his villa one morning polishing his medals, he said to his wife Carlota, "Look here darling, says here in the paper they're looking for an emperor to rule Mexico. Doesn't that sound like fun? Just think of all the lovely parades."

I'm afraid that might not have been too far from the truth. Maximilian viewed Mexico as a country full of simple peasants who would adore him for his benevolence, and he was totally unaware that there were powerful political forces at work inside and outside of Mexico that would very happily grind him into a bloody pulp, if it served their purposes. Apparently the lessons of the French Revolution and the hazards associated with being an aristocratic bimboy were lost on poor old Ferdinand. When it came to the art of diplomacy, "Can't we all just try and get along?" was as sophisticated as Ferdinand ever got.

The conservatives in Mexico consisted primarily of the hacienda owners and the Church. In 1861, Benito Juarez, a full-blooded Zapotec Indian, started to make life uncomfortable for them when he was elected president and immediately passed the Reform Laws, effectively nationalizing vast quantities of valuable land belonging to the Church. The conservatives welcomed Maximilian with open arms thinking that he would do his best to undo this evil deed. But Maximilian, in an attempt to be loved by his adoring masses, refused to get involved. (He was also very busy organizing all those annoying little masked balls and attending to Carlota's growing list of palace renovation projects.) So, for starters, Maximilian had the conservatives mad at him. Then in 1866 his friends the French abandoned him when the Americans, who were no longer constrained by their costly civil war, suggested in no uncertain terms that the French should really go home now and mind their own business. (Another reason historians have suggested for the departure of the French, and I didn't make this up, was because Napoleon III had developed terrible stomach ulcers and the withdrawal of the troops was ordered by his doctors as a way of relieving his stress.)

But wouldn't you know it, Max's biggest problem wasn't all this geopolitical manoeuvring that was taking place all around him. No. His biggest problem was his mother. He had begun to sense that things weren't going well and was actually contemplating abdication and a return to Europe, which would have meant his salvation, when his mother apparently told him something of which he had been hitherto unaware:

"Habsburgs," she declared, "never abdicate."

Well thanks a lot Mom, nice timing!

Without French support, Maximilian's regime was doomed, and on June 19, 1867, on a hill overlooking Querétaro, he was executed in the manner most befitting a person of his high rank: by firing squad. For his last request he asked that they please try not to hit him in the face, he wanted his mother to see him at his very best. (Honestly, that's really what he said.)

As for Carlota, she returned to her birthplace, Belgium, and lived in seclusion for sixty years until her death in 1927. The Encyclopaedia Britannica says that she suffered a "profound emotional collapse" (Britannica-speak for "went totally bonkers") after the execution of Ferdinand and it has been said that she spent much of those sixty years rowing in circles around her castle moat, trying to return to her beloved Mexico. Comparatively speaking, our current flock of royal twits, the Windsors, actually look pretty good.

We got off the bus in the neat and tidy little city of Querétaro and stood there on the sidewalk like two lost sacks of potatoes. You see, the night before, back in San Miguel, I had carefully cut out the appropriate pages in our guidebook covering Querétaro so I wouldn't have to bring the whole book, which weighed about as much as a medium-sized turkey. Then, in the morning, instead of packing them in my bag, I had left them there on the kitchen table. Since I couldn't phone them up and ask them where the hell we were supposed stay in Querétaro, we just stood there, packs on our backs, looking as if Scotty had got the co-ordinates wrong when he'd attempted to beam us down.

Then we made another mistake: we asked for directions to a cheap hotel. After a very nice lady who'd probably never been to Querétaro before in her entire life gave us some directions, we found ourselves heading back out of town towards the highway. Apparently I had neglected to make it clear to her that we wanted a cheap hotel *and* we wanted it to be in Querétaro. At any rate, after inquiring at one hotel on the outskirts where they told us a room would cost about $200 more than we wanted to pay, we turned right around again and headed back into town.

Our packs were heavy; it was hot; we didn't pass a single hotel on our way back into town; we dared not ask anybody for directions again. Somewhere between the Fifth of May and the Sixteenth of

September – both names of avenues – we had what Hercule Poirot would have called a "crise de nerfs." We basically suffered an emotional meltdown. There was a little torta place on a nearby corner and it was all we could do to slowly drag ourselves over to it and flop down despondently at one of their outside tables. It took several fresh, greasy, ham and cheese tortas and a few ice-cold bottles of Coca-Cola to nurse us gradually back to life, but we finally did recover somewhat and mustered the strength to turn to the man at the table next to us and ask, one last time, for directions to a nice cheap hotel. We took him at his word and immediately hopped into a cab.

It didn't delight me that the cab to our recommended hotel appeared to be taking us right back out of town again, and it was frustrating that, on the way out, the cab was driving right past dozens of exactly the sort of hotels we were looking for, but we were past caring. After the cab driver deposited us on the outskirts of town again, in front of an overpriced American-style motel called the Flamingo Inn, we just walked straight up to the front desk and got ready to say whatever was necessary in order to get ourselves a room.

"Can I help you?" said the clerk.

"Yes."

"Do you want a room?"

"Yes, yes."

"Can it be any room, even an awful, loud, smelly one?"

"Yes, oh yes, thank you."

"Will you pay an outrageously large amount of money for this horrible stinky room?"

"Oh God, yes. Yes. Yes."

"Sign here, please."

Our room was fine as it turned out, and after a brief lie-down, we went out to see the town.

We decided to each do some exploring on our own and then meet back at the Museo de Arte, a stunning piece of architecture originally built as a monastery back in the 1700s.

Unlike San Miguel where the cobblestones are imbedded right into the crumbly ground, Querétaro has used tiles stuck in cement as its basic road surface, and so Querétaro has avoided the excessive dust so prevalent in San Miguel and other Mexican towns. So I decided to take advantage of the clean air and the sunny day to walk out and have a look at a couple of Querétaro's most interesting attractions: the Aqueduct and the Ex-Convent of Santa Cruz – Maximilian's final residence.

When I eventually reached the Aqueduct lookout, I gazed out over it and was both impressed and disappointed. The Aqueduct itself was a magnificent thing. There were seventy-four arches in total, spaced fifteen meters apart and standing as high as twenty-three meters tall, and they were strung out in a straight line eight kilometers long. The arches stretched diagonally across a plain and looked like a column of marching giants carrying a long mythical serpent. But unfortunately, the view was almost completely destroyed by the clutter of unrestricted urban sprawl that overwhelmed it. It looked like an L.A. freeway, not a national historic treasure. Very sad.

The guy who built it was called the Marqués de la Villa del Villar del Aguila (Juan to his friends), and everybody thought he was nuts to even try. The locals called it "Don Juan's Folly" behind his back.

Back in the 1700s, if you wanted to build a great big, gold-encrusted church in town, even though they already had twenty or thirty others, no one thought anything of it. But if you wanted to build an aqueduct to bring desperately needed water to a parched town like Querétaro, people laughed at you. The Marqués never let his determination flag, however, and in addition to paying vast sums of money for the project, he also supervised the construction and even put in time laying a few of the stones himself.

Anyway, on October 17, 1738, twelve years after the Marqués began his great project, the town of Querétaro erupted in a frenzy of celebration as the town's twelve public and sixty private fountains all began to gush and gurgle from the plenteous flow of water that now surged into them. Unfortunately, poor Juan never made it to the party. He died just before the Aqueduct was completed.

The Ex-Convent of Santa Cruz was right next to the Aqueduct, so I walked over to take a look. (The term "ex-convent" reveals much about the prickly relationship that has existed in Mexico for decades, if not centuries, between the Church and the State. After the 1917 Constitution, convents officially became ex-convents in order to make it perfectly clear how the State now felt about the Church. Churches and Church properties were nationalized and heavy restrictions were placed on many aspects of their activities. Priests, for instance, were not allowed to appear in public dressed in their vestments.)

I really wanted to see the tree inside the ex-convent that apparently had cross-shaped thorns and was said to have grown from the walking stick of a saintly priest, but the big wooden door of the main entrance wouldn't budge when I pushed against it. A sign attached to it said, "Closed Mondays."

"Well worth the visit," my guidebook had said. "Open Monday to Friday, 9 to 6; Saturday and Sunday, 11 to 6," my guidebook had said. You know those pages I tore out and left on the table back in San Miguel? Fire starter.

So now that I am racked with guilt about not being able to tell you one darned thing about the inside of the ex-convent, I will try and appease your testiness somewhat by offering a couple of little stories instead.

On this site, in 1531, the Otomi Indians, armed with bows and arrows, were on the verge of being massacred by the Spanish, armed with blunderbusses and cannons, when the Indians made a perfectly reasonable suggestion, from their point of view:

"Say, why don't we just settle the whole thing by fighting with bare fists?"

But when the Spaniards said, "No thanks, we'd rather just blast you all to smithereens," suddenly, Saint James made one of his rare public appearances and materialized in the clouds above the battlefield with a red and gold cross in his hand. Well, that was all a bit too much for the Indians, I'm afraid, who then followed their pragmatic instincts, said, "Okay you win," and decided to convert to Christianity en masse, right then and there on the spot.

There's also a little Maximilian Moment tied to the ex-convent as well. Dear old Maximilian used the convent as his headquarters and fort during his last stand against the forces of Benito Juarez in 1867. The story goes that during the fighting, he used to sit on a curb outside the convent hoping that some lucky sniper's bullet would hit him and award him the glorious military death he (and no doubt his mother) yearned for. Max didn't really get the war thing.

After walking back through town, I found myself sitting on a concrete step, with my back against the Museo de Arte, waiting for Robyn and thinking what a nice day this had turned out to be after all, when a pigeon with real issues maliciously unloaded a deluge of pigeon poop onto my head, shoulder, arm, hand, and camera. In retrospect, it was a stupid place to sit. In retrospect one should always be vigilant when in urban centres not to stand beside buildings where pigeons roost. But I live in the country, so what do I know? The thing about it is that one feels so utterly insulted by such a thing, and retribution is damn near impossible. Have you ever noticed there never seem to be any pigeons around when *you* want to dump on *them*?

I had cleaned up most of the revolting mess by the time Robyn arrived, and, bless her heart, she did try admirably to assuage my pouty mood, but when it became clear that I was having none of it, she dragged me across the street to a pretty little restaurant in hopes that a nice cup of tea might have better luck than she did.

Instead things just got worse. Their first attempt at tea arrived in the form of a cup of lukewarm milk with a tea bag dangling in it. For an encore, the scowling waitress brought me a cup of hot water with a bag of *cinnamon* tea in it. Since they were obviously in cahoots with the pigeons, and the kind of retribution I had in mind would have been a very bad idea indeed, we left in a huff, and headed back to the hotel.

A traveller's life is not always a happy life. Sometimes it can be a bit trying. But when things get rough, and you find yourself yearning to be anywhere else but where you are, I have discovered there is one last desperate measure you can take to get yourself back on track. You must follow the recipe exactly:

-order in pizza

-and watch an Ally McBeal rerun. (Go figure.)

And that's what we did.

Journal, December 19

After a disappointing day yesterday, breakfast at the Cafe Fondo is a real find. It was the hypnotic smell of fresh-ground coffee beans in the street that lured us to it. Inside, it has the bare elegance of a cheap but clean boarding-house room in Paris. No matter where on the planet you are, whenever you find bare light bulbs and sparse decor, combined with high ceilings, chandeliers, classical music and good coffee, an irresistible magnet seems to form that draws intellectuals and students into its grasp. Querétaro appears to be no exception to this rule; we are surrounded by such people.

Our waitress is stiff, but polite, hallmark characteristics of a true Mexican.

New visitors to the Mexican interior invariably find the stiff attitude of their servers to be both rude and annoying, I know I did at first. I was more accustomed to the overly broad smiles and familiarity of our own waiters and waitresses back home. But now I prefer the Mexican way. I enjoy the subtle gestures of respect that flow continuously back and forth between the server and the served. It's like an elegant old dance. As for breakfast, it was delicious. Our scrambled eggs were steaming, the coffee was hot and rich, the bread was oven fresh, and the salsa was homemade. In short, the day was getting off to an excellent start.

Our first stop that morning was the Museo de Arte, the place where I had been so ignominiously treated by the pigeons the day before. Built in the 1770s, it was originally the Monastery of Saint Augustine and basically looks like a pile of arches balanced on a pile of arches around a central patio with a pretty fountain in the middle. In the courtyard there was a small army of serious-looking young people standing on scaffolds who were very carefully repairing the cherubs that adorned the arches. Judging by their gleefully happy but mischievous faces (the cherubs' that is), they were delighted at having been given a new lease on life. Each of the columns supporting the arches resembled the shaft of a kind of baroque totem pole of leaves and cherubs. Perched at the top of each one was the face of a very surprised individual in a headdress, blowing on a long piece of pipe with his arms raised as if he'd just been turned to stone in the midst of a holdup. Quite wonderful really.

The paintings were less wonderful, however. They were mostly modern. One batch showed landscapes with floating spheres drifting across them that had other landscapes painted inside; another consisted mostly of skulls painted inside skulls. There were also several rooms devoted to a collection of very large, old, cracked European works mostly depicting adult saints with children's faces. They may have been great works of art for all we knew, but the juxtaposition of those young faces on those old bodies just gave us the creeps.

We then headed over to the Museo de Ciudad, just a couple of blocks away. As we walked in, the sound of our footsteps apparently disturbed the sleep of the toothless old woman attendant who was nesting on a chair piled high with newspapers just inside the door. She leapt off of them onto the floor as soon as she noticed us and immediately began babbling her prepared spiel starting, I'm sure, from whatever point she had left off at with her last visitors. It felt a little as if we'd just woken up Rip Van Winkle's mother.

Being about the height of a young child, her standing up actually made her shorter than when she'd been sitting on the newspapers, but her presence was no less commanding all the same. She made quite an adorable picture standing there with her old-fashioned, floor-length skirt all fanned out like a pleated lamp shade while she prattled on in impeccable English about someone called Sr. Obregon. Once started, she was apparently impossible to stop, but we were in no rush, so we gave her full rein.

From her point of view, Sr. Obregon was a kind of modern-day saint. One whole section of the museum, her section, had been converted into a sort of shrine to him. It wasn't that he healed the sick or saw visions of the Virgin Mary or anything. No, his greatness was based on the fact that he was a hometown boy who had made it big by becoming the president of Coca-Cola for Mexico. In Mexico, for some reason, the presidency of Coca-Cola has become an office of quasi-mystical proportions, second in importance only to the presidency of the country itself. Indeed, the current president of Mexico, Vicente Fox, owes much of his popularity to the fact that he, too, was once the president of Coca-Cola.

But our little old lady then said something that may have shed a little ray of light onto why Coca-Cola and their presidents should be held in such high regard. According to the old lady, the original Coke formula was bought from a poor Indian near Morelos for a pittance by an American who then took it to the States and made his fortune with it. This has, in fact, become a very widely held popular myth in Mexico, and probably owes much of its longevity to the emotional sense of injustice that it engenders. The theme of Americans as exploiters is an often-recurring one in Mexico.

But like any good myth, the strength of it lies in the fact that it could actually be true. The recipe was first created by a morphine addict called John Styth Pemberton in 1885, who said he based the recipe on a famous drink of the day called Vin Mariani. But he did fight in the Mexico-American wars and so he could very easily have picked up the recipe in Mexico during that period.

When she finally came to the end of her spiel, we thanked her, got her to pose for a couple of pictures, and then left her sitting there on top of her newspapers like a little troll doll. For our part, we were off to another museum, this time the Museo Regional de Querétaro.

On entering this museum we were greeted by a guard with a sub-machine gun, which, I can tell you, sure impressed the hell out of me. Then we turned the corner into the main hall and were stopped in our tracks by the sight of a room full of priceless ceramics from Mexico's pre-Columbian past. It was actually like a scene straight out of *Mission Impossible*. The pottery was all displayed out in the open without the use of any glass cases and we could have reached out and touched some of them had it not been for the plethora of infra-red light beams that criss-crossed the room (and that other little problem of the guy with the sub-machine gun). So Robyn and I were standing back at a discreet distance enjoying the impressive display of around fifty or sixty pieces when another couple came in behind us. I was quite engrossed in my very respectful viewing of the pottery when I happened to hear off to one side the man explaining to his wife with great glee about how the infrared light beams worked. I then turned my head to share a little cordial smile with them and saw with abject horror that his finger was slowly wiggling like a curious worm towards one of the pots as if it were guided by some demonic force. My mouth opened, my eyes popped, and I was about to rush over and haul him to the ground, when an ear-shattering alarm went off and the guy with the gun came running across the room full tilt. As the stunned gentleman with the wandering finger was frozen to the spot by these events like some poor victim of Mr. Freeze's laser-powered cold gun, the guard could see that the artifacts were in no immediate danger and ran off to deal with the alarm. He returned a few moments later with his gun in his hand (guns bring such clarity to everything) and gave a little reprimand to our petrified transgressor, but by the look on the guy's wife's face, she had every intention of dealing with him big-time later on, herself.

This little episode out of the way, we moved on to the next section of the museum where there were several excellent and very realistic dioramas of the early Indians busily preoccupied with the daily battle of keeping body and soul together six thousand years ago. In particular, there was a fine display of gleaming, black obsidian arrowheads and knives with plaques set alongside them that outlined in detail how the control of the obsidian market was a major source of power for the Aztecs. They were written in Spanish only, as is the habit in most of the museums in Mexico, but it was very interesting stuff if you could muddle through the translation.

Then farther along the hall we came to an incredible room full of photographs of Indians taken just prior to their first contact with Europeans. My first thought, never my best, was how lucky for posterity that one of them had a camera. My second thought, a considerable improvement over the first, was that unless Joseph-Nicéphore Niépce, the man who invented photography in 1826, took a wrong turn somewhere in the fourth dimension, these pictures couldn't have been taken prior to the arrival of Cortés (1519), and were probably taken more like around 1920.

And that's the thing about Mexico. You can take a two-hour drive south from the most advanced high-tech civilization in the world, the United States, and still find people living in Mexico pretty much the same way they did thousands of years ago. Take a trip to a small rural village anywhere in the heart of Mexico, and you'll still find people grinding their corn with primitive stone tools, pressing their tortillas by hand, and cooking them over simple wood fires.

I was looking at another set of photographs, art photos of Mexican urban life in the Thirties, when herds of costumed children with parents attached to them started streaming past me on their way to an auditorium next door. Evidently, they were on their way to a Christmas pageant – but by the looks of it, a Christmas pageant

Mexican-style, meaning they would probably be putting Baby Barney into the manger and having him visited by the four wise Mutant Ninja Turtles.

But what was really stunning about this whole scene wasn't how the *kids* were dressed, it was how their *parents* were dressed. These were not your average Mexicans dressed in cowboy hats and jeans; these people were wealthy. The way they walked, their finely tailored clothes, and I'm sure their cars as well – all attested to the fact that they were from the privileged class.

The contrast with the museum photos showing the primitive living conditions of the Indians of Mexico around the turn of the century, conditions that still exist to this day, was startling. In the rest of North America, the classes tend to blur at the edges a little, to change more gradually from one group into the next. But in Mexico, the rich and the poor are sharply defined and rarely ever even come into contact with one another. For the traveller who ventures into the barren, interior regions of Mexico, it's a little hard to figure out where these rich people can extract any wealth from at all, but they do, and their wealth is considerable.

In recent times, the Mexican elite have obtained most of their wealth from a very short list: oil and tourism. Manufacturing in the maquilladoras on the northern boundary with the U.S. is gaining rapidly in importance, but it is still dwarfed by the other two. But the reason for the existence of the super-rich in Mexico isn't just that oil and tourism are successful industries. It's also that the wealth from them has been allowed to concentrate in the hands of a small elite because of Mexico's policy of centralization.

For decades, until the arrival of Vicente Fox on the scene, the president of the country belonged to the all-powerful PRI party and he would usually handpick the PRI candidates who were chosen to run for the position of state governor. These men were invariably cronies of the president, often with no connection at all to the state they were intended to represent. All the money from the regions – Chiapas oil money and Yucatan tourism dollars are good examples – was concentrated back into the hands of a small elite, an elite based in Mexico City. Another example of this centralization is that, until recently, it was practically impossible to fly anywhere within the boundaries of Mexico without first flying into Mexico

City. This ensured that most of the high-paying airline industry jobs stayed right there in the capital city. The wealth of the privileged in small cities like Querétaro, almost invariably can be shown to be the result of the connections those people maintain with influential friends and businesses in Mexico City.

Using the regions as a source of wealth is, of course, nothing new. Spain used Mexico in the same way, and of course, in the ancient world, all roads led to Rome. But in the absence of a strong and legitimate democracy, the situation can become both absurd and obscene. And that is what has happened in Mexico.

We finished the museum's loop tour, very impressed with everything we'd seen, and walked outside and caught a local bus to the main terminal at the edge of town. We were resting in front of a TV monitor in the cafeteria, mustering strength for the long bus ride back to San Miguel, when a game show called *How Many Stupid Things Can We Make My Boyfriend Do Before He Pulls Out AN AK-47 And Wastes Us All* was interrupted, and the network switched to live coverage of the great volcano, Popocatépetl, in the midst of a violent eruption. We were getting a little freaked out by the pictures and probably could have worked up a real good panic attack given a few more minutes of flowing lava, when the folks back at the TV station, who after all know what their audiences like best, switched back to the boyfriend show where, because he had guessed the wrong answer to a question, he was now having to dance alone in the centre of the stage with his pants pulled down around his ankles. I would happily have enjoyed a little lunch and watched the rest of the show, but Robyn insisted on dragging me off. Apparently our bus was about to depart.

Chapter 11

Journal, December 20

Got home to our apartment and practically froze to death last night. Apparently, it's time for drastic measures.

I probably can't adequately express to you how deeply and thoroughly the bitter cold of San Miguel had penetrated our bones by the third week of December. I suppose somewhere deep in our chests there was still a minuscule, pea-sized piece of flesh that was still slightly lukewarm, but I assure you that the rest of our bodies were like frozen stone. Our thought processes were functioning so badly, and on such a primitive level, that simple things like turning a door knob in order to get through a door required a degree of cognitive sophistication that we no longer possessed. Thus you would often see us around town pushing and pulling angrily on recalcitrant doors. We wore everything to bed – every toque, scarf, shirt, sock and jacket – and still we froze.

It was useless to go out and buy a heater for our room: it would have been like trying to heat an airplane hanger with a candle. Wood for our fireplace was far too expensive and the heat would have gone flying out of all the unclosable windows anyway.

It occurred to us from time to time that *IF WE'D WANTED TO BE COLD, WE COULD'VE STAYED HOME IN CANADA!* But alas, even that rant was poorly conceived. We would have been warmer back in Canada. There, people had insulated houses and efficient heating systems. In San Miguel, people didn't heat their houses, and instead of a wind-chill factor to contend with, there was a concrete-chill factor instead, from all the concrete in the floors and walls. I'd take a log cabin in the Yukon over a concrete icebox in San Miguel anytime, believe me.

And the other problem was that there was no relief from it. Everything in town was cold. The restaurants were cold, the shower was cold, our beds were cold. Basically, we were in big trouble. A pair of electric blankets would probably have gone a long way towards fixing the problem, but none of the stores had any, and I know this because I tried them all. (I later discovered that most of the local gringos owned electric blankets on the sly, but for fear of the riots that might ensue if the information leaked out, kept absolutely mum about them.)

So Robyn and I found ourselves hanging out at the Laughing Muffin a lot, where there was at least a slight residue of warmth emanating from the ovens. One morning we were drinking mugful after mugful of coffee, the caffeine in our blood reaching levels never before attempted by anyone, when our brains had a brief moment of lucidity, and we hatched a plan to leave San Miguel on January 1 and spend a month, anywhere hot, somewhere on the coast.

Billy, the owner of the café, was sitting with one of the regular old hands at a nearby table when I beckoned him over to join us for a minute so I could tap him for suggestions on where we should go. Billy was a very nice, child-like guy in his late twenties from Kentucky who was under the misguided perception that he could some day turn his little café into a money-making proposition. He had that kind of forced Yankee optimism that announces to one and all that any hare-brained idea can succeed if you just want it badly enough. Meanwhile, Billy had a lousy location in a small niche market for a low-priced product that took too much time to prepare. I am reminded of a Peanuts cartoon where a very serious and dignified Lucy shakes hands with Charlie Brown after he tells her of his latest scheme, and she says flatly, "That was my good-luck-you're-going-to-need-it handshake, Charlie Brown," and then walks away.

But for information about budget holiday destinations in Mexico, Billy's your boy – and *that* he gives away for free.

He sidled over to our table and gave us one of his sly, sexy smiles – the ones that made him look as if he was about to goose somebody.

"So you're looking for a little fun in the sun."

I stopped my teeth from chattering just long enough to say, "Please boss, help us."

"What kind of a place are you looking for?"

"Something very cheap, and warm but not too horribly hot."

"Hey, a bowl of soup would do that for you. Have you tried our— No, huh? Okay. But this place I'm going to tell you about is very, very special. I expect you guys to be very, very respectful of it. Okay?"

"Yez boss."

"Okay." He pulled out a piece of paper and started writing on it. "There's a beach almost directly west of here called Paraiso – it'll take you about a day to get there by bus. There are only two hotels and the one I stay at is called the CIA, as in the spy dudes, and it'll cost you about $10 a day." He clandestinely passed the paper across the table to me.

"It used to be called the Valencia and its name was painted across the front wall of the hotel in large letters but a few years ago half of the hotel collapsed, just fell away, disintegrated, and now all that remains of the name are the last three letters, C-I-A. You'll like it."

"Is it warm?"

"Oh yes, and there's a big black sand beach stretching out in both directions as far as the eye can see."

"But it's warm right?"

"Oh yeah, and you can watch the pelicans diving for fish, and there's phosphorescence in the water at night."

"It's warm, you're sure it's warm?"

"IT'S WARM, ALREADY!"

I turned to Robyn, "He said it's warm."

She cracked a feeble smile, "I think you're right, I think that's what he said. Sounds good, eh?"

"Sounds warm."

As I folded up my precious bit of paper with the word "Paraiso" on it ("paraiso" is Spanish for "paradise") and stuffed it in my wallet, I felt like one of those pathetic refugees from the movie *Casablanca* who'd just been given one of the prized letters of transit. Finally, we would be freed from San Miguel's icy grip.

We informed Isadora that although we were going away for a month, we would return in February, and so as to avoid any possible screw-ups, I paid her in advance and got a receipt. Nothing cheered Isadora up quite so much as being given money, at least nothing I had been party to, and all aglow with her newfound wealth, she invited Robyn and me to join her and a few friends to a pot luck dinner on Christmas Eve. I told her I wouldn't miss any party of hers for all the tea in Mexico, and she beamed with satisfaction.

I spent much of that last week and a half wandering the streets of San Miguel with my camera, soaking up as much of it as I could before we left. Robyn was deeply immersed in one of her craft projects – the latest one being the construction of an elaborately decorated papier-mâché teapot – so my absences went largely unnoticed. Boredom had been a big concern of ours on such a long trip as this, but happily it rarely reared its head. And for that we also had to thank San Miguel itself, for the city was truly awash in art and music and festivals and restaurants and interesting people, and I would think even a head of lettuce would have had trouble getting bored there.

Most of my wanderings were guided by the lists that periodically materialized in my notebook. These lists usually consisted of such earth-shatteringly important items as fresh tortillas, a #2B pencil, two bags of peanuts with lime, and a Cadbury's chocolate bar. It quite delighted me to think that, with Mexico's help, we had cast off the complexities of our former lives and managed to pare down our needs to a handful of these almost child-like "essentials." The ability to live simply was, so far, the greatest gift we'd been given by this place.

There are little shops all over San Miguel that all look much the same when you first visit them. They are little general stores with lots of junk food and a few of the basics like eggs and bread. But in fact, each one often has something that is their particular specialty. The short, stocky, grey-haired guy in the shop across the street had excellent fruit and veggies, a good assortment of chips, and an entertaining parrot named Pedro, but he didn't usually have much else that was on our list. He had an almost military brusqueness about him, always answering my enquiries with the sort of clipped response more often associated with boot camp. I would ask him if he had something, and he, with a very serious look on his face and a moustache to match, would stand there at attention behind the counter and declare emphatically, "Sí, señor!" God, I never would have thought buying an avocado could be such a lift to one's self-esteem.

For our chocolate bars we had to walk a couple of blocks down a very steep street called Hospicio. This little store was usually attended by a rather plain-looking and very reserved teenage girl who would always look at me with absolute terror in her eyes when she realized that I, a gringo, was to be her next customer. She would remain absolutely straight-faced as I mercilessly butchered her language in a lame attempt to tell her that I dearly wanted to buy the two precious Cadbury's chocolate bars that were right there on the rack behind her. Then, after I'd finished my speech, leaving nothing but a few twitching adjectives languishing on the floor, she would blush and break into a lovely, shy, forgiving smile, as if she had just watched me dancing with my jeans pulled down around my ankles like on one of those stupid game shows we'd seen in Querétaro. It was a smile that made me feel as if I must have one of my baby photographs stuck to my forehead by mistake.

Then we would do our little bit of commerce and I'd be on my way. But the real transaction between us occurred when we traded those smiles of mutual embarrassment. The chocolate bars were really just an excuse.

For chickens, I always went to the central mercado or market. Most of the gringos in San Miguel shop at a nice sterile supermarket on the outskirts of town called Gigante, and although we did go there occasionally, we preferred the mercado, where things were a lot livelier: visually, sonically, and microbially. Several years prior to this, it would have taken a lot of nerve for this Canadian boy to purchase and later consume his first dead chicken that had been lying around in the Mexican heat on an open counter for God-only-knows how many days. But since that time, I had rationalized that even at home our chickens were chronically contaminated with one damn thing or another, so if we were vigilant, and always cooked the bejesus out of everything, we should be okay.

To get to the mercado from our place, I had to first pass through the centre of San Miguel – a very safe and touristy place full of chichi restaurants and expensive gift shops – and then all of a sudden, I'd round a corner on one of those narrow raised sidewalks, and I'd find myself surrounded by a crush of busy Mexicans going about their day's work in a totally different universe.

The market district of San Miguel was always packed with people: people piling onto smoke-spewing buses; lining up at the butcher's; clogging up the sidewalks with carts of produce; policemen directing traffic with whistles that blew so constantly you never knew what they indicated; old people begging; beautiful teenagers in school uniforms laughing; people selling sunglasses; people selling electrical extension cords strung around their bodies like snakes; everybody eating; everybody selling; people with small bags of salsa-soaked jicama; people hauling big sacks of puffed-up cheesies; hands holding tacos spilling over with lettuce and beef; hands gripping big plastic cups filled with fresh-fruit licuados; children's faces packed with suckers and gum. The market felt, smelt, and sounded like a living organism and it was strange to think that while this kind of colourful organized chaos was playing itself out all over Mexico, back home in Canada people were cruising smoothly through their antiseptic shopping malls to the hypnotic sounds of mindless Muzak.

Some days when I arrived at my favourite chicken stall, I was so nauseated by the smell of the place that I must have appeared almost as pale as one of the chickens lolling there on a table before me. I would smile feebly at the old lady standing behind her counter – all four feet two of her – and as my eyes strayed to the mighty wooden chopping block, which, like her, was covered in chicken bits, blood, and grease, I did my best not to pass out from the incredible stench. Fortunately for me, since all she sold was chicken, it was unlikely my limited Spanish would get me into too much trouble. I could probably have said, "I'll have a stool sample to go please," and she still would have given me a chicken.

I must admit, though, I was a little thrown the first time I asked her for a chicken because she came back at me with a whole barrage of questions that sounded like a chicken anatomy quiz in

Spanish. But by wiggling and pointing to my various body parts (a performance much admired by the band of giggling onlookers), I managed to convey to her that I wouldn't require the chicken's head or its feet or its feathers or its gills, or its overnight bag even, since we were just planning to eat it anyway thank you very much. When she plopped the chicken into a plastic bag and tossed it down onto the counter for me, her old face crinkled into a smile, and it made me feel more like a busker getting a tip than a shopper making a purchase.

Journal, December 22

Went to Florence's for lunch. She told us that she'd spent the past couple of years caring for her dying mother with whom she'd always been very close.

"But things got a little testy towards the end," said Florence. "I used to try and get her to eat a little something for breakfast, she was starting to waste away, you see. But no, she never seemed to want whatever I had on hand – she always wanted something else – and you know, I was getting pretty strung out with all the work that was involved in taking care of her all on my own. So one morning I couldn't take it any more, and I just said straight out to my very prim and proper mother, 'Do you want fucking eggs or not?'

"My poor frail little mother slowly lifted her head up, and then, with the slightest little twinkle in her eye, said, 'I think some fucking eggs would be lovely, dear, thank you.' "

Journal, December 23

Yesterday morning, I discovered that I had not yet entirely overcome my adolescent fear of being spurned by members of the opposite sex. There is a nice young lady (visualize a teenage, Mexican, Xena the Warrior Princess with braces) who gives me a huge smile every morning from her post at the entrance to her family's pottery shop. I wanted to ask her whether she would consider reading to me in Spanish if I paid her fifty pesos for an hour of reading, and yesterday I got up the nerve to approach her. Hard to believe a grown man would go beet red and start fidgeting nervously with his fingers in a fairly innocuous situation like this, isn't it? But that's what I did. After a few painful moments, I finally managed to spit out my request, and, to my great relief, she didn't reject me outright. She told me to come back later in the afternoon for her decision. Somewhat pleased with having at least partially accomplished my mission, I said that would be fine and started to leave. And then she added that by then her father would be home so she could ask him for his permission.

Permission? Oh God, what a lot of fuss. I didn't ask her to marry me or anything. Did I? Oh dear. Maybe my Spanish was worse than I thought.

Well, as it turned out, not as bad as all that. But when I arrived at the door of the pottery shop around four-thirty, Daddy did have a surprise for me. For my fifty pesos, I would get to spend one enchanted hour in *his* company rather than in his daughter's, and *he* would be the one doing the reading, not her. Well, that would be okay. But I did have one more little thing that was worrying me. The book I was going to ask him to read for me was . . . well it was a Spanish version of a Harlequin Romance. The cover depicted a sexy woman in a negligee and a guy in a tux who was salivating on the woman's shoulder while one of his hands was clearly about to make a mad dash for one of her breasts. I had intended to tear off the offensive cover, but unfortunately had forgotten. I handed Daddy the book and for several long, painful seconds he stared at the lurid picture with the sort of stern expression one usually associates with the likes of Mike Tyson or Adolph Hitler.

My reasoning for choosing that particular book had been that I wanted to learn the common, everyday language of the street, which I figured the Harlequin would provide. I hoped that if I made a tape of someone speaking in that manner, and listened to it repeatedly, I might acquire the knack of separating out individual words from the hail of gunfire that usually flew out of people's mouths. The phrase books I'd been using were fairly useful I guess. But how far into a person's psyche can you really delve with stuff like "The wash-basin is clogged" and "Do you charge for the baby?" Mind you, the Harlequins have their limitations too, I suppose. As an opening line to a stranger in a bus depot, "Your father's guilt or innocence has nothing to do with how I feel about you" also holds a certain risk.

I decided to break the excruciatingly stony silence by explaining my theory to him, and then suddenly his face relaxed, and without further ado, he took me into the back of his shop and we sat down side by side at his very large dining room table.

"I am a cellist," he said. "I understand the importance of training the ear."

Daddy's real name was Rafael, and I have to say, Rafael would not be considered by most people to be an average Mexican. Completely Mexican in his features, he dressed like a bohemian poet, sort of Sancho Panza meets the Left Bank. He wore an old crumpled white jacket, baggy khaki pants, and a very stylish, bright purple shirt. And on his head he wore what looked like a straw version of a park ranger's hat. Rafael did, in fact, play the cello exquisitely; I'd seen and heard him playing many mornings as I passed by his shop.

Well, the scene I had chosen for Rafael to read was one where the two principal romantic characters are meeting for the first time, and Rafael played both parts with great theatricality and conviction. When he spoke the words of the stiff, embittered, single dad, Caleb Reynolds, who was bringing his traumatized son, Adam, to a new daycare after the tragic death of his mother, Rafael's voice was deep and you could feel his anger and his pain. He pounded the table with his fist when he needed to drive home a point. When Rafael reverted back to the female voice of Caitland Rourke, the insecure but sensitive owner of the daycare who was trying to reach out and help these two wounded souls that fate had so unexpectedly dumped on her doorstep, his voice became soft and feminine and higher in pitch and you could feel Caitland's earnest desire to rise to the occasion and make a real difference in someone's life. Rafael became overwhelmed with emotion. The two of us were close to tears.

Ain't it grand the way a simple Canadian boy on holiday in Mexico for five months can end up in the back room of a pottery shop being read a Harlequin Romance by a cello-playing Mexican wearing a Smokey the Bear hat?

I'm sort of sorry I never asked him to teach me how to dance.

Journal, December 31

It's New Year's Eve, and I'm sitting on a bench in the jardín with

Robyn. We decided to take one last walk around it before starting out tomorrow for a month at the beach and hopefully some relief from the bone-chilling cold weather we've been struggling with throughout December. I remember how stunned I was the first time I visited San Miguel's jardín at night because it was darker and quieter than most of the others I'd seen in Mexico. Voices have no echo here and sounds are deadened like in a richly carpeted symphony hall.

Tonight, six pretty teenage girls from Mexico City are standing on the low cement wall that skirts the square while a teenage guy, presumably a friend, takes pictures of them. He is deftly juggling a whole armload of cameras at once and snapping one picture on each of the girls' cameras for them. Their laughter and their playful pushing and shoving make me think they're having more fun taking the pictures than they will ever have looking at them. A second ago, a young boy of about eight on one of those brand new metal scooters flew directly towards us at full speed, and then suddenly veered off at the last moment, like a swooping bird trapped in a house.

"Don't you think a stroll around the jardín would be nice?" I said softly to Robyn as I got up from the bench.

Knowing a rhetorical question when she heard one, Robyn smiled. "Yeah. Sounds good."

The trees in the jardín were trimmed short and square like hedges and they formed a dense canopy overhead completely blocking out the cold, wintry night sky. We were walking into the dark, cave-like heart of the square, a place that was treacherous at sunset when the birds amassed in droves and intimidated everyone with their hysterical Alfred Hitchcock-style screeching. It was quiet now, but a little spooky all the same, a little Gothic. Once inside the tomb of laurels, we found our way by the dim light of Chinese paper lanterns. On either side of us there were nuzzling lovers, each pair a seemingly immobile black form growing like a sculpture out of the black benches. San Miguel is a place simply awash with artistic images. When you leave a San Miguel art gallery and walk out onto the street, it sometimes feels as if you have never really left the gallery at all; that the door leading from the gallery to the street is just another door inside the gallery, leading to another section, another exhibit.

Deep in the very centre of the jardín, there was an ornate wrought-iron gazebo, and inside it, a large nativity scene had been created. These displays are highly revered by the Mexicans, and their devotion to them is a reflection of their kind natures and their deep spirituality, but to me I'm afraid, the scene was very macabre. The baby Jesus was a plastic doll with its eyes closed, and it had the bizarre and somewhat dead appearance of an undressed department store dummy. Angels were hung all around on wires, not entire angels, just severed heads with wings attached to their cheeks. On the one hand I regretted the gulf between a Mexican's perception of these things and mine. But on the other hand I was beginning to realize that the Mexico I experienced in my own head was the only Mexico I'd ever know anyway.

We left the jardín and on the way home we passed by our favourite street vendor, one that sold hamburguesas. I loved watching him work because he tossed and twirled the ketchup and mayonnaise bottles like a Mexican Tom Cruise in the movie *Cocktail*. I looked at his stand carefully because it was one of the many memories of San Miguel that I wanted to take with me to the beach. Two gas lanterns turned his stand into a brilliant pool of light in the midst of the muted voices and soft dark shadows that engulfed the jardín. The people sitting on stools around his stand watched his gripping performance as if they were watching a performer on TV and devoured his burgers with great gusto. His stand was covered by an awning, and printed across it's front was the word "Wonder," a bit of advertising from the supplier of his hamburger buns, but in my mind, a word that summed up the spirit of this strange place perfectly.

Chapter 12

The next morning we found ourselves sailing gracefully up and over beautifully eroded, gold and dusty-green hills in a comfortable Primera Plus bus, while San Miguel slowly faded away behind the overlapping edges of the distant landscape.

We were excited at the prospect of the new adventures that lay ahead of us, and we were quite content to lay back in our seats and let the bus do all of the hard work of travelling for us. We imagined ourselves as pampered passengers on a cruise ship being allowed to lounge on our deck chairs and just take in the day's events as they unfolded, while someone else dealt with all the unpleasant chores of getting us to our destination. Since the risks involved in travelling on a Mexican bus are about on a par with base jumping, a little flight of fancy once in a while serves as a very useful diversion.

We got as far as León, a large industrial town so dismal that the guide books don't even talk about it, when Robyn realized that she had forgotten to bring any Dramamine. Calmly, she explained to me that without some sort of chemical assistance, she would soon be projectile vomiting on everything within a five-foot radius. Since that would very definitely include me, I rushed out into the station, not knowing if I had ten minutes or ten seconds before the bus was due to leave, and I ran madly from shop to shop looking for one that might remotely pass for a drugstore. Finally, a woman running a newsstand directed me towards the baggage-check counter where a young guy who looked about twelve years old had obviously found himself in a job completely beyond his scope. He was irritating several customers at once by trying to get them to see the virtues in the suitcases he had chosen to return to them, even though the suitcases weren't theirs. After what seemed like days and weeks of negotiations, the mêlée finally subsided and the entire mass of suitcases and people made its departure, trundling and grumbling as it went. At last, it was just the kid and I alone at the counter. When he looked across it and saw that I was a gringo, he immediately picked up a broom and tried to sweep his way out of the shop.

I spoke up quickly, "Puede ayudarme, por favor?" (Could you help me, please?) There was no way I was leaving there without a pill. Sheepishly, he inched his way back behind the counter.

I could see through his glass countertop that he sold a selection of about seven different pills and beside each one there was a little card with the name of the pill typed on it. There was no pill beside the Dramamine card.

"Tiene Dramamina?" I said.

He looked into the case and shook his head.

"Tiene algo similar?" I asked hopefully.

At this point, the young guy looked at the various pills in his display and I think I heard him saying under his breath, "Eeny, meeny, miny . . ." His finger would linger on one for a while and then he'd shake his head and say, "Hmm, no, no . . ." and move onto another. I'm sure he would happily have gone on like this all day, but I was starting to panic at the thought of getting back to the platform and finding nothing but a slowly settling cloud of dust where the bus had been, so I asked him if he could be a little quicker please. Very tentatively, the young guy picked out one of the pills. He did it in much the same manner as a person trying to guess which of the shells has the pea under it. With considerable misgivings, I bought it from him.

Now I know you're going to think I was being irresponsible buying a pill from a twelve-year-old baggage clerk when neither of us had the faintest idea what it was for, but in Mexico you rarely get exactly what you're looking for, anyway. A person could spend a profoundly pathetic (and most likely very lonely) couple of months just looking for the right deodorant. So pill shmill, hell they're all supposed to be good for something, right? I ran like mad and got back on the bus and as it was groaning its way out of the station, I turned to Robyn and handed her the pill.

"They didn't have Dramamine, but the guy said this one would work just as well."

And then my dear, sweet, trusting friend Robyn swallowed a pill that for all I knew was for growing bigger, fuller moustaches, and suddenly, I was terrified about what I'd done.

Within about ten minutes, Robyn started to look quite content, and after about twenty, well, she looked more contented than I'd seen her in years, actually. So I turned my head, leaned it against my window, and decided I'd stop worrying and instead spend a little time gazing out at the hilly scrubland we were passing through. After a few minutes, I spotted an extraordinary sight.

"Robyn, look at that huge flock of black and white birds!"

Having slumped down slightly in her seat by now, she leaned into me to have a look, and with her eyes half-shut and a looped-out-of-her-mind grin on her face she said, "Oh yeah, I think they milk that kind don't they?" And then her head flopped over and she fell fast asleep.

I spent much of the rest of the journey engaged in self-flagellation, which is not nearly as much fun as it sounds.

It took us ten hours to get from San Miguel to the Colima state border. Robyn, thankfully, had partially regained consciousness by then and the two of us spent the remainder of the drive into Colima City being bowled over by the spectacular scenery. In the foreground of our view, the terrain was so deeply folded it looked like a giant piece of corrugated cardboard with the outer sheets stripped off. In the distance, set against a clear blue sky streaked with pink and amber sunset clouds, was the dramatic Colima Volcano, complete with plumes of white vapour trailing from its tip. It was spectacular. Apparently God had been buying *his* medication at the León bus terminal as well.

I had spent a good deal of time during our bus ride poring over our guidebook looking for the most highly recommended but still dirt-cheap hotel in Colima. When the book described a place called the Flamingo by saying something like, "If you enjoy listening to ambulance sirens and squealing tires, and don't mind the occasional dead body flying past your window, then this is the place for you," I figured it was our best choice. Everything else in our price range sounded even worse. So, when we reached the bus terminal, I wheelbarrowed Robyn over to a cab, and off we went.

And you know it wasn't too bad. It was a small high-rise-style hotel about five stories tall, probably built in the 1960s. Admittedly, the scowling old woman at the front desk with the cigarette stub glued to her lower lip was so intent on tapping away at her archaic adding machine that she only grudgingly stopped long enough to slap down a key and snatch away our money. And yes, when I asked if she could call someone to give me a hand carrying my bags up the three flights of stairs to our room on account of my having a severely damaged back, she looked up briefly, said no, and then returned to adding up her figures. But there were some definite plusses about the place as well. There was plenty of hot water, the beds were comfortable, and – something which I think merits more research than we have time for here – the stains on the curtains turned into funny faces if you stared at them long enough.

When Robyn's head hit the pillow, she was out like a light. I, on the other hand, didn't sleep a wink and can report that although the guidebook was bang-on about the sirens and the squealing tires, to my knowledge, the dead body never fell. I may, however, just not have noticed it, since I did have to leave once or twice to investigate some unusual screaming in the next room.

By around eight o'clock in the morning, I realized there was no point thinking about sleep anymore so I started to watch Robyn, hoping to see signs of life. For a whole hour I watched her, my dread growing by the minute, because she lay there absolutely motionless – no breathing, no twitching, no nothing. Oh my God, what have I done!? What if my dear, sweet Robyn never wakes up!? And then my sleep-deprived mind had another frightening thought: What if they think *I killed her*? They say spouses are always the prime suspects in a murder, and Mexican prisons are not exactly noted for their congeniality. I've been told that the inmates knock your teeth out when you first arrive so they can use you for sex and not risk having anything important bitten off in the process. Now there's a lovely thought.

But then suddenly, as if to rescue me from the depths of my despair, Robyn's eyes opened up, a big happy smile spread across her face, and she said, "Now that's what I call a good night's sleep."

She's alive! She's alive! My pounding heart positively kicked up its heels with delight! My sweetheart was alive!

Never have I ever enjoyed brushing my teeth as much as I did that morning – every last precious one of them.

We hastily packed up our stuff and took a cab back to the Colima bus terminal, excited to be continuing along with our journey to the beach. We would have to take two more buses, the first one to a small town called Armeria, and the second one to tiny Paraiso.

The drive to Armeria from Colima was gorgeous, and it was noticeably warmer now than in San Miguel. The bus took us along the edges and into the valleys of a dramatic range of mountains called the Sierra Madre del Sur that were carpeted continuously in a green, woolly, sheep-like coat of dense, jungly vegetation. This was volcano country, the result of a struggle of biblical proportions between two opposing subterranean forces: one cheekily called Cocos and the other called the Caribbean.

The Cocos tectonic plate, a shifting mass of rock and lava moving east out of the Pacific, at first appears to be losing this battle. That's because after ramming up against the Caribbean Plate on which this part of Mexico sits, Cocos is pushed underneath it. But Cocos is ultimately resurrected like a phoenix from the ashes in the form of molten lava that is pushed by this collision up to the surface and expelled out through the openings in local volcanoes. The volcanoes of Japan are produced in exactly the same way, except in their case, the Pacific Plate is pushed under the Eurasian Plate. The resulting landscape from this sort of geological activity is usually stunning and this part of the state of Colima was no exception. Think Bali – minus the tourists.

The small, two-lane highway we'd been travelling on eventually ran right into the little heart of Armeria. Our bus hauled over alongside a hardware store and unceremoniously dumped us there before zooming back into the traffic to continue on to its next destination. Several inquiries and a few false turns later, we ended up at Armeria's little local bus terminal and sat down on a concrete barrier to wait for our bus.

Right away, you could tell Armeria was another one of those inexplicably happy little Mexican towns – a lot like San Luis de la Paz, actually, only smaller. If they could just figure out how to package the stuff, the relaxed sleepiness of these places would be worth a fortune. Everywhere I looked, people were happy. There were no crowds, it wasn't noisy, and the air was warm and fresh. Economic activity in this region – as in San Luis – was primarily based on farming. In the town itself, the only businesses were a small coconut-packing plant and about thirty-five small shops supplying the basics. It was enchanting.

After about twenty minutes, the bus to Paraiso pulled in. In some former life it had evidently been a school bus. It was very small and banged up and looked as if some kid had left it too long in the sandbox. Our journey from San Miguel had started in one of the most stylish and complex cities in all of Mexico, and bit by bit, bus by bus, we now found ourselves in a far simpler world, and – as we were about to discover – a far less elegant one as well.

When we climbed onto the bus there were five people already seated and the bus driver had not yet arrived. Because Robyn and I both decided to keep our luggage beside us at our seats, we had to sit separately: Robyn sat on the right side of the aisle, and I sat on the left. In front of me sat an elderly blind woman and a small boy, about six years old. Across the aisle from me sat Robyn and – *The Others*.

After Robyn and I exchanged friendly shrugs about not sitting together, I noticed that – two rows up from Robyn – there sat a woman. Behind that woman – one row up from Robyn – sat another woman, very similar in appearance to the first, only younger. I gathered they were mother and daughter.

The fingers, mouths, and chins of both women were coated and dripping with an orange-coloured oily substance, the result of plucking slices of salsa-drenched cucumber out of the plastic bags that were sitting on their laps, and then eating them. They were like a pair of synchronized swimmers moving food from lap to mouth with a precision and a syncopation that screamed out to be put to music – Strauss's *Blue Danube* from the early part of the movie *2001* would have been perfect. For the entire half-hour of our wait there in the depot, not once did their hands ever stop moving food from their laps to their mouths. Well, that's not entirely true. Periodically, there was a brief pause when, having finished a bag, one of them would take a moment to throw the thing out the open window onto the bus depot tarmac, and then start another. The fronts of their light cotton dresses were so covered in orange dribbles – they looked like children's bibs.

Behind them sat Robyn, completely motionless, her horror at the sight of these two women evident to me from her ramrod-straight back and the deer-in-the-headlights look in her eyes. She also appeared to be trying to keep her butt about half an inch off the seat for fear of what might be sticking to it. Behind Robyn, there sat a skinny, giddy, and somewhat twisted-looking, devil child.

The kid, who was about eleven, was being kept very, very busy hustling out onto the platform to make sure there was always a continuous supply of new fodder for the two women; he reminded me a bit of a trained monkey. But that wasn't his only role. He was also their court jester and would intermittently break out into fits of maniacal laughter, amusing the ladies and, I suspect, rattling Robyn.

Suddenly a look of hysterical glee came over the kid, unbeknownst to Robyn. He took from his pocket one of the ladies' used plastic bags, a small fee for his service I presume, and started blowing it up like a balloon. Pinching the top together, he then started to twist the bag around and around and around. As he did so the bag got tighter and tighter and his smile got eviller and eviller and although I should have seen what was coming, I didn't. Pausing just momentarily to look regretfully into my eyes, the kid slammed the bag – BANG! – between his hands. Robyn, caught totally off guard by the loud, piercing pop, flew about three inches into the air off her seat. I was expecting her to turn around and wallop the little twerp, but instead, and without missing a beat, she landed silently right back down on her seat again in exactly the same spot, just as bolt upright and rigid as before. A pretty cool customer, our Robyn.

The crowd loved it. The Drooling Salsa Girls giggled and wiggled without ever breaking their hand to mouth rhythm; the six-year-old in front of me laughed rapturously; and even the blind old lady beside him let out a cackle and slapped her knees with delight. One sensed that for the regulars, this was a much-anticipated treat.

The driver eventually arrived, and in an effort to show solidarity with his esteemed clientele, he proceeded to spill a plastic bag full of something drenched in orange salsa all over his pants as he sat down on his seat. Mercifully, we then pulled out of the depot before anyone else could hop on.

In spite of the foredoomed start to our bus ride to Paraiso, within just a few short moments of hitting the road, it transformed into a completely different experience. There was no place in the world we'd rather have been than on that funky old school bus on the way to Paraiso Beach; no better feeling than that of the hot, humid, spicy air blowing right through the bus with all its open doors and windows; and there could be no better sight than those legions of lofty palm trees that seemed to completely encircle our bus as we cruised merrily along. That bus ride, at a cost of just four pesos, seemed truly like a ticket to Paradise.

Even I would have trouble getting lost in Paraiso. A road map of Paraiso would show one broad avenue of black sand running parallel to the ocean, and that's about it. On the seaward side of that avenue there were rows of very primitive restaurants called *ramadas* that were basically thatched, palm-frond roofs held up by palm-tree posts. On the landward side was a motley collection of establishments I would loosely describe as restaurants, snack stands, and small motels. I say loosely, because the presence of a table was the only clue to a place being a restaurant, and a door with a number dangling from it was all that signified a motel.

Before Robyn and I left Canada, we had felt very pleased with ourselves for choosing small suitcases on wheels as our principal luggage accoutrements. I thought of them as the next logical step in the evolution of luggage – eventually destined to replace the long-suffering backpack. Well, I was wrong. All the extra hardware needed to attach the retractable handle and the chintzy little wheels makes them too heavy to carry, and they don't work worth beans in sand.

So there were Robyn and I, stepping off the bus at the only crossroads in little Paraiso and feeling like the biggest celebrities to hit the place since Bob Hope went by on his yacht in 1953, and we had to resort to dragging (plowing would be more accurate) our spiffy new suitcases with their totally useless wheels along the strip of sand they called the main street while being scrutinized by a small fleet of mystified stares from the local residents. It looked as if all the people in town, all fourteen of them, had come out to have a good gape. ("And will ya look at that, Manuel? Suitcases specially designed for dragging. What'll they think of next?")

We found the CIA, and its remaining half didn't look much more habitable than its fallen half. It looked as if it had only just barely survived the war in Bosnia, and a room there cost more than twice what we wanted to pay. It was also right next to a dilapidated ramada restaurant that played exceptionally loud music in a fruitless attempt to draw in customers from the all-but-empty street. I was beginning to think maybe Billy the muffin man's advice was worth exactly what we paid for it – nothing.

We went upstairs to see if we were missing something and we came across the hotel's only two guests: a couple of very large and scary-looking Mexican thugs. They didn't look at all pleased to see us, and they didn't laugh even a little when I told them jokingly that we came to Paraiso to hide out from the DEA, so we decided it would be prudent to take our custom elsewhere, and with much foolish smiling and a surfeit of hand-waving, we made our way back to the hotel's entrance and beat a hasty retreat. (We were in such a hurry to leave we actually ran straight into one another a couple of times and even bumped our heads together like Curly and Larry in a Three Stooges routine – entertaining for the locals perhaps, but we were getting right ticked off.)

It was frighteningly hot and humid. I was so drenched in sweat that I looked as if I'd just come in from surfing with my clothes on. The town looked desperately poor and there was garbage all down the centre of the road. The words "Big Mistake" seemed to be looming in the wings, preparing to make their grand entrance.

We walked along the road a little farther and eventually came to a place where it went down into a dip and became wet, slimy, and frankly, off-putting. But with nowhere else really to go, we barged on across it. When we were halfway across I looked inland to my right and saw a large Everglades-like lagoon complete with a sign saying, "Danger, Crocodile Zone." We picked up our pace a little after that.

Once across the slimy patch, we noticed there was an odd, wrong-side-of-the-tracks feeling to this particular section of town. It felt creepy and a little dangerous, as if we'd accidentally stumbled into a ghetto. The first tourist accommodation we encountered was a completely derelict and abandoned campground right next to the crocodile sign, where the only remaining structures were some horribly primitive toilets, now toppled and without doors. My brain, which has a tendency to misbehave at the best of times, imagined this devastation being caused by hundreds of rampaging crocodiles running amuck, their tails flicking and their teeth flashing, while dozens of terrorized campers, madly fleeing in all directions, made a frenzied attempt to escape their snapping jaws. I sensed there was no need to ask Robyn what she thought of the place so far.

Then, a little farther down the road, seeming to materialize out of nowhere, there appeared a tidy little motel called, El Bucanero. A couple of women, obviously staff of some kind, were sitting at the front of the motel under the shade of a pretty terra-cotta tile roof. When we walked up to them, their conversation stopped, and their shocked expressions told me that from their point of view we were the ones that appeared to beam down out of nowhere. I was starting to feel as if we were a couple of very misplaced characters, who had somehow ended up in the wrong storybook.

I asked if they had a vacancy and one of the ladies gave me a nod and proceeded to lead us over towards the rooms. It's hard to read the signals of Mexicans because they tend to always be so stiff at first, but I thought I detected good vibes from this lady, so I was greatly encouraged.

The room was lovely. Two comfy beds, very clean, toilet worked, shower worked, and by the looks of things, we would have the whole motel to ourselves. She said the price was 180 pesos a day, but when I offered her 120 a day if we took it for three weeks, she snapped up my offer without even a pause. So, that was that; we'd found ourselves a home. I paid her right away and we collapsed in our room for the rest of the afternoon.

Just before dinner, I walked the hundred yards or so to the beach. Standing there, I gazed over to my distant right, and there I saw black sand as far as the eye could see. The white surf crashed hard against it and sent plumes of diaphanous spray up into the air that then swept across the beach and disappeared into the adjacent palm groves. Closer by, I watched as the bubbling, boiling water rushed up the beach in a mad panic to distance itself from the fury of the giant waves that were smashing themselves to smithereens out in deeper water. As the rushing water finally neared its farthest reach up the gently sloped shore, it became a thin veneer of foam, pure white, like fancy lace. It skimmed along the black sand and formed beautiful overlapping arcs that slowed down, bit by bit, ever so slowly, until the white edges stopped for an instant to pose against the black background and then rushed back down the slope like the last suds in the sink after the plug has been pulled. The wet sand that was left behind when the water receded was speckled with tiny crab holes, and I watched with amusement as they blew thousands of little perfect bubbles in a gracious salute to the ocean's stately retreat.

Chapter 13

The next morning we awoke re-energized and agreed that we had to apply ourselves to the task of stocking up on basic supplies – the main one being coffee. So, we got dressed, locked up our room, scooted nervously past the crocodile lagoon, and hopped onto the bus back to Armeria.

Our bus driver was a friendly, stocky old guy, with thick, well-groomed, grey hair named Juan. He was clearly the captain of his ship, and he had just finished cleaning his bus top to bottom when we arrived. His bus had a lovely long red horn that perched proudly on the hood of the engine like a mermaid figurehead on the prow of a ship, and as he swung himself into position behind the wheel, he gave the horn one long continuous blast. The sound it gave off seemed perfectly suited to this sleepy little seaside resort. It was a relaxed sound, more akin to the sound of a far-off, mournful fog-horn, than to the curt, impatient beeping of its over-worked city cousins.

Pulling out of Paraiso, we passed through a small section of the mangrove lagoon and, as if on cue, a perfect white egret lifted off in slow motion from the shore directly beside us. According to the locals, there really were crocodiles in the lagoon, and just the thought of them lurking there in the shadows was enough to imbue the place with a special kind of mysterious beauty, one both enticing and threatening at the same time.

A few seconds later, out the side windows of the bus, we watched respectfully as row after row of tall and majestic coconut palms, seven stories high, swung past us like giants on parade. Banana trees were planted in between the palms, and their lush green plumage took full advantage of the leftovers of light that filtered down to them after the palms had taken their fill.

The clean, fresh wind rushing noisily in through the open windows and doors of the bus went silent and still as the bus came to a full stop beneath a canopy of those looming trees. Juan peered intensely off into the dense forest and once again gave his horn a blast. Like ghosts walking out of the mist, several men then suddenly materialized out of the dense vegetation and slowly made their way onto the bus. Juan greeted each one with a smile and a little friendly banter. To me they looked far too old to be plantation workers, but their machetes and sweat-covered brows said clearly that that's what they were. I marvelled at how the sense of unease generated by those vicious-looking hacking instruments was so quickly dispelled by the workers' own relaxed and jovial manner.

A few hundred yards further along the road, we passed a jalapeño field. There were several groups of hunched-over farm workers moving across the field at a relaxed pace, presumably harvesting the crop. A lovely viny scent reminiscent of fresh basil wafted off the field and blew into our faces through the open windows of the bus.

We finally built up a good head of steam and veritably flew up onto a highway overpass where we were lifted to a level high enough to see over the tops of the feathery palm groves. From up there we had a clear view of those exquisite, green, woolly mountains, and once again they were embracing their role as the perfect backdrop to a beautiful scene. Coming down the overpass, Juan shut off the engine to save fuel, and we glided the rest of the way into Armeria. Just at the edge of town, the bus shot past a dirt field giving us a brief glimpse of a jumble of chestnut-skinned teenage boys in red, green, and blue soccer uniforms who were chasing frantically after a cloud of dust.

We took a couple of rights and lefts along the narrow streets of the little town, and then Juan stopped unexpectedly at an empty intersection. He leaned out of his seat towards the open front door of the bus and started to wave and smile at someone. I turned my head to follow his line of sight and to try and figure out what was going on, but I couldn't see anyone that he could be waving at. It wasn't until

I gave up looking and my gaze dropped down far enough to take in the pavement near the edge of the bus that I spotted him: a little boy, who couldn't have been more than about three years old. He just stood there on the corner, looking quite bewildered. Finally, after much waving and prompting from Juan, the little guy started to wave back, but not with the common everyday "Hi, how are you?" kind of wave – nope, this kid was using the kind of wave used to guide vehicles through an intersection. He was the closest thing to a traffic cop Armeria had, and Juan had no intention of disobeying his directions.

Juan leaned back in his seat with a satisfied smile on his face, and after giving the little guy a friendly, thank-you salute, carried on towards the depot. Juan played this game with his little friend every single time we drove with him into town, and sometimes there would be quite a delay waiting for the little fellow to start waving. But nobody ever complained. It was a game enjoyed equally by all. Nobody ever said, "Hey, hurry up! I'm going to be late!" This was small-town Mexico, and here people always made time for such things.

The prime motivation for our trip to town that morning was to handle our coffee problem. You see, Mexicans, dear souls that they are, really don't get the coffee thing. Once you leave the large tourist meccas of Mexico behind, if you can get coffee at all, what they usually give you is a mug of lukewarm water, and a jar of Nescafé. Don't even try asking for cream. So when we travel in Mexico, we always brew our own.

We make it cowboy-style in our hotel room in a plain saucepan placed on top of something called an MSR campstove. These wonderful gadgets come with instructions that say they can be run on almost any kind of fuel imaginable: white gas, kerosene, gasoline, or – and are you ready for this – jet fuel. Now just what kind of overachieving, Harvard Business School graduate was trying to impress his new boss by suggesting they add that one to the list? I figure his name had to be Nigel. And just where am I likely to be able to obtain jet fuel, Nigel? "Excuse me, sir? When you finish filling that jumbo jet, would you mind squirting a half a liter in here, please?"

On a previous trip to Mexico, I looked up the Spanish for "white gas" in my phrasebook. Nothing there. I think Nigel probably wrote it. Now I admit, white gas isn't on every tourist's list of travel essentials, but Nigel, you gotta get out more. Did you know, Nigel, that telling people travelling in Mexico how to say, "Do you have some change for the parking meter?" is completely useless because there aren't any parking meters in Mexico? And has anyone ever gone on holiday and had to know how to say, "Please sir, will you clean my watch?" Well, yes, you have, Nigel, but you see that's my point. You're strange, Nigel, very strange.

The search for white gas in Mexico is complicated by the fact that Mexicans don't camp. Life is pretty close to camping for most of them already, so what's the point? So the problem is this: not only do you have to ask the shopkeeper for something you don't know the word for, but the shopkeeper doesn't have the faintest idea what you want to do with it either.

Looking for white gas once in La Paz, a street vendor told me that what I wanted was called *petróleo*. Thinking that petróleo sounded an awful lot like petroleum I told him no, I didn't want gas for my car. At which point, he said if I wanted gas, meaning propane, I should get it from the Calorgaz man. In the end I went along to a shop down the street and bought a liter of petróleo, but it wasn't white gas either; it was kerosene.

All right, so where do you buy white gas in Mexico? (Are you paying attention, Nigel?) In a paint store, of course. Mexicans use it as paint thinner.

While Robyn was off looking for coffee, I walked into the next best thing to a paint store in little Armeria, a *ferretería*, or hardware store.

It was cool, dark, and hushed inside the store. There was one long service counter running the whole width of the store and most of the merchandise was stacked on shelves behind it. If the year had been 1901 instead of 2001, I'm sure this store would have looked almost exactly the same. Most of the small stores in Mexico run on this old model where the customer has to go up to a counter to make a request for what he wants, and then the item is retrieved for him by the shop's clerks. Until this century, most stores the world over operated this way, and, I must admit, I rather like them. It makes it very simple to purchase something because you don't have to wander around for hours trying to find it, and it lends a nice air of polite formality to the occasion as well.

There were about six workmen ahead of me in line who were waiting patiently for their turns, and there were about twenty-five pretty young ladies working energetically behind the counter, retrieving the orders. My arrival, however, triggered a barrage of quick sideways glances and giggles all around. This was a good sign, actually. As I've said before, the best cities in Mexico are the ones where the young women laugh at you. It means you're seen as a welcome novelty, as opposed to a plundering imperialist.

When it came to my turn, I think they held a little secret lottery with their eyes to see who would have to serve the funny gringo. One brave soul finally stepped forward.

"Do you need something, sir?" she said politely, her hand firmly on the hammer in front of her just in case.

"Do you have gasolina blanca?"

"Yes, sir."

I resisted the urge to fly across the counter and embrace her, and instead, like a nurse requesting a urine sample, I handed her my empty bottle.

"I would like a liter please."

She was gone for quite a while and I was dearly hoping that they hadn't discovered they were out of the stuff and were busy trying to decide amongst themselves what they could substitute for it.

She finally brought back my bottle all filled up with something, and when I looked happy, she was clearly relieved. But when I sniffed it, it smelled like turpentine, a distinctly different odour from white gas, so I tried to explain to them that I thought they had put something else in the container by mistake. Oh God, here we go, she says to herself gripping the hammer more firmly. The poor girl called over the manager, a big, scary, Russian general of a woman, who then gave the bottle her official sniff, and declared emphatically that it was absolutely without any doubt gasolina blanca. I sniffed it one more time myself, and although I was again convinced it was turpentine, I looked across at all those pretty young faces on the other side of the counter, all fearfully clutching their hammers, and I realized – it didn't really matter. Hell, if it gives off fumes, our stove can probably burn it. I decided I'd rather pay the dollar for the stuff, just to bring back all those nice friendly smiles, than bother making a fuss.

"Thanks," I said. "It'll be fine."

Twenty-five frightened faces across the counter from me lifted simultaneously into smiles of relief, and twenty-five hammers were quietly returned to their racks.

I met back up with Robyn to continue the search for coffee, and after two failed attempts, we, or I should say Robyn, stumbled onto some really fine-smelling, freshly ground coffee in a little corner grocery store. It's amazing how difficult it is to find real coffee in Mexico. They look at you as if to say, "Oh no dear, we haven't seen that old stuff for ages. We're not so out of touch as you might think. We know all about instant. Been using it for years." So although the proprietor swore proudly that it was instant, the discriminating and not-to-be-questioned faculties of Robyn's nose said otherwise, and we loaded up with four bags of it. It turned out Robyn was absolutely correct. It was Colima coffee – grown on the slopes of the very same volcano that had appeared so picture-postcard perfect to us a couple of days ago when our bus was nearing Colima after the long journey from San Miguel – and it's considered by many to be Mexico's finest.

We got back on our bus loaded up with coffee, turpentine, eggs, cheese, bread, and instant noodle soups, and soon we were off again along that lovely road to Paraiso.

This time round the bus was filled with an entirely different cast of local characters: beach vendors. It seemed that there was a whole menagerie of these folks that travelled out to Paraiso every day to flog their wares, and today they were all on the bus, squeezed in right next to us.

They were not, however, the annoying jewellery and blanket hawkers so commonly seen at the up-scale resort beaches of Acapulco and Cancun. These guys were Mexicans selling to Mexicans, and a merry old bunch they were.

There was one dapper old fellow, not at all Mexican in appearance, who was wearing khaki trousers and a rakish straw hat whose twinkly blue eyes and kindly smile looked so familiar, I almost blurted out, "Uncle Mort! After all these years, it's you!" He was selling unshelled peanuts. Periodically, he punctuated our bus ride with quiet little outbursts of his sales pitch, "Cacahuates," (caw-caw-what-ays) which he always said in a very soft, sing-song voice as if he were trying to carefully waken a baby. I sensed that although his fellow vendors knew he was several cupcakes short of a tea party, they refrained from mocking him because he was, after all, one of them. One wondered if he ever stopped; if while alone at night in his room, his mantra just kept pouring out of him – an old familiar habit to keep him company and send him gently off to sleep.

A good deal of the space in our little bus was taken up with a fairly scruffy group of travelling musicians in cowboy hats. I knew from experience that their particular musical niche was probably the style of music commonly found in these parts. It's a style that floats adrift somewhere in the murky realms between mariachi and country. Their instruments – a guitar, a couple of fiddles, a trumpet, a tuba, a snare drum and a double bass – reclined gracefully beside them on the seats as if modelling for a Salvador Dalí painting.

There was a dark-skinned guy whose sunglasses and smile of gold teeth scattered sun sparkles around the bus whenever he twisted in his seat, which was most of the time. He wore an old wooden yoke across his shoulders that had a gourd dangling from one end and a large plastic jar dangling from the other. Judging by the swirling and sloshing that was going on inside the jar, he was a purveyor of some sort of beverage.

There was another guy who had a weird little metal box hanging off one of his shoulders that looked like something he'd constructed for himself out of a collection of wires, dials and switches he'd found at the dump. For a small fee he would let you grasp the two pieces of copper pipe that were wired into this thing and give you an electric shock. Now is that scary enough or what? ("Feeling a little psychotic today? Try a little of my electric shock therapy for people on the go, and save yourself the hassle of line-ups at the asylum.") He also carried with him a pocketful of mysterious inventions, things he'd made out of magnets and springs and things, and although I was curious to know what they all did, I wasn't going anywhere near that little metal box. He might want to give away free samples.

What was really delightful about the group, though, was how

happy everyone seemed. Judging by their looks, these folks weren't exactly getting rich doing what they were doing. But there was a lovely cheerful mood in the bus anyway, and I suspect it was because all of us were looking forward to a nice day at the beach, with music and balloons and peanuts and drinks and, hey, even electric shock therapy – and it just doesn't get much better than that, now does it?

Journal, January 6

It's about our fan. It hangs in the middle of the room just a couple of inches above my head. The first time I experienced the mighty gale-force winds blasting down from it, I went outside to see if the rest of the airplane was sticking out of the roof with its tail in the air. The thing is terrifying, but we need it: to cool off the room, and to keep the mosquitoes at bay.

My biggest fear about the fan was that one day Robyn would be standing under it, forget about the damn thing because it was on all the time, and then suddenly raise both her arms and break into a rousing rendition of that perennial wedding favourite, *YMCA*, chopping off both arms at the elbow instantly. (In Robyn's case, the odds of this happening were not as low as you might think.)

So, we talked about the fan and agreed to be careful, and every morning we went through all our various chores and ablutions trying to remain calm and relaxed, and yet all the while we were really shuffling around like a couple of nervous, arthritic, Irish clog-dancing penguins with our arms firmly affixed to our sides.

I was watching out of the corner of my eye one morning as Robyn proceeded with her own very special ritual of re-making the bed that the maid had already made for her, when I saw that she was rapidly approaching that moment in all bed-making when the person flings the sheet up into the air in a vain hope of getting it to lie evenly across the bed. Not wanting to nag and hover over her ad nauseam, I waited and prayed that she would find another way to spread out the sheet. But when I saw with horror that her wrists had moved into the pre-flinging position, I started to panic. Thinking maybe she had become so caught up in the whole process that she had forgotten about the fan, I just plain lost it and screamed, "No

Robyn! No! Don't move!" Of course my yelling then made her jump six inches into the air anyway, putting her even closer to the fan's blades, and so I yelled out again, "Get down, get down, watch out!" and, as you might expect, this completely freaked out poor Robyn, who ended up crouched down and quivering on the floor.

Not for long though. Big Robyn was soon back full-bore, assuring me that she and I would both have a far better chance of surviving this holiday if I would keep my frigging mouth shut about the fan. Sensing a certain hostility in her tone, I went for a little walk on the beach.

The fan also had a terrible squeak. It finally got to me so much that one night I actually up and moved in to the empty room next door. The room was no great prize, but at least the fan worked well. My enjoyment was short-lived, though. Before very long, the fan in that room started clicking. I was just contemplating the idea of spending the rest of the night ripping out every stupid bloody fan in the entire motel, when I had an epiphany. It came to me spoken in one of those husky, echoing whispers, like the way "Rosebud" was whispered in *Citizen Kane*, except for me the words were "vegggetable oilll."

I went back to our room – it was about three o'clock in the morning by this time – and marched directly over to our supply table. I grabbed the plastic vegetable-oil bottle, turned the fan off, and poured about half a cup of oil onto it. When I started the thing up again, to my utter shock, and Robyn's utter delight, there was nothing but a quiet, oily hum. It was sheer bliss. I almost jumped for joy, but the thought of my decapitated head bouncing jauntily onto Robyn's lap persuaded me to forego such displays of exuberance until a later date. Instead, I just turned off the light and climbed into bed. With large smiles of contentment spread across our faces, the two of us drifted off to our first really decent night's sleep since arriving in Paraiso.

Journal, January 11

I've always thought that maybe heaven is right here in front of us like some parallel universe, but that most of the time we can't see it because it's a little out of sync with our normal reality. Maybe you have to acquire a certain knack for seeing it. Enjoying Paraiso takes a certain knack as well.

Paraiso was either a grand and glorious tropical paradise full of exhilarating and uplifting sights and sounds – or it was a gringo's worst nightmare. Take your pick. Certainly Nigel would have hated it. We loved it.

My camera didn't get Paraiso at all. I'd walk along the beach transfixed by the long stretches of black sand scalloped by large, lacy, white whorls of foam; and all my camera could see was dirty black sand and hot hazy skies. I would delight in the fact that a smiley young waiter with a baseball cap on backwards would, for the price of my Fresca, bring me papaya and cucumber snacks and then let me sit all day long at his table watching long sparkly waves change from blue to celadon green as they curled over and went thump on the shore; and all my camera would see was a bunch of derelict shacks and a few bits of plastic blowing across the sand. No. Paraiso was definitely not for everyone.

Certainly not for Mel and Trudy.

One day Robyn and I were sitting in the little open-air restaurant at our hotel, having a cup of tea made from our precious and diminishing supply of Twinings English Breakfast, when a strange sight walked by: two towering backpacks on legs. Obviously these two had taken a wrong turn at Kathmandu.

Now since our hotel was in the middle of nowhere surrounded by a wasteland of crumbling shacks, and we hadn't seen a single gringo for days, I simply couldn't let them pass by unaccosted.

"Hey there, friends, you look lost."

The backpacks halted abruptly, and as they turned to face us, two pairs of eyes emerged.

"Well, holy mackerel . . ." said the tall, male backpack now sporting a big grin, ". . . fellow travellers." His accent sounded familiar.

They approached.

I smiled back and said, "You guys aren't Canadian by any chance now, are you?"

"Sure are," he said. "I'm Mel and this is Trudy. You Canadian, too?"

"Absolutely."

"Well, I'll be damned."

"So," I said, "where abouts are you from?"

"Port Alberni, in British Columbia."

"Oh . . ."

Now normally at this point in a conversation one looks for something good to say about your new acquaintances' hometown. And Port Alberni is only about a three-hour drive from where we live, so I know it pretty well. Problem is, there is almost nothing nice to say about Port Alberni. It's a pulp-mill town, filled with substandard housing and surrounded by clearcuts. Even the almost nice things sound like insults. Things like: "You know, the landscape around Port Alberni must have been one of the prettiest on earth once upon a time. Too bad they had to spoil it by putting that town right in the middle of it all."

So I just said, "Oh," again and smiled lamely.

"So where are you from?" he asked.

"Oh, pretty nearby. We're from Hornby Island."

He paused and he paused and he paused. I soon realized that he had about as much good to say about Hornby as I'd had about Port Alberni. We might as well have been talking about East and West Berlin, that's how much the two communities had in common. To me, Port Alberni was symbolic of bad forestry, rednecks, and trailer parks. But then I suddenly realized that to him, Hornby represented hippies, marijuana plantations, and welfare bums.

He said, "Oh," and smiled lamely.

Hoping to find some common ground somewhere, I asked him what he did there; hell, maybe the guy ran a health food store.

Sensing our mutual desire to connect, Mel just shook his head and looked down rather despondently, saying, "I'm a logger." But then he suddenly brightened and blurted out hopefully, "But I smoke a lot of marijuana!"

My turn to shake my head. "Gee that's nice, uh, I don't."

Sighs all around.

Then Mel said, "Hey, we're lookin' for a place to stay, something nice and not too expensive. You guys have any ideas?"

I shrugged and waved towards the Bucanero, "This place is great. It's clean and it's the cheapest I've seen. Why don't you have a look? That lady over there's the owner."

Mel and Trudy didn't speak a word of Spanish and our landlady didn't speak a word of English, so after a few moments of listening to the two Port Albernians trying to communicate with her by inventing a new type of Spanish which is just English with an additional "ito" added on to the end of everything, the poor Mexican woman turned and looked imploringly at me to come to her rescue. My sympathies are always with the Mexicans in a case like this, and I couldn't believe the two Canadians hadn't even taken the two minutes it would have required of them to learn the Spanish for "Can I see your rooms?" Although, to be fair, if their phrasebook was anything like ours, Nigel had arranged things so they first would have had to thumb through at least a hundred and fifty pages of totally useless tripe covering everything from girdles to ski-lifts before they would have found it.

It only took about three Spanish words from me and the landlady understood what was wanted. She immediately led the two backpackers off to have a look at a couple of the rooms. They were gone for about ten minutes, and when Mel and Trudy arrived back, I expected them both to be pretty impressed by the place. Instead they waved goodbye to the landlady and looked ready to depart.

Mel looked a little sheepish, and Trudy was trying to smile as politely as she could.

Finally Mel said, "Don't any of the toilets in this town have toilet seats?"

At that moment the little crack between us and them opened out into a great chasm. This is what I wanted to say:

You guys are spending two weeks hitch-hiking in a Third World country with sleeping bags, camping gear, and a tent. You have accidentally stumbled onto a spotlessly clean, inexpensive, secure motel where everything works including the electricity, the shower, the toilet, the door, and all (oh all right, almost all) of the windows, and you're unhappy about the fact that the toilet doesn't have a little plastic flip-up seat! What the hell are you doing here!!!?

But I didn't say that. I just said with another limp smile, "Probably not."

And after a few shrugs of regret all around, we said our farewells, and off they went.

Later that day, in the dimming light, as the sun was sinking into the Pacific, I saw Mel and Trudy standing on the road at the little T-junction in the centre of town. They were all alone, not another soul in sight. They appeared to be slowly sinking as well, sinking into the sand under the burden of their gigantic knapsacks. They looked utterly lost. Not geographically . . . conceptually. They were up to their necks in the wrong Paraiso. I decided to reach out and make one more attempt at helping out a couple of my floundering countrymen.

I approached them casually with a smile, and they looked up, a little surprised to see me.

"Listen, you two. You guys need to put down your packs, have a beer over in one of the restaurants, and take a room at our little hotel for the night. It's clean, the people are nice, and it's cheap."

They began to waver. They looked extremely tired after carrying around packs all day. They looked into each other's eyes and sent secret messages back and forth. Then Mel smiled politely and said, "Thanks anyway, Stephen, but I think we're going to get a cab and try another town."

In search of toilet seats no doubt.

After we said goodbye, I sat down by the sea, listening to the rhythmic swoosh of the waves on the black sand and watching the pink-orange glow in the distance, out where the sky met the sea. I began to think how maybe Mel and Trudy were just doing what we all do most of the time: live right next to paradise, in our own little parallel universes, and never realize that the thing we want the most is right there beside us all the time. We're all just too damn busy looking for toilet seats to notice the really good things we already have.

Life at Paraiso was full of that slow-paced sanity that Mexico does so well. It was like a health spa for the mind.

One evening, I was standing on the beach while a giant red balloon of a sun was slowly floating down and coming to rest on the horizon, washing me and everything around me in a pink and golden glow. The wind had lost its daytime gustiness and had now settled down to a steady but strong exhalation of warm air coming straight in off the Pacific.

I looked to my left, back down the beach towards the main mass of ramadas, and saw a gathering of about two dozen men beside one of the large sea-going open boats called *pangas*, the kind the fishermen use. They were waiting for the tide to reach far enough up the beach to make the launch of their boat as easy as possible. Since these folks don't have much in the way of labour-saving devices, whenever time or nature offers to step in and lend a hand, they readily accept the offer.

And watching them got me to thinking.

People in this part of the world have always used time as a tool. They used it in the construction of their pyramids; now they use it to launch their ships. This waiting, this acknowledgement of the value of time as a useful thing, in and of itself, may be the most important thing that differentiates the Mexican from the gringo. I think Mexicans live in a world where time's accomplishments are deemed to be sacred. Their respect for the accomplishments of time outweigh their respect for man's own artificial timetable. I think this respect grows out of the habit poor societies have of using time – cheap and relatively plentiful to them – to accomplish their everyday tasks. So it matters neither a pip nor a squeak if Juan is a little late arriving at the bus depot in Armeria on account of his playing with a kid on a corner. Time itself has not been wasted; it has been used as it was meant to be used: to derive a benefit, and in Juan's case, a distinctly non-financial one. People in my part of the world, on the other hand, seem bent on destroying time – along with everything else.

When the tide reached an acceptable height, the two dozen or so men braced themselves alongside the twenty-foot-long panga like a crew of Olympic bobsledders and waited. Suddenly, on someone's command, the beast started to slide resolutely towards the water. The boat and the men resembled one desperate creature – a giant turtle with centipede's legs – trying to evade the jaws of death by making one final death-lunge towards the sea. Then, anticlimactically, they stopped, and had a short rest. Again, a voice yelled out, and again the beast hurled itself forward, this time making it all the way to the water's edge before it stopped.

And again they waited. They needed the water to thicken a little in front of the boat; it was still just a few inches deep. They also wanted to wait for a wave that crashed as far out to sea as possible.

That way they could push the boat off the sand, get the motor running, and have a few precious meters in which to gather up speed before they smashed up against the huge wall of surf that separated them from the open ocean.

There was one final push from the crowd of men, and then the lone fisherman on board gave a couple of quick jerks to the motor's pull-cord and eased the roaring prop down into the water. The bulk of the helpers now wandered back onto shore, but one of them remained in the water right next to the whirling blades of the propeller, and kept on pushing. He pushed the boat into deeper and deeper water, and when the water got too deep for him to remain standing, he hauled himself up into the boat with the other man, and the two of them headed off straight for the crashing surf as fast as they could. When they hit the wall of water, the boat was angled upward at a frightening 40-degree pitch, and only the very back of it around the engine seemed to be still in the water at all. The bow of the boat was pushed up so high by the onslaught of the crashing wave that it looked as if the boat would surely be flipped over backwards, dashing the bodies of its two occupants onto the shore. But the engine roared and the helmsman persevered, and the boat eventually rolled over the huge curling wave and came down onto the gentle sea that was waiting on the other side. Then, still looking alarmingly precarious at a 30-degree angle to the horizon, the boat went cruising off to the fishing grounds, with both young men standing, maybe in order to see their way more clearly over top of the boat's elevated bow, or maybe because the wind and the ocean air felt so damn good against their proud, happy faces.

The time in Paraiso was a gift. We spent a lot of our time watching things: the shore-fishermen who stood on the beach and cast their nets into the surf, happy to go home with the five or six bony little fish they hauled in; the pelicans that flew in formation, parallel to the shore, just skimming the tops of those long, gently curling waves; the swooshes of red, pink, and blue, candy-floss clouds that filled the sky every evening with their playful swirls; and the setting sun, leaking its orange ink into the blue-black sea as it gradually sank into the dark, syrupy water.

Paraiso had its sounds as well. We grew so accustomed to the endless sound of Mexican oom-pah-pah music that when there was a power failure one day and the music died, it felt as if the town had stopped breathing. Intermittently, pickup trucks would cruise past our hotel selling vegetables or propane or collecting aluminum cans, and the loudspeakers they used to announce their arrival always sounded as if they were ordering us to evacuate before some sort of alien invasion. There were so many others. There was Juan's bus horn, the repetitive circus tunes of the ice-cream carts, the rhythmic swoosh of our room fan, the soft chatter of the maids and the dry scraping of their brooms – and of course – the many sounds of the sea.

We became quite good friends with that dark-skinned beverage seller with the gold teeth and the wooden yoke as well. His name was Eduardo and he was a very happy guy. He told me that the beverage he sold was a palm-flower nectar called *tuba,* that he collected fresh every day by scaling a few palm trees that he owned. One day, just for the hell of it, I decided to ask him something.

"Eduardo? What is your favourite word?"

He looked at me with an embarrassed smile.

"Oh, Estevan, this is a children's game, no?"

"Sí, Eduardo."

He gazed off towards the ocean for a moment, and then turned back to me and said, "Amistad," the Spanish word for "friendship." It was a touching response, exposing more of his inner self than I'd expected.

"And what is your favourite sound, Eduardo?"

The shy grin on his dark face erupted into a sparkling smile of gold teeth.

"Oh Estevan, this is getting too hard!"

"Come on, Eduardo, it's just a game. What is your favourite sound?"

He looked thoughtfully down at his bare, knobbly feet, as if hoping they might offer a useful suggestion. With the sound of the Pacific Ocean crashing all around us, and music being pumped out of several restaurants along the beach, I was expecting him to choose something from our immediate surroundings. Instead he lifted his head and said in a soft voice, "The sound of the wind in the hills."

On January 24, reluctantly, we left Paraiso, and started our trek back to San Miguel.

Chapter 14

We decided to make optimal use of our journey back to San Miguel by stopping off at two of the places we'd rushed through in our haste to get to the beach: Colima and Guadalajara.

We arrived at the Colima bus station around three in the afternoon on Wednesday, January 24th, and immediately hopped into a cab and headed for the Flamingo Hotel. Now why, you may well ask, would two perfectly sane people choose to return to a hotel like the Flamingo, having already learned that the place was a complete dump? Well, disregarding the sanity assumption part of your question for the moment, the reason was – because it was cheap, okay?

In a moment of insensitivity loud enough to be heard halfway round the world, I asked the one-eyed man at the front desk of the Flamingo if he could help me up the stairs with my rather heavy suitcase, on account of my having a bad back. As if to say, "I'll see you one bad back and raise you a game knee," he inched his way over to the key rack and motioned to the cane that had been standing there in plain view the whole time.

"Me too," he said with a little smile.

It was no contest. This poor guy was in way worse shape than I was. I asked him if there was anyone else around who could possibly take my bag upstairs for a couple of bucks, and after a few phone calls to several different floors he finally tracked down someone: an androgynous-looking maid who I think was a man trying to look like a woman trying to look like a man. Whatever. He/she did the trick quite nicely. We got everything up to the room, I thanked the maid with a two-dollar tip, and we closed the door behind us and collapsed on top of our beds.

We tried turning on the room's table fan, a great battered old leviathan of a thing, to try and get a little air moving in the place, but quickly shut it off again after hearing the incredible racket it made. Finally, we managed to cool the place off just by opening the balcony door, and for several very pleasant and peaceful hours after that, we simply lazed about the room. It was just beginning to look as if we might actually have one of those very rare experiences – a quiet night in Mexico, the kind that usually only happens after power failures – when all hell broke loose.

An infestation of young students took over our entire floor, every hallway and every room, and proceeded to scream, whoop, bang and slam on and at every surface they could find. In accordance with the Mexican law that states that mayhem with music is always to be preferred over just plain mayhem, they then cranked their fleet of sound systems up to levels designed to once and for all rid the world of all people over the age of thirty-five. Robyn and I dove across the room to our suitcases like a matched set of flying squirrels and in a mad frenzy of zipping and unzipping finally laid our hands on the four precious objects that we so desperately desired: our ear plugs.

Unfortunately, the earplugs, although a big improvement, were not good enough at their job to block out everything. We could still hear enough noise through them that whenever there was an unexpected crash, pop, or shriek, books and drinks flew out of our hands like a family of flying trapeze artists whose catchers had momentarily stepped out for a smoke without letting anybody else know.

And then I had a moment of divine inspiration. I walked over to the fan and turned it on. Instantly, the jarring sounds of the students' drunken revelry were extinguished, drowned out by the exquisitely loud and steady droning of the fan. Brilliant! A sound-cloaking device disguised as an ordinary room fan. With the flick of a switch our room had become as peaceful as a Trappist monastery. It was almost as good as listening to the soothing crash of waves on the Paraiso beach! Zamfir eat your heart out. We found our bliss at the Flamingo Hotel.

After a few more, well-deserved minutes of self-acclaim, we lay back contentedly on our beds like a couple of Cheshire cat grins, and slowly drifted off to sleep.

The next morning we were unable to use our beloved MSR stove to make coffee because it was in about seventy-five pieces, I having dismantled it for the bus ride between Paraiso and Colima. (Assembling it was no mean feat, considering its preference for reconfiguring itself as a replica of a Russian Sputnik satellite). So, as soon as we were washed and dressed, we headed out onto the streets of Colima, clearly focussed on the idea that our first mission of the day would be entitled *Stalking the Elusive Latté in the Wilds of Nescafé Mexico.*

We had pinned our hopes on a small café Robyn had discovered in our guidebook called La Arábica. Our route took us across an incredibly beautiful, sun-streaked plaza called the Jardín Nuñez – a wonderful place full of fountains and palm trees and lovers on benches. It stood out immediately from other run-of-the-mill jardíns we'd seen elsewhere in Mexico because it was spotlessly clean and extremely well kept. Most big Mexican cities have to contend with the problems associated with pollution, dust, garbage disposal, and poverty. But apparently not Colima. All of those problems were notably absent here. There was something unusual going on in Colima, something that warranted further investigation.

"Did you notice that all the palm trees have numbers on them?" said Robyn.

It took a moment for my mind to resurface from its total absorption with two young lovers who were passionately groping one another on a bench a few meters ahead of us. "Uh no, I hadn't noticed that."

Robyn's narrowing glance told me she sensed my distraction but was willing to let it pass. "Why do you suppose that is?"

"So they know if any are missing? Being the state capital, there are probably dozens of bureaucrats in an office somewhere whose sole purpose in life is to catalogue every tree, rock, and blade of grass they come across. They probably work for the Ministry of Stationary Objects."

Robyn looked doubtful.

We crossed the street leaving the jardín behind us and discovered with the help of our map that we were on the main street of town, Francisco Madero. Again I noticed how different it looked from the other cities of Mexico we'd been to. The street was newly paved and lined on both sides with bright, modern shops selling shoes, clothing, furniture, and ice cream. There wasn't a tortilla or a fruit stand in sight. And you know, it was kind of nice for a change. I guess we'd been gone from Canada for about three months by then, and we were about ready for a little urban sanitization. Mind you, there was no mistaking the place for anything other than Mexico. For one thing there were Mexicans everywhere, a bit of a giveaway that, and for another, the majority of the shops were selling shoes, a Mexican obsession.

We walked around in circles for a while trying to find La Arábica, and we were just beginning to get a little frustrated when Robyn's incredible nose came to our rescue by locking onto the alluring aroma of freshly ground coffee like a bloodhound in hot pursuit of its prey. With me following closely on her heels, panting hard and trying to keep up, she sniffed us all the way to the coffee bar's front door.

Most Mexican shops have those front doors that are more like garage doors, so when they slide them out of the way, the whole front wall of the place is open to the street. La Arábica's was like that. One of the things that's nice about these doorways is that they are conducive to a wonderful sense of continuity from shop to shop, and they enhance that feeling of collective space that is so prevalent on the streets of Mexico. They also give things a nice relaxed feeling because people flow easily from one shop to another like warm and gentle tropical breezes. Best of all, they make your little journeys around town more interesting because you can see what's going on in the shops as you walk by. Like the breaking down of the "fourth wall" in theatre, you feel privy to events not normally seen.

I was buying some ham once in San Miguel from one of these wide-open shops and I ended up getting considerably more than just the ham for my money. The little shop consisted of a single square room split down the middle by a big glass deli-cooler, and there were three or four cute young girls set up behind the cooler taking and filling the orders. While I was waiting for my turn, an old pickup truck drove up alongside the front of the shop, practically brushing up against the crush of customers inside, and it idled there momentarily, waiting for the traffic to move. The young guy driving the truck took one look inside the shop and was immediately smitten with one of the girls behind the counter. His head and torso hanging out of the truck as far as they could go, he started courting her right then and there, pleading with her to tell him her name and to agree to meet him after work. I should add, this was no ooh-lah-lah-babe-how-about-it kind of courtship either. He was courteous and respectful towards her. In turn, the girl, who was busily tossing large greasy slabs of ham from cooler to scale and back again, responded with a coy little smile and a face flushed with embarrassment. We, the customers, were caught right in the middle of it all and turned our heads in unison, like spectators at a tennis match, intently following every thrust and parry of the ancient ritual in which we had inadvertently become involved. I think the sense that he might have to leave at any moment if the traffic started moving added considerably to the tension. And you know what? After much imploring from the young man and much encouragement from the young lady's co-workers, she said yes! She agreed to meet him after work. The entire shopful of people, behaving very much like a bunch of self-congratulatory aunts and uncles, erupted in a sea of beaming smiles at this most romantic of all outcomes. Then the traffic suddenly started to move again, and in an instant the young man and his truck were gone. We all gradually settled back in to the more mundane tasks at hand, namely, the buying and selling of different kinds of ham and cheese, but I'm sure that when that little piece of human drama inserted itself so unexpectedly into the ordinary routines of all the people in that shop, it brightened everyone's day. I know it did mine.

And that's the thing about Mexico. You end up feeling as if you're a part of things, and simplistic as I know it might sound, I think one small part of the reason for that is those lovely, big, wide-open shops.

We walked in to La Arábica, sat down at a little table, and were instantly overwhelmed by the intoxicating smell emanating from the freshly ground coffee haze that hung over the pretty little coffee bar. We ordered two cups of coffee, and after a few minutes of loud, dental-suction sounds from their very spiffy espresso machine, the waitress brought them to our table. Robyn has a particularly sublime facial expression that she keeps in reserve for two of her greatest pleasures in life: an excellent cup of coffee and a shot of fine tequila. That exact expression, kind of like Cookie Monster's during a quiet, blissed-out moment, googly eyes and all, was spread out across her entire face after she took her first sip. Clearly, Robyn was in java-java heaven.

Conversation being a bit of a lost cause during episodes like this, I quietly drank my coffee and whittled away the time perusing the entertaining assortment of funky old black and white photographs that graced the walls. One in particular held my gaze. It showed Emiliano Zapáta, the moustached Mexican revolutionary, armed to the teeth with bullets and guns, sitting at a coffee bar around 1918. He was calmly relishing his morning cup of coffee, presumably before setting out on another day of blood and mayhem during the Mexican Revolution. If I ever get offered a free ride on a time machine, I think that's one destination I'd like to skip.

We strolled over to the magnificent Jardín Libertad and were again struck by how gorgeous Colima's plazas were. This one had a pretty, curlicue, wrought-iron gazebo in its centre, a colourful profusion of flowers and shrubs all neatly arranged in borders, and a liberal sprinkling of tall, stately palms. I looked at the people all sitting there relaxing on benches, their kids playing quietly at their feet, and I remembered Robert Frost and his lovely line about children swinging on birch trees: "One could do worse than be a swinger of birches." Wistfully, I thought: One could do worse than be a sitter on benches.

I wanted to speak to someone at the Ministry of Tourism because I'd had the brainwave that maybe these guys would be a useful source of information for a travel writer who might just be able to encourage a whole whack of Canadian tourists to come down here for a holiday and spend lots and lots of money. I clearly misunderstood the purpose of the Mexican bureaucracy. But, that aside, I was also thinking they might feel inclined to give me some free stuff, and that would be kind of neat too.

When we arrived at the office, we were greeted by a very attractive woman who informed us that the person who could find out if we could see the person who knew whether the minister had finished lunch yet, wasn't free just then, but we could wait if we wanted to. After a brief consultation, Robyn and I concluded that our next urgent appointment was probably not until about March 2051 (my one-hundredth-birthday party), so what the hell, we may as well wait. And besides, there were brochures to read, one of my favourite things.

After about twenty minutes in the waiting room (and about twenty-five elbow pokes from Robyn regarding the numerous snorts and chuckles that erupted from me while I marvelled at the creative English translations used in the brochures), we were informed that if we returned the next day at nine, we would be able to speak to the minister then. I consoled myself by stuffing my pockets with as many brochures and tourist guides as I could fit into them, and after thanking the young lady at the desk, and answering her question on the rare and often abused use of the subjunctive in English, we headed back out into the glorious Mexican sunshine.

The next day started off with another round of pure ecstasy in a cup at the Arábica coffee bar, and afterwards, Robyn and I decided to go off in different directions, with a plan to meet up again around four o'clock at the Jardín Libertad. She wanted to see the University Museum of Popular Arts where they apparently had an incredible mask and native-costume collection, and I wanted to see if there really was a Minister of Tourism.

Well, I got to the Ministry of Tourism a little early and sat down on a bench outside. At nine o'clock precisely, the doors were flung open and a herd of important-looking men in suits stampeded into the Ministry of Tourism offices. At about nine-o-five, they stampeded back out again. When the dust finally settled, there were just two people left. I was one; the other was Ambrosio. Judging by the deep rings around Ambrosio's sad eyes, he was the only government official in all of Mexico who was ever expected to do anything. The rest of them were always off having lunch. He did have his own office though, so he led me into it, and we sat down at either side of his desk.

Now although Ambrosio is the only government official in Mexico who ever does anything, that does not mean he actually accomplishes anything. Ambrosio's idea of helping me gather information about Colima was to read brochures out loud. Not wanting to make any waves in case he really did have some free stuff to give me, I listened politely. This went on for the better part of an hour, during which time he told me nothing I didn't already know about Colima – well, except for two things: he told me why Colima was so clean and he told me why they numbered the trees.

The reason why Colima was so clean was quite simple: it was the state capital of a wealthy state. That meant that there were both the desire and the means to keep it looking good. As for the trees, according to Ambrosio, if you got up at the crack of dawn in Colima, and went for a stroll through one of the many beautiful palm-treed plazas of the city, you would see dozens of supple little men shinnying their way right up to the top of the palms, eager to obtain their day's supply of tuba – that same watery nectar of the palm flower that Eduardo had been selling at Paraiso. Then, like caterpillars, these guys would undergo some sort of metamorphosis a little later in the day, and re-emerge in scattered locations around town dressed in all-white uniforms and dangling gourds of ice and tuba from yokes stretched across their shoulders. The trees have numbers because each tree is licensed to a specific *tubero* for a fee, and, of course, there is a whole department of important men in suits who spend their time rushing in and out of their offices all day in order to ensure that the government receives it. But, the useless bureaucrat thing aside, I thought it was a terrific idea. Those beautiful palm trees weren't just so many pretty faces – they were hard-working income generators for a whole bunch of local small businessmen. And big business was prevented from destroying these little enterprises by a law that required that the person who walks around selling his nectar on street corners has to be the same person that scales the trees every morning to harvest the crop. Beautiful urban plantations for the people. Delightful.

I did finally get some free stuff from Ambrosio, although it wasn't exactly free, as I did have to sit and listen to him read brochures for an hour. I got two glossy promotional magazines; a letter from the minister, complete with disgustingly garish letterhead and an extremely pretentious seal that told everyone in Mexico to be nice to me; and two tickets to the Ballet Folklorico on Saturday night. There was no secret de-coder ring or membership card included, but, all told, it was still a pretty good haul. The tickets to the ballet were a treat, but the letter was the real prize. Now, whenever I was in a situation where I felt a little inadequate or insecure, I could wave my letter about like Louis XIV's handkerchief, and I might actually get a little attention. No more restaurant tables next to the kitchen for this guy. Waiters would be *forced* to bring me water when I asked! Wow. Think of it. Respect at last. I thanked Ambrosio with a dignified handshake, pulled on my sweat-stained Tilley Hat, aimed my dirty old sneakers towards the door, and strutted out onto the street feeling every bit the emissary of His Excellency, the Minister of Tourism himself. There'd be no stopping me now.

You know that insulting, chauvinistic, xenophobic cliché about the useless and corrupt Mexican bureaucrat? Horrible, isn't it? It's totally true. But according to my guru on these matters, Alan Riding, the important thing to keep in mind about the Mexican government is that without the existence of one specific article of the Constitution, it would be a whole lot worse. Hopefully, knowing this will make you feel better next time you're shelling out twenty-five bucks to the guy with the portable "No Parking" sign.

Here's the gist of Mr. Riding's thesis.

Most of the corruption in Mexico has stemmed from one-party rule. Between 1929 and 2000, the year Vicente Fox was elected, Mexico was ruled by the PRI. Elections, although ostensibly democratic, were so well orchestrated by the party that they were always foregone conclusions. The Mexican attachment to hierarchical systems also played a role in the PRI's firm grip on the reigns of power. Mexicans (both men and women, by the way) believe in the value of hierarchy, they've done so since time immemorial, and the president of Mexico is viewed as all-powerful, a true heir to the Aztec emperors and Spanish kings of the past. And why do they prefer their hierarchical beliefs to more modern ones? Because it's safer than the social chaos that has always ensued when the hierarchy has been toppled. But isn't the price paid for such stability unbounded corruption? Corruption, yes; but unbounded, no. In the case of Mexico, says Riding, the political system has a built-in mechanism for limiting the growth of corruption.

The reason things are not even more corrupt than they are, according to Riding, is because a president can only have one six-year term, and each new president brings a slightly different arrangement of the hierarchy in with him when he takes the oath of office. In order to maintain absolute rule, the various leaders have had to agree not to rule absolutely, if you catch my drift. The style of the typical Mexican leader has always been, by and large, the style of the country itself: hierarchical and gifted at negotiation.

Each new president makes a big deal at the beginning of his mandate about the fact that, during his tenure, there will be significant change – and in fact there usually is. Not because there's any major shifting of power from the political right to the political left, exactly. No, in Mexico, power is negotiated and then shuffled between the five major groups – media, labour, business, the Church, and the army – and the knowledge that this shuffling will invariably happen sometime in the future has had the effect of keeping folks in line over the years. Alliances of mutual corruption between the bureaucracy and the Church, for example, just turn into useless liabilities during the reign of a president who is bent on curbing the Church's power. So, according to Riding, it's the six-year term that has limited the corruption.

To fill in the time before I was due to meet up with Robyn, I walked over to the Museo de Historia de Colima on the Jardín Libertad to have a little look. Once inside, I wasted no time testing the efficacy of my letter from the minister. After just a brief moment of dangling it in front of the face of the man at the door in lieu of the entrance fee, I was whisked off to the upstairs office. I was absolutely stunned by the response. They were actually impressed. The woman in the office sent me off with my very own security guard to attend to my every need. I had my own little entourage; the only things missing were the hat boxes from Harrod's.

It's just as well my entry was free, however, because although the museum had a few charming ceramic figurines of some very jolly-looking local blokes from around 1200 A.D. sitting around on benches drinking moonshine, the fee was exorbitant. I don't remember how much, but it was way too much.

Spurred on by my success at the museum, I decided to walk over to the other side of the jardín and try my hand at waving my letter around at somebody from the lovely Hotel Ceballos in hopes of landing us a free night or two away from the Flamingo. I have to admit, I was really starting to get a feel for this corruption thing.

Built in 1880 and the survivor of numerous earthquakes (including a 1941 quake that all but levelled the city), the cream-coloured, palatial Hotel Ceballos is an imposing sight that holds court over the adjacent Jardín Libertad like a benevolent old patriarch. It's a two-story, square building, with a front face that consists of a long colonnade of fourteen scallopped Gothic arches on the lower level; and a row of fourteen wrought-iron balconies, each covered in its own trim little awning, running above the arches on the upper level. It's the kind of place that makes you feel important just walking into it.

Once inside, I finally tracked down the manager. He was a stout, cheery fellow called Ernesto, and Ambrosio had said he was a personal friend of his and would treat me well. I presented him with my letter, and he proceeded to take me upstairs for a little tour.

The steps to the second floor were made from a beautiful black volcanic rock dug from local quarries, and all around the stairwell there were delicate, hand-painted floral designs, some of them the originals from 1880. When we reached the top of the stairs, we walked along an impressive twenty-foot-wide hallway and out onto one of the little balconies overlooking the plaza. I felt like Evita Peron out there and was momentarily moved to give a little regal wave to the oblivious masses below. You never really know just how awful a place like the Flamingo is until you've been to a place like this.

After Ernesto showed me a couple of very impressive empty suites with high ornate ceilings and furniture lavish enough for the Sultan of Brunei, I got quite excited about the idea of staying there for a few nights. But alas, it was not meant to be. Ernesto was evidently a little more savvy than the folks over at the museum. He took one look at my scruffy attire and told me they were full up – a Mexican's way of politely telling you to take a hike.

I met Robyn at the jardín as planned, and after returning to the Ceballos for a cup of wonderful coffee in its courtyard restaurant served by men in white coats and accompanied by the romantic tinklings of the hotel's very own resident pianist, we faced up to our pathetic economic reality and started hiking out to the outskirts of town to a more affordable restaurant called VIPS (pronounced "Beeps," which is also my preferred spelling). Our guidebook told us it was a real American-style restaurant selling hamburgers and fries, but the brief description in the book didn't really prepare us for what we found there, namely, Walmartland.

Beeps is part of a complex in an outlying section of town owned and operated by Walmart, and there is a slightly sinister quality to the whole place. It feels a little like a modern-day Trojan Horse, purporting to be bringing the benefits of the good life to these supposedly needy people, when really its controllers are only interested in conquest. And, judging by the fact that Walmart did not display its name anywhere on the exterior of the building, the generals in charge were well aware that the locals might be hostile. Walmart culture and Mexican culture are just about as diametrically opposed as two cultures could possibly be.

On walking into Beeps, I noticed signs hanging from the ceiling stating that if our waitress didn't smile at us, we'd get a free dessert. Well, I said, rubbing my hands together with an evil little cackle, this should be a piece of cake, as it were.

I figured there were two good reasons for my optimism:

a) Mexican waiters never smile, and

b) The restaurant thinks it'll never have to pay out because Mexican customers are too polite to complain.

My hopes were short-lived, however.

A further look around told me that when we'd walked into Beeps, we'd walked out of Mexico. It looked like a Barbie restaurant. Everything was new, clean, bright, and stinking of efficiency. The tables and booths and floors and walls and air were all either made out of brightly coloured plastic or made out of real stuff that had been made to look like brightly coloured plastic. The waitresses all wore Waitress Barbie uniforms. And they were all smiling – constantly. It was like a sci-fi movie directed by Andy Warhol where the small town is invaded by an army of cloned aliens that all look like smiling, plastic, Waitress Barbie dolls. It was terrifying. I had apparently underestimated the power of Walmart to brainwash and indoctrinate their new recruits.

My burger was fine. Robyn's grilled cheese was fine. And our waitress at Beeps never stopped smiling at us the whole time we were there. We didn't feel much like dessert anyway.

We paid our bill and went over to Walmart to take a look. Well, there's no use describing it, you know what it looked like. It looked like every other Walmart in the world, except that all the "sales associates" were Mexican. I hate to admit it, but we cruised around the store for quite a while. It was strangely, almost hypnotically, pleasant to listen to the monotonous Muzak and let my eyes gaze fondly down aisle after aisle of familiar merchandise. I got a buggy, not really necessary to transport my purchase of 200 grams of ham, but a thrill all the same, and I wheeled it up and down each and every aisle, sporting a silly, contented grin on my face. Robyn eventually tracked me down.

"It's time to go home now, Stephen."

"Ah, do we have to?"

"I think you're scaring people. And you know how you feel about Mexican prisons."

"Right you are then. Just once more round Ladies' Lingerie and I'll meet you back at the check-out counter." I was gone in a flash, leaving nothing behind but two parallel streaks of smoking buggy-wheel rubber in my wake.

The Cashier Barbie automaton at the check-out had the same model of pasted-on smile we'd seen at Beeps and was very quick and efficient with our meager purchase of ham, tuna, and rolls. And then it got a little weird.

Not only did the cashier accept my large denomination bill without even a cringe, which as you may recall almost never happens in central Mexico, but she then proceeded to dole out the exact amount of correct change right down to the last centavo. I don't know where Walmart gets its centavos from, because Mexicans just don't use them anymore, but the point is that a centavo is worth only one tenth of one U.S. cent. It appears that Walmart, as an institution, is simply incapable of comprehending the idea that some amounts of money are really not worth bothering about. It's a long time since those frugal Pilgrims landed at Plymouth Rock, but their values live on in Walmartland. And the funny thing is, you'd expect that it would be the people in a poor country like Mexico that would be more inclined to count everything down to the very last fraction of a penny, rather than those from a wealthy country like the U.S., where people can afford to be generous. But in fact, it's the complete opposite. More than once in Mexico, I've been given a gift by a merchant operating a small business – a merchant with much less money to throw around than me – and, I swear, it was for no other reason than as an expression of his or her good will.

Now a casual observer of Colima's Walmartland might say, "Look, Mexico is succumbing to American values, it's all over for Mexico." Hah, I say. If you look carefully behind the painted-on smiles of the waitresses and scratch beneath the surface of the indoctrinated cashiers, I guarantee you'll find a stern, dignified, and entirely illogical Mexican underneath. Companies like Walmart have attempted to brainwash these folks in some kind of sensory-deprivation boot camp somewhere, but they'll never pull it off. This culture is just too strong. Like every other invader of Mexico over the centuries, Walmart too will eventually be absorbed and transformed by these people. And Walmart will never know what hit them. (If you sense here the kind of vitriolic bluster usually associated with those who are about to go down to an ignominious defeat, you may be right, but let's hope not.)

Thirty minutes later, our cab pulled up in front of the Flamingo Hotel and thirty minutes after that we'd showered and were lying on our beds, pleased to be back in Mexicoland. Walmartland is okay, but I wouldn't want to live there.

We spent several more blissful days in Colima, I guess you sort of figured out that we liked the place, and much of our time was just spent bench-sitting. Bench-sitting is really just a variation on two of our other favourite pastimes: hammock-swinging and anchoring. (Anchoring, for those of you who have never done it, is where you take a boat out to a nice bit of quiet water, throw out the anchor, and lie back and watch the ducks drift past. The ducks themselves frequently engage in this sort of activity using tiny little anchors that are very difficult to see. It's very Zen, very fishing-without-a-rod.) But there are three wonderful things I absolutely have to tell you about before we bid farewell to sunny Colima: the Museo Universitario de Artes Populares (a folk-art museum), the Ballet Folclórico, and Sunday nights in the jardín.

If I could send you to only one museum in all of Mexico, Colima's folk-art museum would be the one. On the ground floor there was a wonderful collection of native costumes, most of which had actually been used by the local Indians as part of the various religious and traditional festivals that occur regularly in the nearby villages. Most of the costumes were extremely bizarre – lots of sequinned and mirrored veils covering faces, and fancy robes covered in embroidered images of spiders, beetles, and snakes. One extraordinary costume, which should have been titled *I Never Saw the Alligator Coming, Honest*, was displayed on a freestanding papier-mâché figure of a Mexican peasant and gave him the appearance of having been speared with a six-foot alligator, the head protruding from his crotch and the tail sticking out from his butt.

But the really neat stuff was upstairs. The entire second floor was crowded with glass cases absolutely crammed with the kind of crafts poor Mexican artisans make out of whatever they have lying around, articles they hope they can flog for a few pesos to passing tourists and little kids. There was a tiny nativity scene made entirely out of corn-husks. The whole thing was about two inches across; the crèche no bigger than an ant. There were teeter-totters and boxers that came to life by swinging the little paddle on which they sat, and little wooden people who danced in a gazebo when you turned the primitive wooden crank. There were shelves overflowing with little amusing portraits modelled in clay of every conceivable traditional Mexican occupation: bakers, butchers, tinsmiths, and more.

I think the museum offers people a kind of survey of the Mexican soul. The downstairs of the museum is full of demons and magic and has a certain threatening quality to it, while the upstairs gives viewers a vivid insight into the Mexicans' love of play. Surely it's this intriguing blend of the frightening and the sweet that lies at the heart of so much in Mexico. To me, the museum's a real gem, but then I'm the kind of guy that finds anchoring fun.

Robyn and I had been told that the Teatro Hidalgo had once been Father Hidalgo's home, so when we first walked into the theatre to see the Ballet Folclórico, my initial reaction was, "Whoa, dude, groovy guy to live in a place like this."

A dizzying number of tiers of boxed seats rose straight up from the main auditorium, only stopping when they reached the elegant ceiling high up above. There was no setback at all from tier to tier, so each one felt as though it was close and intimate with the stage. If you unrolled the Leaning Tower of Pisa out into one long rectangle, and then rolled it back up again with the stacks of pillars on the inside, and added a lot of velvet and brass, that's what it felt like to me, standing there on the auditorium floor looking up. Turns out, my image of Hidalgo living here as some Mad Priest of the Opera pounding away feverishly on his giant pipe organ and belting out a litany of inspiring revolutionary slogans was a bit incorrect. Hidalgo never lived in this exact building at all, although, in a sense, he did live under it. He was banished to a home on this site in 1792 by his church elders. They had hoped they were getting rid of the little troublemaker once and for all – him with his silly ideas about justice for the oppressed. The theatre was built on top of Hidalgo's old home in 1883. It was one of President Porfirio Diaz's flights of fancy, built with the money Americans and Germans were pouring into the country in the last years of the nineteenth century. Poor Porfirio, so many theatres, so little appreciation. In 1910, the ungrateful common people of the nation showed their dissatisfaction with him (and showed an appalling lack of understanding of the importance of opera in their lives) by setting off the Mexican Revolution.

As for the Ballet Folclórico, we were provided with an evening filled with stunningly beautiful costumes and proud youthful faces, stamping and swirling to the music of a small but excellent orchestra. For two hours I was completely lost in the colourful fantasy world of chivalrous love between beautiful young men and women from Mexico's rich cultural past. It was an extremely polished, high-octane performance. And that was *especially* impressive when you consider that the performers were all students from the University of Colima, who were probably planning to party all night long in the hallway outside our room.

In the town squares of the more traditional Mexican cities, you'll often see Canadians and Americans sitting around with silly grins on their faces as they feed and nourish themselves on all that sweet ambience of an older culture, a culture still steeped in the romantic notions of a bygone era. Those people are bench-sitters too, just like Robyn and me, and you'll occasionally spot them in the jardíns of Colima.

On our final night in town – a Sunday – we went to the Jardín Libertad. Every Sunday night, they light up the ornate little gazebo in the centre of the jardín, and they stuff it to overflowing with an orchestra playing old Glenn Miller tunes. When we got there, Mexican couples were already dancing together in the shadows around the edges of the gazebo, and Robyn and I took a seat. Pretty soon, we were in moonlight and stardust heaven.

That last night in Colima, the jardín was warm and soothing, with a gentle breeze shushing through the palms and blending in with those relaxed, jazzy dance tunes from the Thirties. Knowing we were soon going back to San Miguel, we just sat and tried to suck it all in – the band, the couples dancing, the kids climbing like monkeys on the wrought-iron railings. And yeah, we had silly grins on our faces too.

For one precious evening, it felt as if maybe romance hadn't thrown in the towel quite yet after all. Maybe romance had found a plaza in Mexico to try and make one last stand.

Chapter 15

On Monday, January 29, the cab driver dropped us off at Avenida Madero 218 in Mexico's second largest city, Guadalajara, our last stop on the journey back to San Miguel. I was expecting to find a sign on the door saying, "Posada San Pablo. Welcome to our humble but comfortable inn. We are located on the second floor, so please ring the buzzer and someone will be happy to come out and wait upon your every need. We carry bags cheerfully, we massage feet enthusiastically, and we always have tea and cookies on hand for the weary traveller."

That was what my guidebook led me to believe I would find. Instead, we stood there confronted by a locked door, no buzzer, and no signs, none of any kind at all. The door remained completely indifferent to my yelling and my pounding. Responding in any way to such bad behaviour was apparently beneath its dignity. I was forced to face the reality that there was no longer an inn at this address. Would anybody like a big heavy guidebook on Mexico? Some signs of violent, physical abuse, but can probably take lots more.

Robyn's patience with hotel hunting lasts about a minute. Then she'll take whatever comes next – a Hyatt Regency honeymoon suite for $1000 a night or a Salvation Army skid-row dormitory for a hymn and a prayer. Makes no difference. I may have been at least partially the cause of this state of affairs. You see, I have been known in the past to engage in secret experiments on her to try and discover just how far down the Grunge Scale (my own personal hotel-ranking system) a Canadian woman would go before breaking under the strain. I know it must seem cruel, but how else is mankind ever to know?

So, the way we handle the hotel thing most of the time is that we park Robyn someplace where she can be comfortable, while I head nobly off on a sacred quest for the perfect hotel. In this case, we found Robyn a little Fifties-style diner called the Café Argentino, where, for the price of an espresso, they very good-naturedly let her camp out surrounded by all our things.

About an hour later, after a fairly successful campaign from my point of view, we checked in to the Hotel Las Americas. Its chief attributes were that the rooms were very civilized, quiet, came with cable TV, and cost only $25 a night. Its drawbacks were that it was in a part of town that looked a lot like bombed-out Beirut after the Lebanese Civil War, and that most of the cars passing within inches of the front doors were going at speeds of up to 130 mph thus becoming airborne as they flew past due to a sudden uplifting of the road at that point. Like I said, a veritable coup.

Since, at $25 a night we were splurging a little, I decided we could save a few bucks if I put together our MSR stove and cooked us up a little something I call Ramen Salmon.

Ramen Salmon

The key to much of the finest in French cuisine is the simple cream sauce. The same can be said of many hotel-room dishes. But unlike its French cousin, the Hotel-Room Cream Sauce owes its delicate flavour and smooth consistency to the degree to which the ramen noodles are ground. The finer the grind, the smoother and sweeter the sauce. This lovely creamed-salmon dish is best served on or beside a fresh, crusty roll.

Step 1-Using your Swiss Army knife, open the can of salmon, drain it into the toilet (so as not to plug the sink), and set it aside to breathe.

Step 2-Take one of your small Melamine travelling plates and place anywhere from 2 to 5 tablespoons of ramen noodles from any of the commonly available ramen soup brands onto it. (Instant Lunch, which comes packed in styrofoam cups, is often the most readily available). Take one of your hotel-room glasses and grind the noodles as finely as possible. The more finely you grind, the less you need to use. If there are pieces of insect in your noodle flour after grinding, you can do one of three things: pick them out, start again with a cleaner glass, or stay in better hotels.

Step 3-Bring the milk and a spoon over to your work surface, and clear away all flammables from the immediate area. Remember to place the MSR aluminum windscreen UNDER your stove when working on wooden tables or chests. The open flame of these little stoves probably won't do as much harm as all the cigarette burns that have preceded it, but burning down hotels should always be avoided where possible, especially if you're in it at the time.

Step 4-Now you can start up your MSR camping stove. Always remain calm while using a campstove in a hotel room. A few minutes of slow regular breathing as in meditation is a very good idea. Some people like to pray. Tie back long hair, especially if frizzy. Dreadlocks tend to ignite rather like children's sparklers, only more so, so a hair net might be a good idea.

Step 5-To start the stove, turn the valve and fill the little fuel reservoir half full. Ignite the fuel with a match. In warm climates white gas vaporizes very quickly so you can probably light the stove from a couple of feet away. Never throw the match. If the flame reaches three feet in height, you have overfilled the cup. This is when the benefits of your breathing exercises should become obvious.

Step 6-Place 3/4 of a cup of milk in a saucepan and heat briefly. Pour in the noodle flour and simmer 5 minutes or until thick. Add the salmon, cook another 5 minutes and serve with fresh rolls.

Step 7-Turn off the stove and dangle it out an open window for a minute or two. This will reduce the smell of unburned gases in the room while you dine, and if you're lucky enough to have a window facing the interior of your hotel, it will also give you an interesting view of the other sorts of activities people pursue in hotel rooms while away on holiday.

Bon appétit!

*N.B. A note to my mother (and to anyone else for that matter): This last bit about using a campstove in a hotel room – it was just a joke, honest. I didn't mean any of it. You know, Mom, I would never do *anything* as foolish as that. And to those people contemplating trying such a thing themselves, I have a little piece of

advice: please don't.
S.A.

By the way, the modern ramen noodle, also known as Maggie Mee in the Philippines, was invented in Japan by Mr. Momofuku Ando in 1970. For those wishing to embark on a life dedicated to the blessed noodle, I recommend the book, *Book of Ramen*, (Turtleback Books, 1993, Friday Harbor, U.S.A.) and The Official Ramen Home Page at: http://mattfischer.com/ramen. Some believe that Gandhi's favourite mantra "ra-ma, ra-ma" may really have been "ra-men, ra-men," although so far my attempts to verify this have proven unsuccessful.

Jalisco's most famous artist was the painter José Clemente Orozco, and some of his greatest works are in Guadalajara, the state capital. On Tuesday, we set out to have a look at them.

Orozco was a muralist. He painted without the use of his right hand and right eye, which were both lost in a school science experiment when he was a young student. He, Diego Rivera, and David Alfaro Siqueiros were known in the Mexican art world as "Los Tres Grandes" (The Three Great Ones). The Mexican Muralist Movement, to which they all belonged, was the most important art movement to come out of Latin America during the whole of the twentieth century. But it had a significance that went way beyond the realm of artistic style – it was profoundly cultural as well.

In the years following the end of the Mexican Revolution (which lasted from 1910-1920), the artists, philosophers, and politicians of the day made a concerted effort to overcome, once and for all, the Mexican people's deep-seated sense of inferiority. The mestizos and Indians of Mexico had the psychological damage from four hundred years of conquest and servitude to work out of their systems, and the Mexican Muralist Movement played a significant role in initiating the cleansing process.

Although entire books have been written on the cause of the Mexican Revolution, actually the reasons were pretty straightforward. The dictator, Porfirio Diaz, who ruled Mexico from 1876 to 1910, had created an economic boom in the country on the backs of the poor. When he threw open the doors to foreign investment, he created the environment in which mining and agriculture could become hugely successful endeavours. The price paid for agricultural success was the appropriation of land from the peasants. The price paid for mining success was the government's turning a blind eye to the existence of new forms of slavery. Workers could be tied to their owners by their debts to the company store, or falsely imprisoned by collaborating local authorities and then sold off to corporations in the form of chain gangs.

So although the Mexican Mural Movement started in the 1930s, it was in fact a direct spin-off of the Mexican Revolution. The Mexican Revolution may have begun in 1910, but the path it followed from there was both tortuous and tortured. It wasn't until the presidency of Lazaro Cárdenas in 1934 that the Revolution's real goals – land reform for the benefit of the average Mexican, and the entrenchment of a Mexican identity (Mexicanidad) – began to be acted upon in earnest. Cárdenas worked vigorously to promote the interests of the common Mexican, perhaps at least partly because he was himself a mestizo with Tarascan Indian blood in his veins.

The 1930s in Mexico were a time when philosophy hung thick in the air like smoke in a bohemian café. A philosopher called José Vasconcelos was Cárdenas's Minister of Education, and he wrote often about his idea that the Mexican people were a "cosmic race," harbingers of a future world where Eastern and Western sensibilities and features would blend into one global race. For Vasconcelos (and for Alan Riding), the Indians, with their distant origins in Asia, would be the source of the spiritual characteristics of the new race; and the Spaniards, with their European roots, would be the source of the technological traits. He took it upon himself to invite the finest Mexican artists to paint murals on the walls of large public buildings with the intention of both educating the people about their noble Indian roots and showing them vividly the degree to which they had been exploited by the technologically advanced Spaniards.

The three great Mexican muralists are often discussed in the same breath, but in fact, they all left quite different imprints on Mexican society. Rivera was a man whose personal life took on almost mythological proportions, but his work, although powerful as narrative, was flat and expressionless in its portraits of people.

Siqueiros was a raving, gun-wielding politico who spent more time stirring up the masses than actually painting. Orozco, to my mind, was the greatest painter of the bunch, capable of creating an endless wealth of intensely moving and profoundly powerful images.

It's important to realize how deep was the feeling of Mexican inferiority that Orozco and the others were trying to obliterate. It's also important to realize that in present-day Mexico, to a large extent, the feelings persist.

Octavio Paz, one of Mexico's greatest writers, deals at length with this subject in his book, *Labyrinth of Solitude*. His way of trying to rid the Mexican people of this feeling of inferiority that they carry around with them like a ball and chain, is to explain it away by calling it something else: solitude:

> Our sense of inferiority, real or imagined, might be explained at least partly by the reserve with which the Mexican faces other people and the unpredictable violence with which his repressed emotions break through his mask of impassivity. But his solitude is vaster and profounder than his sense of inferiority. It is impossible to equate these two attitudes. When you sense that you are alone it does not mean that you feel inferior but rather that you feel you are different. Also a sense of inferiority may sometimes be an illusion, but solitude is a fact, we are truly different and we are truly alone.

His words remind me of a father who, after yelling at his child, says that he is not angry. The truth is he does not want to be angry, and he hopes that by saying he is not, that that will make it so. Paz's weak attempt to sweep this sense of inferiority under the carpet by his clever use of rhetoric, to me only serves to emphasize the power it holds over him.

Feeding on that great upwelling of national pride that followed the Revolution, the muralists fought like Titans to establish a sense of pride in the Mexican people. View the murals in this context, and they send chills up one's spine.

We reached the entrance to the Instituto Cultural Cabañas, home to many exquisite Orozco murals, only to be told by a very resolute security guard that I wouldn't be allowed to take my tripod inside. I had specifically brought a tripod to photograph the murals because I knew they were located in a huge, dark tomb of a building (oddly referred to as "The Chapel"), where flash units were not permitted on account of the fading that they cause.

"Señor, if you won't let me use a flash, then I need to take a very long exposure with my camera, and unless I want the murals to look as if they were painted by Jackson Pollock, I need to use a tripod for that."

"Sí, señor."

"So can I take in my tripod?"

"No, señor."

I asked him to take me to his leader. He led me into a large office where I was greeted by a very short, charming young lady with the words "No, No, and No" tattooed on her forehead. She listened politely to my point of view and then told me in the nicest possible way that it would require a letter from someone very, very important to disregard the rules. When I asked her who exactly that person might be, she said she had no idea. Fearing that she might at any moment pass me along to a whole series of officials whose job it was to say "No" in increasingly polite and sympathetic ways, thereby condemning me to a Kafkaesque nightmare of days and weeks spent wandering the hallways of the Mexican bureaucracy, I gave birth to a brand-new baby idea.

I reached into my pack with an attitude just one step removed from gloating, and triumphantly pulled out my letter from the Minister of Tourism of Colima, with all its seals, signatures and important sounding names. Then, with one impressive flourish of my hand (it's all in the wrist), I dropped it onto her desk.

There was an intense silence in the room as she carefully perused the letter.

"This is a very handsome letter, señor."

"Why yes, thank you."

"You must be very proud," she said, handing it back.

"Yes, I treasure every moment with it. So, do you think I can take the tripod in now?"

"No, señor."

"Right. Thank you then," at which point I had no alternative but to skewer her with it.

We entered the chapel through a pair of massive side doors. Directly overhead was a magnificent, simple, barrel-vaulted roof with semicircular stone arches placed at equal intervals along its length to act as ribs to support it. The curved spaces between these arches were where Orozco did his painting.

Considering that most paintings are painted in the hopes that people will actually be able to see them, could Orozco have possibly found a more awkward place to put his paintings than on a ceiling? I suppose on the underside of a kitchen table would have been a little more awkward, but not much. In order to view them, Robyn and I and the half-dozen or so other people in the chapel had to walk around with our Adam's apples pointing straight up and the back of our heads flopped over and resting between our shoulder blades. This was all very well for contortionists like Robyn, whose favourite party trick used to be to bend over backwards until her head appeared between her legs facing forwards again. But the rest of us there that day spent much of our time in a great deal of pain, bouncing off the walls and each other like a bunch of heavily drugged, sleep-walking whiplash victims.

I did eventually find a most excellent solution to this problem. Long, perfectly flat benches without backs ran the entire length of the floor, and you could lie on these things for as long as you wanted and gaze peacefully up at any one of the grand panels. (And if you happened to nod off for a few minutes, nobody'd be any the wiser, right?)

The murals are grim affairs, but moving. The Church is depicted in one panel as Death himself. Death is wearing a friar's robe, and, instead of a scythe, he is carrying a pointed cross, which is aimed directly at the naked Indian crouching down around his feet. In another, a ruthless-looking Spanish nobleman is using a large wooden cross to carry a monarch's crown. Another shows a train-like mechanical horse carrying a crown and crushing peasants as it lurches ahead, out of control.

It's easier to understand how Orozco arrived at some his images if you remember the politics of the times in which he was painting. The Thirties and Forties were highly charged decades in Mexico on account of the fierce, pitched battle that was being fought between two diametrically opposed groups: the fascists on the one side and the common working people on the other. Not only did Orozco use the obvious symbols of the cross and the crown to represent the traditional oppressors of the Mexican people, he also used the swastika as a way of tying in the Mexican struggle against injustice with the struggles of workers the world over. All told, it makes for a heady brew, and the fact that they're painted on the inside of a house of worship makes their impact all that much more powerful.

We returned to our hotel room, Orozco's traumatic images still firmly etched on our minds, and turned on the TV where there was a Mexican show in progress that was entirely devoted to playing videos of people with their pants falling down. The whole show. It must have been called *The Pants Falling Down Show* because there wasn't a single video where anything else happened. Actually, that's not entirely true, there was a bit where a very frisky little monkey was squeezing some lady's breasts as if testing them for ripeness, and one where a guy was lighting farts through his pants, but for the most part – pants falling down. I had no idea pants could fall down in so many ways, affecting so many people, and in so many circumstances. Many of these memorable moments were concluded by the appearance of a little cartoon devil guy who would blow a neatly timed raspberry every time somebody's butt was exposed. Robyn was in absolute stitches. In fact, after a few minutes of non-stop, gagging laughter, her eyes started to take on that wide-eyed, almost choking, please-somebody-help-me-I'm-dying-here look. A guy bends down to pick up some candies and his pants split – Robyn cracks up. A guy is helping carry a bride's train as she leaves the church, and he grins mischievously and lifts it right up to reveal her butt – Robyn cracks up again. Soon she was clutching her gut and wheezing, desperately trying to suck in a little air between laughs. In response to her garbled plea, I turned the TV off.

That silly show had succeeded in completely flushing Orozco's murals from our thoughts. Poor Orozco, there he was hoping to bring about change by grabbing the world's attention with all his profoundly significant images, and it turns out that a better way to truly engage people's attention is just to show them pictures of people with their pants falling down.

Before leaving Canada, Robyn had said to me that she would go almost anywhere and do almost anything with me on this trip, as long as I made her one promise: that she could make a pilgrimage to one special place, and pay homage to the divine beverage that was made there. The next morning, after stocking up on chocolate donuts and sandwich supplies at Gigante, we took a city bus over to what is known as the "old" bus terminal and then got on another bus destined for the quaint little town of Tequila.

The first half of the bus ride out to Tequila (a ninety-minute trip) was taken up with the task of getting out of Guadalajara – normally, you would think, a tedious business. But in fact we were entertained constantly by the onslaught of pedlar-merchants that got on and off the bus with the kind of snappy regularity more often associated with vaudeville. One guy hopped onto the bus dressed very snazzy-like in a black and white striped shirt and proceeded to sell us on the merits of his book of mathematical formulas and conversion tables.

"Never again be perplexed by the square root of the number 2! Impress your friends at parties with how quickly you can convert milliliters to fluid ounces! Confronted by strangers while walking alone on the street at night, confuse them with the formula for compound interest, $P=A\div[(1+(R\div100))n]$, and then get away while they try to figure it out!"

He was good. He sold one in less than a minute. I was busy trying to think whom I might buy one for, when he suddenly vanished. Pity. Just the thing for Aunt Millie and Uncle Mort.

For the last forty or so minutes of the trip, we drove up and over and around gently rolling hills of spiky, blue agave plantations, whose changing geometric patterns had a beauty about them that verged on the mildly hypnotic. Then, as so often happens when travelling in Mexico, we were abruptly wrenched from our cocoon-like reverie by being dumped into the thick of a bustling little street scene. Robyn had made it to Tequila at last.

Although the brief glimpses of cheap bottles of no-name tequila in the souvenir store windows did slow our progress momentarily, we couldn't quite imagine the genitalia motif that was used on all the glassware and pottery fitting in with our décor, so we plowed our way through the crowds, setting our sights on the main distillery district, a few blocks away.

It must have been the off-season or something because when we got out near the large entrance gates of the José Cuervo and Sauza factories, the streets were completely quiet and empty. However, this did lend an air of sanctity to the surroundings, which was entirely in keeping with Robyn's pilgrim mood. You know, I think she was only partly kidding about the idea of this being a pilgrimage. I think there was a level on which she was channelling her female connection to nature and its cycles into a deep interest in the mysterious alchemy that could transform a humble desert plant into the mind-altering substance known as tequila. And there were certain elements around that were fortuitously supporting the almost spiritual nature of her journey. There was the lovely, musty smell of fermentation everywhere, not incense exactly, but almost. And the streets were strewn with agave pulp, not the sweet grasses common in Mexican processions, but near enough to give a similar effect.

We arrived at the Cuervo factory to find it was closed to visitors. Same with the Sauza. Not great planning on our part, but it wasn't as if there was a recreation co-ordinator at our hotel that we could have consulted or anything, and don't even think about the guidebook. All it said about Tequila was that it took twenty minutes to get there – and it even got that wrong.

So we went for a little amble along one of the town's pretty little, twisty streets, and just resigned ourselves to enjoying the sunshine and knowing that nothing was urgently required of us. We passed by an old broken-down doorway that was open just a crack, and I poked my nosey nose inside. It appeared to be an old abandoned distillery. My camera looked up at me and started begging, "Could we go inside please Dad, could we, could we huh, could we?" and I relented. Robyn followed cautiously behind.

We passed through the doorway and came out into a bright but desolate-looking open area surrounded by large, ram-shackle buildings. Slowly making his way over to us was an old man walking with a limp. He told us his name was Alberto, and when he discovered we were tourists interested in the process of making tequila, he offered to take us on a tour.

The old factory had been known as Tequila d' Reyes (Tequila of Kings), and as Alberto led us inside the main building, it looked like the boiler room of a World War II destroyer that had been bombed to smithereens by enemy torpedoes and then spent the last sixty years rotting on the ocean floor. There were dozens of great big greasy gears, the size of tractor wheels, that looked like part of a crusher that squeezed the juice out of the steamed agave hearts, or "pineapples" as they are called. I figured the crusher was probably steam-era technology, maybe mid-1800s or so. There were six badly damaged, giant, copper distilling vats, twenty feet tall, with pipes and gauges and lots of just stuff tangled all around them. They looked as if they were the result of a battle between two groups of plumbers with very differing views on plumbing theory. There was an oven for cooking the agave hearts prior to crushing, that was nothing more than a big old, crumbling brick room with openings.

Alberto led us from the main building back out into the brilliant sunshine and then over to another smaller building that was cool and dark inside. It took a few moments for our eyes to adjust, but we could see right away that the floor was wet. As our eyes gradually adapted to the light, we found ourselves inside a large, high-ceilinged room that was filled with hundreds of barrels of tequila, stacked one on top of the other. Some were leaking.

I said to Alberto, "I guess it's been many years since you last made tequila here. Do you think you'll ever be able to get the place up and running again?"

"It's running now, señor. Not today, because this is our day off, but tomorrow, we continue with the work."

Oh. Right. We're not in Kansas anymore. No, we're in Mexico now, where people use a tool until all that's left of it is the splinter you got in your hand the last time you used it. This is a place where, if you need a bolt, you don't go to a store that sells every size of bolt imaginable; you go to a store that makes you the bolt by welding a head onto a piece of threaded rod. Nothing gets thrown out by Mexicans until every single possible ounce of usefulness has been sucked out of it. Hell, even Alberto was in bad shape, but not so bad that they were ready to throw him out yet. I wondered if that was partly why I wasn't getting much sympathy from anybody about my back problems while we were in Mexico. Things just aren't expected to remain in perfect condition forever here. Breaking down is just part of the normal course of events. Join the crowd, my friend, we're all a little damaged around here.

When Alberto finished taking us around, he offered us a sample taste before leaving. I get headaches from booze, so I declined graciously, but Robyn was enthusiastic enough for two. She watched keenly as he poured a generous quantity of the crystal-clear liquid into a little ceramic souvenir cup. Ceremoniously, he handed it to her. That such a pure substance could be produced in this dirty, rusty, greasy, medieval torture chamber of a factory was indeed some kind of miracle. She sniffed. She swirled. She sipped. Then she knocked the whole thing back in one quick toss and closed her eyes. I felt as if we were watching someone taking Communion. Alberto and I waited for a few moments to see if she was going to start speaking in tongues or ululating or something. But there wasn't a sound – only a look of blissful satisfaction spreading across her face. It was that googly-eyed, Cookie Monster look, all over again.

I thanked Alberto on Robyn's behalf, since she had apparently been rendered speechless, and we walked back to the main entrance. I noticed Robyn had a little momentary stagger as we passed back out onto the street. I suppose she was still slightly overwhelmed by it all.

We started back the way we came, and as we got to the gates of the massive Sauza fortress, we noticed some activity around the ticket window. I made a few enquiries of the man behind the glass, and he said if we wanted to have a tour of the factory, we could probably tag along with the package-tour group of Americans who were just about to begin one. We leapt at the chance.

There's no need to describe the Sauza tour; it was really a very run-of-the-mill affair. I suppose it was a very nice factory as factories go. I mean, it was clean with lots of stainless steel and men in white coats and hard hats and everything. But I kept looking for the missile silos. The guy giving the tour was young and buff and cool, and performed his well-rehearsed spiel as if he was doing a stand-up routine in a popular nightclub. Like good little sheep, we followed the Sauza guy around and laughed at his jokes and stared vacantly at large shiny autoclaves while he recited meaningless numbers about the zillions of gallons they could hold, and by the end of it all, I was bored to tears. I preferred Alberto. He was old and he limped and he was real. The Sauza place just had no soul, certainly no Mexican soul. And soul's a large part of tequila. Hell, they operated the Sauza factory twenty-four hours a day, every day of the year. Now just how Mexican is that? Mexico is all about holidays and rust and dust and traditions and mystical rites (and sombreros, amoebas, banditos, cucarrachas, and bad trumpet playing, but let us not venture too far off the designated course). And it's all about tequila, the kind that comes from scruffy little distilleries like Tequila D'Reyes.

Mexicans themselves have always placed great significance on tequila and its role as a powerful symbol of their culture. The Nahuatl Indians, who produced the precursor to tequila called *pulque*, considered the maguey plant from which it was derived to be divine. They considered the plant to be the earthly representation of the goddess Mayaheul, a lady amply endowed with 400 breasts. (It took a few pulques to see all 400, I'm told.) Also, the state of intoxication itself had a spiritual value for the Indians because it was seen as being related to the dream state, a thing of profound importance in their culture.

There does seem to be something uniquely Mexican about tequila. Maybe it's partly because the smoky, spicy zest in its flavour conjures up the scent of the Mexican countryside. Or maybe, as anthropologist and writer Alfonso Alfaro observed, tequila is like the Mexican mestizo himself, created through the blending of two cultures. Tequila was born because the Spanish introduced the distillation process into the making of pulque, an Indian drink.

But it was not always so highly regarded by the upper classes in Mexico. The historian José María Muriá observed that during the nineteenth century a strong French chauvinism developed towards tequila (a by-product of the French influence that accompanied their brief reign from 1862-1866), and it was relegated to use chiefly by the masses. But after the Mexican Revolution, anything associated with the masses attained a greater prestige, and tequila soared in popularity across all sectors of Mexican society, coming to be identified with the new Mexican nationalism of the post-Revolution period.

I tried to share all this fascinating information with Robyn while they were plying her with margaritas after the Sauza tour, but she just nodded periodically and stared back at me with that same stoned look our cat has when I'm telling her about my day.

Chapter 16

We got up early on the morning of Thursday, February 1st, quite content to let Guadalajara continue along its road to total urban breakdown without us. Guadalajara has a few beautiful old buildings, but apart from that it's a very noisy, very dirty city in a state of serious decline, and we were only too happy to be leaving it.

Ever hopeful that Mexican realities had undergone a complete sea change while I was sleeping, I went down to the lobby and asked the guy at the front desk if he could help me down with my bag, as once again we had chosen a hotel without an elevator. I have to give the guy credit. He didn't mince words. He just said no. He didn't even have a cane or a limp or anything. He just wouldn't do it. I think it was that not-wanting-to-look-subservient thing again. It was taking me a while to get used to this sort of attitude, but I kept reminding myself that it wasn't really his fault – it was just a cultural thing. I'm not saying the despicable little twerp didn't tick me right off. I'm just saying, I think I was beginning to get it.

I couldn't carry my bag down the stairs; I didn't want to just kick it over the edge and watch all my camera equipment land in a crumpled heap of glass and metal at the bottom; and frankly, I didn't want Robyn to try carrying it because if she hurt her back too, then we might both end our days flopping around on the floor of the Hotel Las Americas while a crowd of curious Mexicans stood around having a good look. So, because the suitcase had to be pushed, not pulled, down the stairs, and because I had to keep my back straight when walking, I ended up having to go down the stairs to the lobby on my knees, pushing my suitcase ahead of me as I went. I looked like a beggar on holiday. As I thumped from step to step, I saw out of the corner of my eye with some satisfaction that a new guest was standing across from the guy at the front desk, and that the two of them were utterly horrified by what I was doing. I think they were caught somewhere between guilt and bewilderment. I was tempted to carry on right out the door that way just to see if I could embarrass them into giving me a little help, but alas, my knees were getting sore, and this was a battle of cultures that I sensed I could not win. So, after the final thump onto the lobby floor, I stood up, declared, "Hallelujah brother, I can walk!" and marched out the front doors to where Robyn was patiently waiting. Through the glass doors I could see the two guys at the front desk still standing there in a state of shock. They continued to watch us with deer-in-the-headlight stares until we finally disappeared entirely from their field of view.

We treated ourselves to two seats aboard one of the ETN buses, Mexico's best, and as always it was well worth the few extra dollars. There is one drawback to consider though if you're thinking of getting on one of these. They seem to have a fondness for showing disaster movies with at least one shot of a Third World bus sailing off the end of a broken bridge and exploding into a mushrooming ball of swirling orange fire. But if you don't mind that, ETN is great.

When we got into San Miguel later that afternoon, we went straight to Violetta's house. We had met Violetta at the Laughing Muffin back in December, when all three of us played Scrabble there as a way of seeking refuge from the cold. We couldn't get back into our apartment until February 3rd, so Violetta had agreed to put us up in exchange for a few games of Scrabble and an occasional saliva-soaking by her dog and surrogate baby, Willy, whom we all adored.

Violetta was similar in many ways to the other expat women of San Miguel. She was elderly, about seventy, and had originally come as a widow in search of fine weather and cheap accommodation, and then just never left. And like so many others, she was both an excellent painter and also a terribly insecure one with regards to her abilities. But where she differed from the rest was in the fact that she didn't have the hard edge of many of the others we had met. She spoke with a lovely Georgian drawl and carried herself with the grace of an old-fashioned Southern belle. She always dressed stylishly and was clearly a woman of refined taste, but she never put on airs. In fact, we discovered with some amusement that carousing at a local bar with a bunch of fairly raunchy drinking buddies (mostly Canadians) was a sacrosanct part of her daily routine.

There were some sad aspects to Violetta's life, though – mostly connected to loneliness and physical pain. She greatly missed the companionship of her second husband, and found herself living a fairly isolated existence in a part of town that was far from her friends. It didn't help, either, that her Mexican neighbour played loud music constantly and continually parked his bus in front of her driveway so she couldn't get into it. Her physical pain came from a variety of sources, but it was often bad enough to prevent her from getting out of bed in the morning. Occasionally she slipped into a mood of despair.

On the Friday morning, I decided to head out early from Violetta's and walk through town over to Juárez Park to take some pictures of Candelaria, an annual flower fair that was supposed to be quite wonderful.

God, it was great to be back walking those streets again. There's nothing particularly grand about San Miguel when you first spot it off in the distance from a bus or a car; it appears to just be a sprawl of human bric-a-brac at one end of a large plain. But when you are walking through it, it's like looking at an old, wrinkled face up close, full of lines and character that echo every laugh and tear that has ever touched it over its long and fruitful life.

Everywhere around me, I was being welcomed back by the charming spirit of this old and twinkly colonial town. I smiled at the wide-eyed cherubs carved into a pair of big old wooden doors, and looked again with amazement at those fanciful brass door knockers cast in the shape of a woman's gracefully dangling hand. The walls of weathered and peeling paint that adorned every street along my route were reminiscent of multi-coloured abstract paintings, only they were even more beautiful because they were so totally uncontrived. A schoolboy in a navy-blue school uniform suddenly brushed past me, probably running home to get something he forgot. Walking in front of me there was a group of cheerful and confident teenage girls with beautiful, café-au-lait-coloured skin and long, shiny, dark brown hair that their proud mothers had tied back for them with clean white ribbons. A neatly dressed, ten-year-old boy in a school uniform was crossing the street, his arms clasped protectively around his little sister, and the two of them, unaware of my presence, almost bowled me over as they hopped up onto the foot-high cobbled sidewalk on which I was walking. He glared at me (and why not, his sister was his charge), and then once they were safely beyond my reach, he noticeably relaxed his grip. An ancient, leathery woman, draped in a rebozo and using a cane, crossed the wobbly street an inch at a time, grimly resolved that if she accomplished nothing else that day, she would make it to the other side. I passed alongside a church and saw two women standing next to it, setting up a stand full of children's knickknacks and candles for the church. The sidewalks were so high and narrow that I felt a little like a mountain goat as I inched carefully around an old chiselled-stone corner, trying not to tumble onto the street below. I stuck my nose gingerly around the corner's edge, in case a kid should come flying around it and crash into me. Just a step or two in front of me, I spotted another young teenage girl; she was wearing a uniform just like the others, but she was walking alone – she was a dwarf, and it jolted me for an instant.

And just then, just as I was about to have an intense personal debate with myself about whether the handicapped were better off here or back in Canada, there was one very bizarre moment, straight out of a Fellini movie, where a man looking decidedly medieval, dressed in a long black velvet cape with ribbons in purple, white, and green trailing from his shoulders, went zooming past on a motorscooter.

The flower fair was a big disappointment. There were lots of flowers, and they were very pretty, but unlike my walk through town, there was no magic there. It looked like an ordinary plant nursery. It was actually very un-Mexican. There wasn't enough clutter; there were no clowns or animals, no loudspeakers, no silly music. I've since been told by locals that it used to be much better, and then someone decided it needed a few regulations. Oh yeah. Those'll kill just about anything. Death by lethal regulation I think they call it.

Journal, February 4

We're back at Isadora's now. We ended up down at La Vida's last night for a drink with Violetta. Met a radio host that I used to listen to in the Seventies while working alone in my studio making pottery. He holds dominion over the bar much like Norm from the TV show *Cheers*. It's strange, but I related to him better on the radio back then when he was a thousand miles away than I do now in person. He was more intimate and personable on the radio. In person he's a little brash, and more inscrutable. He talked a little about his show being cancelled and he was still pretty bitter after all these years. I think San Miguel is a useful sanctuary for some people.

Journal, February 5

We had tea at Florence's yesterday and met Claire. I think Florence is a serial hostess. She is continually picking up strays in the jardín. There's probably a pit full of them in the back yard.

Claire is a Canadian from Saskatchewan and suffers from chronic fatigue syndrome. A friend gave her the idea that San Miguel might cure her, clear mountain air, that sort of thing. Trouble with that theory is, at this altitude there isn't much air, and the air that *does* exist is full of dust. Anyway, if I'd been her friend in Saskatchewan, I would have sent her away as well – she prattled on endlessly. Talking to her, I thought *I* must be the one suffering from chronic fatigue. But she did say one thing that caught my ear. She said she had a really nice apartment in the Colonia San Antonio district. Since they're pretty hard to find in San Miguel, tomorrow I will investigate.

The name of her street was the 25th of January. She was number 30. This is what happens when you ask somebody for directions in Mexico:

"Excuse me, can you tell me where 30 the 25th of January is?"

"No, it's the 6th of February, señor."

"No, I want a street, not a date."

"You're on a street, señor."

"Which street?"

"The 16th of September."

"But I need 30 the 25th of January!"

"No, señor, who's on first."

"Who?"

"That's what I said."

And so it goes, until you have no hair left.

When I got into the neighbourhood of San Antonio, I was faced with the fact that there were no street signs to give me the faintest clue about where I was. I stopped to ask a couple of teenage schoolgirls if they knew where the 25th of January was. They shrugged and politely said no. Okay, fair enough, no is good, certainly it's clear. I walked on a little further and asked a nice young couple whether *they* knew. He was adamant that I should go in one direction and she was adamant that I should go in the other. They started to have a heated argument about it, and so I decided to just leave them there to sort it out for themselves. A group of teenage boys then came bobbing and grooving by and I thought, oh well, it's worth a try, I'll ask *them* where the 25th of January is, and they said I was on it. Seeming quite pleased with themselves, they then gyrated on down the street as if they were practising the latest in football victory dances. But once they were gone, I realized my problem was far from being actually solved: a) because I didn't believe they really had a clue what the name of the street was, and b) because there were no numbers on any of the doors.

Well, to make a long story short, I got hopelessly lost and there was a complete absence of people in the street to ask for help. I had just about given up hope when I passed beside a little grocery store and saw a man inside sweeping. I decided, what the hell, I'll go in and ask him. On hearing me enter, he turned around to face me, and immediately I realized I'd made a terrible mistake. It was very evident from the look of his eyes that he was totally blind. I didn't know what to do. He was waiting for me to address him. If I turned and ran he might think I was a thief, but it also seemed inordinately cruel to cause embarrassment to a blind man by asking him for directions. So I resorted to what I always resort to when all else fails. I started singing *La Vie en Rose*. No, just kidding. I resorted to the truth. I asked him if he knew where the 25th of January was. He smiled, put down his broom, walked to the edge of the street, and proceeded to give me detailed (and, I should add, totally accurate) directions on how to get there. So there you have it; that's the answer I guess. If you get lost in Mexico, there's only one thing to do: ask a blind person for directions.

Getting there was definitely half the fun in this case – all of the fun, actually. Claire's apartment was okay, but no better than Isadora's. I think I must have drifted off at least five times during our conversation – I think we talked about blankets and slippers – and after my head fell into my teacup for the fifth time, I flicked off the last drop of tea dangling from my nose, and hastily departed.

It felt so good to be out on the streets and free again that I decided to prolong the experience by meandering my way home haphazardly, guided only by whatever narrow lane or wall of trailing flowers caught my fancy. As I walked, my thoughts turned to all the times I'd had trouble getting good directions in Mexico. I once asked a worker sitting on a curb having lunch with his friend which way I should go to find a certain address. He pointed straight at a brick wall at the end of the street. I walked obediently up to the wall, thinking that if I did so, all would become clear. I got to the wall and saw that it was indeed a brick wall. Having no idea what to do next, I looked back to the guys on the curb again and shrugged a perplexed "What now guys?" They just pointed right through the wall. I scratched my head, pointed right through the wall and shrugged back to them one more time, just to be sure. Again they pointed enthusiastically at the wall. Again I turned and looked at it. I tried walking into it a couple of times, thinking maybe it was one of those faith things where you just really had to believe in it. To this day I still have no idea what was going on. I suspect I was standing inches away from a magic portal leading straight into the Mexican psyche. I guess I missed my chance. Feeling utterly defeated and ridiculous, all I could do was slink around a corner and ponder the great words on the cover of Carl Franz's, *People's Guide to Mexico*: "WHEREVER YOU GO . . . THERE YOU ARE!!"

"You know, I just don't get Mexicans," said Elisabeth. "Look at those guys over there carrying bricks up to the second floor of that house."

Elisabeth was addressing Robyn, Florence, and me late one afternoon while we were sitting on our rooftop terrace overlooking San Miguel and all getting sloshed on margaritas. We met Elisabeth on the bus coming back from Guadalajara. She had just arrived in Mexico from Los Angeles. She was tall and fiftyish with a haughty way of speaking and looked like a bit of a preppy in her brand-new, perfectly tailored blue jeans. Her lipstick was a shade of red that seemed designed to impress, and she applied it with such precision that I'm sure she had to use masking tape to stay within the lines. It all looked like an elaborate hoax to hide her insecurities, whatever they may have been.

Like so many of the people we met in Mexico, she seemed to be at a crossroads in her life. She was single and had just come into some money after the death of her mother. So, I suspect, like Margaret, she was taking the opportunity to seek out new directions. When she first arrived in San Miguel, she had impulsively flung herself into a stone-carving class at the Bellas Artes art school, only to quit after the second lesson when she realized that breaking a nail or mussing her hair might be distinct possibilities. I think, as with Margaret, the relentless advance of time was weighing heavily on her, and, in a slightly desperate way, she was hoping to squeeze in one last adventure in Mexico. That, maybe, was where her mood of urgency came from. But there was certainly nothing in her personality to suggest that Mexico and she would ever make a good fit. By her own admission, she found the place and the people totally baffling.

She continued, "The top of the scaffolding is about two feet higher than that second-floor window they're using to gain access to the upper floor of the building, and every time they take bricks up, they have to step back down onto the window ledge and then inside. It would be way less work to just lower the scaffolding a couple of feet and then they could just walk right in. A couple of minutes of extra work now would save them lots of work over time." She looked at the three of us. "Don't you think?"

Florence stepped in with her opinion. "Yes, but what's the point in saving time if it means that there will be less work for a cousin or a sister's brother or whoever else happens to be around and needing the money? It doesn't cost much for a homeowner here to hire one more person, and the extra job might help feed a whole family."

Elisabeth looked stunned. This made no sense to her. She thought charities should be charities and work should be work.

I decided to wade in. "And there's another thing to consider. In Canada, and I'm sure in the States, we plan and plan and plan everything down to the littlest detail, and, you know, I think it adds considerably to the stresses that accumulate in our societies. I remember when I first moved to Hornby Island, I was horrified by the way people worked. They would start a project, just start it, and then see where it took them before they made any further plans. The next day if there were problems, they confronted them one at a time. I knew this one potter on the island . . . The smoke from his kiln used to creep into his house and stink the place up. One night when his girlfriend told him that that was it, she'd had it with all that smoke, he went out in the middle of the night in a torrential rain storm and just cut a hole in his roof with a chainsaw to let the stuff escape."

"Didn't the rain come in the hole?" said Elisabeth.

"No, he threw a tarp over it. Kept it like that for years. It blew off on windy days but he'd just put it back up."

"Well, I guess if it saved the relationship . . ."

"No, she left him anyway," I replied, "but that's not the point."

I took a sip of my margarita, a handful of chips, and continued.

"A couple of years after I moved to Hornby, I started to build my workshop with a local carpenter named Roger; there were just the two of us working on it. So we built the floor, it was thirty-six feet long and sixteen feet wide. Then, after scratching his head for a few minutes, he suggested we build three laminated beams, huge things, each one ten inches by four inches by thirty-six feet long, build them right there on the floor. I said, 'Yeah, but Roger how are we going to get them up in the air? They have to be about twelve feet up there to hold up the roof.' He said, 'I dunno. Don't worry about it.'

"So we get the beams hammered together and lying there on the floor, and Roger looks at them for a while. Then he goes home for lunch, comes back, has a coffee and looks at them a little more, goes home again, and comes back later, this time with a crow bar. He shoves the crow bar under one end of the beam and gives the bar one mighty push and says, 'Shove a shim under it, will ya!?' The shim raised the beam about an eighth of an inch. We had twelve feet to go. He can't be serious. But after a few days and a lot of shims and blocks and posts, we had those three beams up there. It doesn't make sense maybe from a time-is-money point of view, but it works pretty well when time is all you've got."

Elisabeth was unimpressed. "I think you're all nuts."

"More than likely," said Florence, "but you know, they sometimes have their reasons for what they do. I have a little San Miguel story that might interest you.

"There's a little Mexican grocery store right in the centre of San Miguel called Bonanza. It's only about twenty feet wide by fifty feet long, but the locals call it a supermarket anyway because it carries a little of everything. It does a pretty good business. It carries a lot of the kind of gringo food that's hard to find elsewhere in town: Duncan Hines cake mixes, Mars bars, Kraft Dinner, Budweiser – the staples of any good North American diet.

"Well, once upon a time, they scored big time when they brought in a little smoked salmon of a particularly high quality to see if it would sell. They had only just barely put it on the shelf and word got around about how good it was. They sold out everything the first day.

"Now, the owner's no fool. He orders more right away. The same amount, because he doesn't know why it sold so well. Maybe there was some weird gringo fiesta like Our Lord of the Sacred Salmon or something. Anyway, he felt confident that he could at least sell the same amount as before.

"The day the salmon arrives, word gets around, he sells it all in one day. So our owner places another order for the same quantity as before. Sure, he's a little cautious, but what if the salmon bubble bursts? He knows people are fickle and he doesn't want to risk having his prosperous little business go belly-up on account of a truckload of salmon that all of a sudden nobody wants.

"Now, there were a lot of gringos in town who apparently planned their lives around exactly when that salmon was due to arrive. ('I'd love to marry you on Saturday honey, but that's the day the salmon arrives.' That sort of thing.) When this latest order didn't arrive at the time specified by the owner, people were furious. The gringo community was thrown into chaos. He told them to be patient; it was on order; it would be here soon, maybe tomorrow. He told them anything he could think of to get them off his back. When it didn't come and it didn't come, the local gringos started to say nasty things about the owner. He was just another incompetent Mexican; he never orders enough; with a little Yankee ingenuity we could turn his store into something that would make some real money, etc., etc. The stories got back to the owner and he became disheartened.

"When the order of salmon finally arrived, the usual thing happened and it sold out within the hour. Later that day, one of the store's regulars, an elderly gringo guy, stopped by and became irate over the fact that he had missed out again on the salmon and that now it would be another month before any more came in.

" 'No señor,' said the owner. 'It will not be another month. It will not be ever. I have decided not to carry it any more.'

"The gringo turned purple. 'What!? You could make a fortune from this stuff! Order in more! Raise your prices! Haven't you heard about the law of supply and demand? You have a copious overabundance of demand, and should be capitalizing on it.'

"The Mexican owner just looked the gringo in the eye and without expression said, 'This salmon has made everyone angry. I have very unhappy customers for the first time in thirty years. It's bad for my business to have disappointed customers, and if I stop carrying it, things will return to normal, and people will enjoy shopping in my store again. It will also be a great relief to me personally.' "

There was silence on our rooftop as the four of us mulled over Florence's tale.

Then Elisabeth spoke, "So you're telling me capitalism doesn't work? That Mexican inefficiency is the best way to go?"

Florence just smiled. "No. They have different priorities, that's all. And you're perfectly free to choose yours."

Journal, February 28 – The Day After Mardi Gras

Sweeping and mopping are clearly national obsessions here.

Mexico is a dusty country and I think the general feeling here is that Mexican dust should be up in the air whenever possible. If it settles for any length of time on something, it is your patriotic duty as a good Mexican to stir it up and put it back where it belongs.

They don't do a real Mardi Gras here in San Miguel. You have to go to a coastal town like La Paz or Acapulco for that, where they celebrate it under the name of *Carnaval.* But they do have a lovely spring mating ritual that coincides with it where teenagers of both sexes go traipsing about town cracking eggs on each other's heads. It isn't as mucky as it sounds, however, because the eggs are first hollowed out and then filled with either confetti or powdered limestone. Both those materials admirably serve the purpose of marking and then ultimately embarrassing their victims. I don't know how many thousands of these things were smucked on the heads of the slow of foot yesterday, but this morning while out for a walk, the plazas and streets looked as if Lex Luthor had succeeded in detonating a Good Year blimp filled with icing sugar over the entire city. And true to form, there were legions of women shopkeepers out and about on the streets vigorously sweeping their little hearts out, zealously intent on getting all that white powder up into the air again before their customers started arriving. For this mildly asthmatic wheezer, it will be a good day to stay home and do some serious sampling of our latest collection of unusually flavoured potato chips.

Journal, March 7

Robyn and I have just lately become aware of the fact that in three weeks or so we'll be leaving San Miguel and heading back to Canada. It's going to feel like leaving a faithful old friend.

I've started to notice that some of my attitudes about things around here have gone through quite a change. I used to think the highly orchestrated, over-sentimentalized Latin pop music we hear all over San Miguel was laughable in its over-the-top romanticism. But now I think the music fits perfectly with the ornamentation and passion of the language, the people, and the surroundings here – and I am beguiled by it.

I'm beguiled by many things, actually. I was coming home from a stroll around the jardín at about nine o'clock this evening and I had a good look at the light cast by the street lamps onto the darkened streets. Each lamp cast a warm, golden glow down onto the smooth, well-worn cobblestones beneath it, and made the stones look like amber-coloured, polished leather. Between each pleasing patch of light cast by the lamps, was another patch of darkness – where threat and mystery hid. As I walked along, I passed into the light, then into the dark, and the rhythm of the shadows kept me alert. The rhythm of my footsteps kept me calm. A lone figure in the distance was just a black silhouette set against a distant light, and the long shadow that spread out behind it as it walked, swished from side to side like a sorcerer's cape. Then it was gone. Carefully, I walked into the trail of shadows it left behind.

Journal, March 8
11 a.m.

Once again we find ourselves in Florence's old blue Renault, this time on the way to Pozos for a return visit with her and Elisabeth. Florence drives her little car as if it were a stagecoach being pulled by wild horses and she its maniacal driver. We just finished racing Grand Prix-style through a little village called Los Rodriguez. As we were passing through, Florence said it was a town of giants, originally settled by a family of very large Italians. She said that when the churches in San Miguel needed Roman centurions for their Christmas plays, they always got them from there.

"They don't look very Italian to me," said Elisabeth. "Just lots of little Mexicans, exactly like everywhere else."

Like many annoying people, Elisabeth is occasionally right. Florence grudgingly conceded that she didn't see any either. I get the feeling the gulf between these two is reaching critical proportions. Elisabeth's world is the world of the pedant. Whereas Florence, like Don Quixote, prefers a world where mythical towns are peopled with Italian giants. They really represent two diverging roads, and, as Mr. Frost says, you really can't travel both. I think I'll stick with Florence's world. She has a lot more fun in hers – and besides – she's the one with a car.

Most Mexican towns welcome new arrivals by exploding the tires and breaking the axles of the poor unsuspecting visitors' cars on speed bumps known as *topes* (topays) that they place at the outskirts of town. Unlike the sort of gently rounded bumps we have in Canada, the Mexican version is more like one of those spike strips police lay across highways to blow out the tires of fleeing criminals, so we're talking major structural damage here. The town of Rodriguez had a dozen of them, and Florence had her own special technique for how to deal with them.

She liked to push the Renault's accelerator right down to the floor and then, just before reaching a tope, jam on her brakes and skid over it, not coming to a stop until several meters past it on the other side. For our part, we, the three passengers, screamed in unison throughout the entire length of the skid, thinking foolishly that such behaviour might just possibly discourage Florence from continuing to drive like that. Huh! Florence beamed with pleasure at the robustness of our screams and, encouraged by what she thought was our seal of approval, proceeded to attack each subsequent tope with even more gusto than the last, and we went – zoom, break, skid-over-bump, stop – over all twelve topes, before finally, thankfully, leaving town.

12 a.m.

Just moments ago, we stopped to take pictures of an enormous flowering century plant, also called maguey, that we spotted off to the side of the road. It had one solitary shoot that drove upwards towards the sky for twenty feet or more from its spiky base like a Saturn rocket waiting on the launch pad to take off. At its top there were small flowers poking out like dishes on a microwave-relay tower. As I was framing Robyn and the plant inside my viewfinder, Robyn bent one knee coyly and waved her arms towards the plant like a 1950s game-show bimbo motioning towards the grand-prize Maytag washing machine, and I snapped the picture.

1 p.m.

I am sitting on a pew inside the main church in Pozos. The fact that Pozos has three large churches (two still in use and one that looks as if it took a direct hit from a W.W.II bomber) is an obvious indication of the wealth that the mines of Pozos must have generated for their owners over the years. It wasn't until I sat down here and started looking up at the soaring vaulted ceiling that I realized just how unbelievably huge this particular one is, especially considering the size of the town. It is cool, hushed, and visually less cluttered than some of the other churches we've seen. Florence has just whispered to me that she thinks the statue behind the altar might be a statue of God himself, an idea so foreign to her Anglican faith, that the devil inside her is clearly tingling with mischievous excitement at the wicked thought.

1:15 p.m.

When we emerged from the church into the blinding light of day, Florence asked the woman custodian sweeping there whether she knew who the statue behind the altar was supposed to be, and the lady told Florence that it was a statue of Saint Peter the Apostle. Florence looked disappointed. It seems her search for God, or at least a reasonable facsimile, isn't over yet.

We bought some bananas from a guy selling them from the back of his pickup truck, and then drove up a steep hill to where there's a local crafts market run by the makers of pre-Columbian instruments who live nearby. Not exactly bustling with activity, there were just two merchants with two tables of merchandise set up in an otherwise empty square. Pozos always makes me feel as if we must be the only ones who didn't hear the evacuation sirens.

Being the only customers they'd probably seen all day (hell we were probably the only *people* they'd seen all day), you might think they would have poured on the sales talk pretty thick, but it wasn't like that at all. They were dignified and proud of their work, and they politely demonstrated all their stuff for us. Occasionally one of them would blow into these beautiful long sensual gourds and out would come some slightly scary, ritualistic moan that seemed perfectly well suited to this odd little empty town. There were clay ocarinas shaped like turtles that gave off a lovely, dry, emphysemic, whistling sound. They had a vast assortment of mysterious-sounding rain sticks with beautifully carved animal motifs on them that made a lovely *shooosh* whenever one of us rotated one end-over-end. And there were wonderful wooden sculpted frogs and alligators that bonked out the swampy, half-drum/half-xylophone sound of a marimba. In spite of having had a wonderful time wheezing and bonking our little brains out, we almost ended up leaving without buying anything. Thankfully, Elisabeth came to our rescue, and bought a very erotic, sixteen-inch long moaning gourd from one of the female artisans. There were several distinctly naughty smiles and twinkles that flashed back and forth between the two of them as they conducted their business, and I must say, it was a bit of a shock. The thought of our very proper Miss Elisabeth even imagining doing something unspeakable with that sixteen-inch gourd . . . was . . . well . . . You know, I think there's hope for her yet.

2 p.m.

Florence was trying to find her way to the studio of an American sculptor friend of hers, and drove us right to the edge of Pozos along a steep, rocky, and little-used dirt road. To our left, there were a few concrete-and-adobe houses that were only one step removed from disintegrating back into becoming part of the road themselves. To our right, the landscape fell away into a shallow gorge, beyond which lay a stunning view of a dappled green desert, a tabletop-flat butte, and a big blue sky painted childishly with puffy white clouds. All eyes and necks in the Renault, including Florence's of course, strained to the right of the slowly moving car to have a look at the gorge, when suddenly a free-standing double arch, the last remnant of one of the grand old haciendas built here over a hundred years ago, slid into view and framed the whole scene perfectly. It was a breathless moment. Florence pulled over to the side of the road and we all got out, all speechless for a change. The haziness that was always so prevalent in San Miguel was completely absent here. The clarity of the light was so pure that everything, near or far, was in sharp focus. The clouds themselves seemed within easy reach. The twin arches were on the one hand sad and pathetic for having fallen into such ruin, but they had also grown to resemble the timeless and wise eyes of an ancient Greek sculpture, a sculpture that was gazing towards us while at the same time gazing out over a view of paradise. It looked exactly like a surrealist painting by René Magritte.

Magritte once said: "When we are moving, it is the tree that becomes the spectator. The tree can watch through its various manifestations as chairs, tables, and doors, the more or less agitated spectacle of our life." It's this kind of topsy-turvy view of the world, this jumbling together of things out of context, this inversion of logic and of time from a so-called "normal" reality into a new and mysterious dream-like reality, that makes surrealism so Mexican. When Magritte refers to the chair or table that watches us go through all our agitated human activities, he could be describing Mexico calmly watching the frenetic modern world burning up its inner workings from its overheated pursuit of "growth." It seems no accident that three of the great surrealists of the twentieth century – Frida Kahlo, Leonora Carrington, and Remedios Varo – all lived in Mexico. And of the three, it is particularly interesting that the lone Mexican of the bunch, Frida Kahlo, actually considered herself a realist. Of course. If you spend your entire life inside a surrealistic world, then that's what's real for you.

Surrealism and Mexico were made for each other. When André Breton came to Mexico to teach the Mexicans about surrealism in 1938, he left after a few months, saying there was nothing he could teach them on the subject that they weren't already living – each and every day.

3:30 p.m.

We have arrived at the Cinco Señores Mine just outside of town.

We have just stepped from the car and it feels warm, wide-open, and free here, like standing on a Canadian prairie in the middle of summer. The air is clean and clear, and the only sounds are of the wind breathing through the empty, eye-socket windows of the ruined buildings and of the crunch of our own shoes on the gravelly ground beneath our feet. Why is it that I find ruins so reassuring? Why is it that they seem to emit such feelings of peace? Maybe it's because they are a monument to forgiveness. After man has finished taking from nature and using it for his own selfish purposes, nature welcomes us back to the fold – in a sense forgiving us our prodigal ways. A line in a wall, once compelled to be straight by an arrogant human hand, becomes irregular as it weathers, and now looks more at home in the natural world. A broken staircase that once led to a second floor, now leads only to fluffy white clouds in a deliriously blue sky. A tree grows from inside a roofless stone house. Mother Nature is taking back control, and everything is going to be all right.

I think the four of us must have looked like a bunch of spaced-out zombies as we floated ethereally through the collapsed walls of the abandoned buildings. We were like ghosts: we had no need of doors. The real trick was not to become permanently ethereal by falling down one of the many open holes that were scattered around the site – all of them unmarked and unfenced. According to local folklore, some of them "go down for miles." If Florence really was a collector of tourists, this would have been a great place for her to keep them.

I saw Elisabeth off on her own, sitting on the scattered remnants of some concrete steps. She suddenly looked very old. Thinking that maybe the gulf between her and the rest of us was starting to wear her down, I went over and sat beside her.

"Are you okay?"

"Oh yeah, I'm fine," she replied without much conviction. "Where're the others?"

"They're over there by that tree, eating their lunch – pop and chocolate cupcakes, I think." She smiled. I thought this might be a good time to delve a bit into just what made Elisabeth tick. "So," I said after a brief pause, "being from L.A., do you get a little scared out here in the open like this?"

"Well, I would never come to a place like this on my own, but I like the wide-open spaces part. For years I made my living by sailing, you know. I used to deliver yachts to their owners. I just can't do it any more. But oh yeah, I like open spaces. At home it's hard to get out of the house. L.A.'s pretty dangerous."

Yachts? Did she really say she used to deliver yachts? I tried to visualize this style-conscious woman sailing a yacht single-handedly across a howling, tempestuous sea, while holding a compact up to her face and carefully applying the correct shade of lipstick for the current weather conditions, and I couldn't do it. I didn't know what to say. Fortunately, I was rescued from this embarrassing moment by the arrival of Robyn and Florence, and we all headed back to the car.

As we walked along, I thought further about Elisabeth's unusual revelation. There could be only two ways to explain it. Either she was making the whole thing up or I had made a huge mistake about what sort of person she was. Not feeling too comfortable with that last option, I decided it would be best just to conclude she was making the whole thing up.

On the way home we stopped at a truckers' café for a coffee. When Elisabeth turned her nose up aristocratically at the only coffee they had – instant – it looked for a moment as if we might have to surgically remove a crazed and flailing Florence from the top of Elisabeth's head. But in the end, Elisabeth relented, and we all survived. We survived the mine shafts of Pozos, we survived Florence's driving, we survived the coffee, and we survived each other.

Chapter 17

Journal, March 12

We walked past Isadora's kitchen this morning on our way out the door, about a quarter to ten, and caught her in the middle of swallowing a large spoonful of peanut butter, and she looked every bit the cat that just swallowed the canary. Poor Isadora. Eating is one of her few remaining pleasures, but if she puts on any more weight, it's only going to make her back pain even worse. She's trying acupuncture now to relieve the pain, but the three-block walk over to the clinic practically kills her, and she says she doesn't have enough money for cab fare anymore.

I peered around the water-filled plastic bag hanging in the kitchen doorway.

"How goes it, Isadora?"

"Ugh, I'm a mess," she croaked. "I'm broke and these acupuncturists cost a fortune. Say, did you know I've started doing portraits of people? If you think of anybody who might want one, let me know, would you? And they're cheap. People like them. Yeah, they do."

"What about asking your son in Seattle for a loan, Isadora? He's an accountant, isn't he?"

"Ugh, he's got less money than I do. His apartment costs a fortune and he does all the bookkeeping for the local food banks and charities; they hardly pay him anything. Ugh! That's what you get for raising a kid during the Sixties in Greenwich Village. He's too kind, I should have raised him to be a greedy, money-grubbing capitalist." She lets out a couple of deep, throaty chortles. "But I'm going to go see him, help him out in his office, answer the phone for him, that sort of thing."

I tried to imagine phoning an accountant and having someone like Isadora answer with that smoky-bar, gravelly voice of hers . . . Yikes. I've met her son; he's a sweet guy. I suspect he knows that she's the one who really needs the help.

"Well, take it easy, Isadora."

"Ugh. Like do I have a choice, already?"

Leaving Isadora and her gloom behind, we headed out the front door feeling pumped with enthusiasm at the prospect of another day of high adventure with Florence. This time round, we were going to search out a couple of very special churches in Yuríria and Salamanca with an Episcopalian minister from Iowa called Bob Dingwall and his friend Barney from New York. We were going in Bob's very posh, super-deluxe, all-dressed minivan, and thankfully (or so I thought), he'd be doing the driving instead of Florence.

Emerging from Isadora's onto the narrow sidewalk, we turned right and headed for Bob's place. The giddy sounds of school kids out on a break tagged along behind us as we went. Our eyes were, as always, glued to the sidewalk in front of us, ever watchful for a gringo trap or a turd. My concentration was so intense and the doors of the houses were so close to the sidewalk that my arm inadvertently brushed across the bosom of a maid standing in a doorway. She smiled and I smiled – and then we were on our way. Such a friendly way to start the day.

We got to Bob's and all piled into his outrageously luxurious palace on wheels. It fell somewhere between a Rolls Royce and a Learjet. The only things missing were the flight attendants and those little packets of nuts.

Whoever deals the cards that make up the various combinations of accidental travelling companions of one's life must surely have the most hilarious job in the universe.

Bob was a large, jolly man – and a very rotund one. He was a man of the cloth who loved to eat, drink, and be merry. Chaucer would have recognized this latter-day friar right away.

His friend, Barney, also had ties to the Church, something to do with administration. The two of them made quite a pair sitting up there in the front of the van. You see, as if in obedience to some law of cosmic equilibrium, Barney was as small as Bob was big. That's not to say you could ever forget Barney was around. Being a clever, feisty, annoying, always-joking kind of guy from New York guaranteed that that would never happen. His greatest joy in life was baiting Florence, and it knew no bounds.

Florence was Florence. Tall, bossy, talkative, and perpetually high on life. Her mother called her the baby bulldog, and who am I to disagree?

Robyn and I, of course, were perfect in every way.

We all got a little concerned when Barney didn't show up exactly on time, but Florence said not to worry, and sure enough he arrived in due course and off we went.

After ten minutes of inching our way through the confusing muddle of San Miguel's narrow and bumpy streets, we were finally breezing our way down the highway with the beautiful rolling desert whizzing past. Barney, who was taking charge of the front passenger seat as if it were his pulpit, proceeded to address the congregation:

"So do you want to know what happened to me this morning?" His voice and his eyebrows were pure Groucho Marx.

"Oh sure, Barney," sighed Bob, "I take it we don't really have a choice?"

"That's right," said Barney followed by a little rapid-fire laugh. "Well, this morning at around eight o'clock, I'll be damned if the phone doesn't ring. I got to bed pretty late last night so I was a little groggier than usual, right? But I thought, gee, it could be something important, that's not the usual time to call somebody. Maybe my mother was dying and wanted to speak to me for the last time or something like that, ya hear what I'm sayin'? So I pushed that ejection button on the side of my head there, and I sprang out of my bed and onto my feet, well sort of onto my feet. You see, I was dragging my sheet a little and it made me trip over a chair there in the middle of the room, and as I was falling I knocked over a cup still half full of coffee, spilling it all over me, right? But before I hit the ground, I lunged for the telephone and got the cord all tangled around me like I was a body just been tied up by the mob and about to be dumped overboard, you know what I mean? Can you picture this Florence?"

Florence made no reply. Very uncharacteristic of her, I thought.

"Now, so far, that's okay. I guess I should be a little more careful, and you know it might be a really important call, right? So it might be worth all that. But you know what? I got to that frigging phone, excuse my language Florence, on the second ring. And do you know what I heard on the other end after I said hello? A dial tone! No kidding. Somebody had called me at eight o'clock in the morning – I practically killed myself trying to get to the damn thing; I'm barely able to twitch I'm so tangled up in sheets and phone cord – and they hung up! Like some kid pushing doorbells for a joke! But I sent off an irate e-mail right away to the only person back home I could think of who was low enough to pull such a dirty, childish prank. Boy, it sure better have been him, though, because I said some really nasty things, and I'd hate to lose a friend because of someone else's stupidity. I knew it couldn't be one of you folks calling to make sure I hadn't slept through my alarm, because you wouldn't have been dumb enough to hang up on me after only two rings. Isn't that right, Florence?"

Still more silence from Florence. I don't think I'd ever seen Florence's face such a bright shade of red.

"Anyway, I'm fine now, I'm over it. So what's good to see in Urethra, anyway?"

Bob tried to look unamused. "It's Yuríria, Barney. Yur-rir-i-a."

"Yeah, that's what I said, Urethra."

We were about ten kilometers from the small city of Salvatierra, when Bob pulled over to investigate a very forsaken-looking hacienda.

We walked through the broken iron entrance gate out of respect I suppose – the walls were certainly in no condition to keep us out. The whole place was a little reminiscent of the disintegrating Xanadu of *Citizen Kane* fame, after its fall from grace, only with a hefty dollop of Zorro thrown on top for good measure. Just inside the gate, there was a school group of sixteen-year-olds in uniforms huddled around their teacher, looking far too happy about being out and about for me to believe they were even the slightest bit interested in what she was talking about.

We had our own tour guide as it turned out – Bob. And since none of us knew much of anything, he was the closest thing to an expert we had. And he knew it.

Leaning back, the way portly men often do, Bob declared, "Definitely nineteenth-century."

Well, good. I'm certainly glad we got that straightened out. I do so like to know exactly where my plinths and apses belong. Our little troupe cast a flickering of smiles at one another, proud of our clever general's vast knowledge.

"Although I'm not entirely sure about that dome over there . . ."

Oh God, our leader was quivering on the brink of indecision.

" . . . it could be as early as sixteenth. Very plain, very functional-looking."

I decided to lend a little support, "Yes, I can see that. Much less ostentatious . . ."

"No. I was right the first time. Definitely nineteenth. Definitely."

Right. Good. Phew. That was close.

We prowled respectfully around for a while, and then, without actually mentioning it, we all proceeded to look for places to urinate. Really. You couldn't turn a corner without seeing one of us either squatting or unzipping surreptitiously. The cloak of civilization we wrap ourselves in seems sadly threadbare during moments like these.

All quite refreshed, we congregated briefly under one of the colonnades, and craned our heads upward in unison trying to emulate Bob's scholarly pose. I noticed that his fly was undone.

"You know," I hazarded, "those balusters look like they were hand thrown out of clay on a potter's wheel."

The hush that ensued was really quite disconcerting. Bob seemed quietly indignant at my outspoken intrusion into his domain. We all awaited his proclamation.

"Mm. Unlikely, very unlikely. Nineteenth-century, though, no doubt about it. Definitely nineteenth-century."

Right. So much for trying to move up a little from my designated position as class fool. Call me petty, but I decided against telling him about his zipper.

The century having been now duly clarified, and with much nodding and smiling about Bob's unquestionable brilliance on things architectural, we started to make our way towards the van.

"I must have a picture of the relics," Bob boomed from behind the lens of his camera when we were halfway across the courtyard. "And I want all of you in the picture. So gather yourselves over there in front of those arches."

We stood there on the debris-covered, old courtyard – grass and small trees now pushing up between the flagstones – and we all stared back at Bob and his little camera. As we stood there waiting for him to take the picture, I tried to imagine what our tattered old group looked like through that lens. Maybe we were the real relics in this picture.

I'd seen photographs of myself taken recently, and it was horrifying how old I was beginning to look. Horrifying how old I felt as well. When I'd been finally able to get up and walk a bit after those four agonizing months of lying helplessly immobile on the floor after I injured my back, I had had to use a cane. The cane had caused people to treat me as if I were old, and so in a way, I had been forced to be old against my will. The sad, defeated eyes I'd seen on my mother's face, when I caught her off-guard one day struggling to lift herself out of bed, had become my eyes for a while too.

These thoughts made me feel an odd empathy with the hacienda. The four of us had walked around this place, analyzed it, peed on it, basically used it for our entertainment, without ever thinking that a place that had once been so noble and new, so full of laughter and life, deserved more respect. We treated it the way some young people treat old people, not realizing that the body wears out, but the person inside doesn't change. Allowing people (and places, for that matter) a little dignity is really the least they deserve. I began to see my own deterioration in the broken tiles and bricks that were scattered around at our feet, and now that I felt a connection with them, I wanted to tell them I was sorry. Silly really, but there you have it.

"Okay, that's it, everybody. Back in the van!"

The main purpose of our trip was to visit the Augustinian convent in Yuríria, built around 1550. *1550?* Do you realize that means the Spanish had only been in Mexico for thirty-one years by that time?

Now think about how incredible that is. Think about going camping back in the Renaissance, six thousand miles from home, and trying to build a stone structure larger than a Home Depot store, with no electricity, no Coleman stove, no Swiss Army Knife, no pizza take-out, no 4-in-1 Adventure Compass/Whistle, and only a few horses to carry your stuff around on. It takes me two hours in the morning just to make coffee and get dressed for God's sake! (I'm much improved by about 2:30, really, I am.) And it's not as if they were building these things in some kind of a Shangri-La with a temperate climate and boundless sources of food and water. Mexico is mostly desert. Clearly, the early missionaries were nuts. I sometimes wonder if the Church just sent the strange ones over here to get rid of them, the same way the English made use of Australia.

Salvatierra, one of a cluster of places in this area with delightfully medieval sounding names – names like Salamanca, Santiago, and Cortazar, was the first town on our agenda. Salvatierra is a great town to go to if you love driving. If you love parking, forget it. We spent a lovely half-hour doing circles around the centre of town trying to find an elusive, but beautiful-looking, two-spired church.

"There it goes again!" we'd all scream as we caught a momentary glimpse of it. After about the third time round, a large crowd had gathered out front to cheer us on as we went flying past – a few of them were trying to start a wave. Bob just smiled lamely each time round and tried desperately to resist the urge to leap into the back seat and strangle Florence, who was quietly repeating helpful comments like "You should have turned left, Bob. I would have" and "Oh! Oops, oh well, you just missed the perfect parking spot. What a shame."

Bob decided in the end to just park illegally and get on with killing Florence. As for the church, it was okay, nothing special. Doors definitely nineteenth-century, the inside probably eighteenth, at least according to Bob. (Churches can apparently be one century on the outside and another century on the inside, just another one of those little cosmic mysteries, I guess.) There was one really cool thing, though: an adjoining courtyard that had a fountain with a two-headed dragon spout in it. It wasn't old, and it wasn't very authentic, but it made a great photo op, so we all gathered round the thing, and proceeded to gorge ourselves in an orgy of wild clicking.

It was about one o'clock when we arrived in Yuríria, having made just one stop to stock up on Pinguinos, those delicious chocolate cupcakes so beloved by Florence, and we parked right next to the Harley-Davidson Funeral Home. That's right, the Harley-Davidson Funeral Home. Just when you think you're getting a bit of a handle on the Mexican mind-set, they throw you something like this. The walls were plastered with giant pictures of shiny new "hogs" and the floor space was covered with caskets. ("Daddy will be so happy now, honey. He's in Harley heaven, riding a brand-new Electra Glide Classic, like he always wanted.") So much for the image of the devout Mexican.

The church was impressive. And it was in incredible condition considering it was about 450 years old. According to Bob, these early churches were called convents, but they weren't convents the way we think of them today, at all. They were huge hotel/forts, primarily designed as instruments of conversion, and they certainly weren't full of nuns – mostly they were packed with friars. Recently, I did a little research on the Internet and according to the only information I could find on the subject, the confusion over the correct meaning of a convent hinges on the fact that it was not gender that defined the difference between a monastery and a convent, but the rules under which they functioned. Monasteries were places of spiritual retreat that had particularly harsh rules, and convents were places where the rules were more lenient. I think in later years convents did begin to function mostly as nunneries, but in the earlier days, monks could live in convents and nuns could live in monasteries – a situation that clearly had its advantages. (Interestingly I gleaned this little morsel from a site devoted to sado-masochism called BDSMcentral, no doubt the same place Bob gets all his information from. There I found an article written by someone called CadetLuke1, who had developed a complex theory as to why some things in life end up on top and other things end up on the bottom, no doubt a subject very dear to his heart. I'd like to thank CadetLuke1 and just tell him that he needn't try to contact me directly about this. I'm really not interested in finding out anything more about S&M at this time. Thanks, anyway.)

Attached to the huge church section was an equally large residence for the staff – the whole complex functioning as one impenetrable fortress. Outside they had large, empty plazas that acted as open-air churches in order to facilitate the conversion of thousands of people at one go. According to Bob, these sessions were so gruelling for the priests that they actually used special supports to hold up their "blessing" arms. The number of conversions was truly mind-boggling – the Franciscans claimed that by 1531, just ten years after the victory of Cortés, they had converted one million Indians.

The rather plain façade of the Yuríria church was a bit of a relief, actually, compared with some of the frenetic ornamentation we'd seen on churches elsewhere. Apparently the plataresque style, as it is called, is typical of the early Augustinian convents in Mexico, and closely resembles the style of the Salamanca University in Spain, built around the same time. As the name suggests, it mimics the work of silversmiths ("plata" meaning "silver"), and looks as if it has been stamped onto a flat surface.

The four of us walked into the main part of the church.

"Sixteenth-century," began Bob, his eyes looking a little wild, as if he were in a trance and about to make contact with his dead Aunt Iva.

"Notice, practically no windows, very Roman. The walls are massively thick things to support the huge barrel vaulting covering the nave. No buttresses you see, they would have taken too long to build. Time here was of the essence. There'd be no tracery or clerestory here."

"Certainly not," I whispered. "But Bob, do you think that a cinquefoil in the apse is worth two in the niche?"

"Sorry, what was that? Oh, look at the wonderful ribbing in the spandrel near the triforium. Oh, my lungs and liver, isn't it exquisite?"

I couldn't see what the hell he was talking about. It was an absolutely gigantic church, but apart from that, rather plain, I thought.

"Gosh, Bob, I don't know. Do you ever get a little triptych right up in your pinnacle there, right near the transept? God those things hurt."

"Huh?" Bob turned his gaze towards me. "Did you say something?"

"No, no, just enjoying it all. It's amazing isn't it?"

"It's like having an orgasm, spiritually of course."

"Uh, my thoughts, exactly," I said taking a step back. I then made my way to the exit just as fast as my little ambulatories would carry me.

One by one, our merry band coalesced again outside the enormous church doors, and then Bob led us over to the residential section. As we stepped out of the blinding sunlight and into the cool, dark interior, we were immediately greeted by a couple of guards whose principal function, it would appear, was to defend the convent from groups of malicious tripod-wielding assailants. I suspect that this peculiar fixation that museums in Mexico have with tripods came about through some unfortunate bureaucratic misunderstanding about what the hell a tripod is, and that the rule might have eventually been rescinded, except that one day, several security guards probably got their heads bashed in by a mob of irate photographers who couldn't get even a vaguely plausible explanation for the absurdly ridiculous rule, and then all of a sudden the rule started to make sense – as a way of protecting the security guards.

Thank you for listening. I promise that's my last word on the subject of tripods.

We walked down a dark hallway and came out into a beautiful, airy cloister. Cloisters are what they call those wonderful, colonnaded, covered walkways surrounding a central quadrangle, or garth. They fill a person walking through them with a lovely sense of calm and relaxed harmony. The light always seems to be soft and golden in cloisters – a soothing, pampering light. Voices inside cloisters are echoed and muffled at the same time, as if they were trying to tiptoe quietly from one place to another. I often think I'd like to park myself in a cloister for a while, to really soak up some of that restful ambience, but unfortunately, they are considered places of transition, and if one were to attempt to take up long term residence, say by lying on a bench or on the floor, passers-by would natter at you, and that would spoil the whole thing.

We snapped a few photos, and then walked through a dark, arched entranceway that led us to a stairwell and up a long flight of stone steps, balustered ornately in old mahogany-coloured wood. The windows that bordered the stairway were covered in thin metal screens that were pierced all over with tattoo-like dots in circular,

Moorish motifs, and they lent an air of mystery, perhaps even danger, to the space.

On the second floor we entered room after room, and it felt very much as if this was really just a hotel for monks. Each room was tiny, but with a glorious view. Bob glowed and said, "I could live here." And I had no doubt.

One room was exceptionally tiny, only large enough for one person to stand up in – the penitence room. We all took turns standing in it, trying to imagine being forced to spend time there. I suspect just its existence was enough to maintain discipline in the convent.

Further down the hall, Bob was standing and grinning outside a door, his eyes just two little raisins in the jolly face of a snowman.

"This room is a perfect Kodak Moment."

We entered the large room. At first it appeared to be just another empty room, but then at one end, each of our minds slowly came to the realization that the eight holes at the far end of the room – were toilet holes.

I walked over and peered down one of the holes. It seemed to go down forever; remember, we were on the second floor of a very large building. This was the stuff of nightmares. Maybe it's just me, but don't you feel when you're sitting in an outhouse, your butt wedged into that cold slivery hole there, that you better get this over with fast because there's probably a honking big, loathsome reptile in there with lots of sharp, snapping teeth that's making his way up to your butt just as fast as he can wriggle? I grabbed firmly onto my glasses, bent my head down over the hole, and wondered how many seconds there'd be before your heard the splat. I wondered what else might have been forced down these holes, never to be heard from again, and how many pieces they'd had to cut it up into. We took all our pictures, half laughing and half shivering with dread, and then eagerly retraced our steps, going back downstairs and out the front door, all quite relieved, I'm sure, to be outside again in the clean, glaring light of day.

There was a beautiful, big grassy park on the grounds behind the convent, and we sat ourselves down there on a little stone wall beside a fountain, underneath a shady tree. Clusters of school kids munching their lunches were strolling past and giggling at us. It wasn't the laughter of ridicule, it was the kind of nervous giggling usually reserved for movie stars, and in Mexico it's a welcome sound and usually a sign that you're in a friendly place, a little off the beaten track.

I watched two young kids kicking a soccer ball our way. When they got within twenty feet, I could see that one of them was carrying the goalposts – two big rocks. He placed them down on an unoccupied bit of grass, and they both entered that zone, that wonderful mystical state where kids become the greatest sports heroes the world has ever known.

The convent looked huge as we sat there in the park; I think the giant's castle must have looked that big when Jack first set eyes on it. Yuríria has never grown large enough to overwhelm the convent, and for a few moments I felt as though I could imagine what an awe-inspiring presence it must have had back in 1550. And I could also imagine that it must have offered a very reassuring sense of security to those poor old lunatic friars in what was still a very threatening world.

Lunch eaten and several packages of Pinguinos later, we arrived in Salamanca.

Sometimes, there's a very good reason why a place is off the beaten track. Nobody in their right mind wants to live there. Salamanca is a place like that. And you know this before you even get there because the stench of the city extends for miles and miles and miles around it.

Here's a list of things manufactured in Salamanca, as proudly reported by the Guanajuato State web site: chemical agents, rubber mixtures, plastics, oils, ground adhesives, enhancers, industrial ammonium reactors, pesticides, sulphate, liquid-carbon candles, and last, but believe me not least – urea.

Not only that, but everything is covered in grime, and the best thing the web site could find to say about the place was that the restaurants were deficient, and the transportation, acceptable.

We parked and headed off in search of another church in which Bob could experience another of his heavenly orgasms (presumably such places are few and far between in Iowa), and I can't tell you how delightful it was to have nothing more important to do than that. There we were, driving around the Mexican countryside, kibitzing with new friends and consuming large quantities of Pinguinos, and the purpose of our great mission was nothing more than that we were looking around for interesting churches. A finer life I can't imagine.

The church we were seeking out was one called the Parroquia Antigua. It was built in 1692, and it was famed for its Churrigueresque façade. With a little practice, even I was getting so that I could recognize one of these. Their trademark is a unique pillar called an *estípite* that narrows towards the bottom instead of flaring, the way any sensible pillar would do. This inversion of the logical is, to me, a quintessentially Mexican hallmark.

We found the church by heading for the old part of town and asking people on the street for directions. Although the façade was very nice, the inside did nothing for Bob – apparently it was totally refurbished in the nineteenth century, a century that turns him on about as much as a blind date with an aluminum door. But all our walking was not in vain. There was a bakery kitty-corner to the church, and we fortified ourselves for our next foray with cookies and doughnuts all around.

On our way back to the van, the ladies were lassoed by a shoe store, putting a sudden and perhaps lengthy halt to our progress. Barney went for a coffee, and Bob and I wandered down the road to have a look at a plain but very old-looking church, called the Templo de Agustin.

Although Bob said of the outside, "Definitely sixteenth-century, a true convent like the one at Yuríria," the inside was eighteenth century baroque all the way, and even I could see that. As soon as we walked in, we knew we'd hit the mother lode. For a true lover of the baroque, there's no such thing as too much. Even the excess should be excessive. Every surface in this church was slathered in gold leaf. I'm sure if a priest had walked by, *he* would have been covered in gold leaf. Full-sized figures of sad-eyed saints in golden cloaks looked imploringly down upon us. Pink, rosy-faced heads of cherubs with blank stares popped out of the walls and were surrounded by curled scrolls of gold, leaves of gold, fish scales of gold, pillars of gold, mantelpieces of gold, X's and O's of gold, and six-foot-wide, giant crowns of gold. The creators of this stuff were clearly not satisfied with the idea that wall art should be two-dimensional. In places it protruded three feet or more into the main church hall, that part known as the nave, almost extending right into the pews. The cherubs stretched their necks out so far from the walls that you could practically feel them sniffing in your ears. Visually, it was almost complete chaos, like a tornado in Las Vegas had lifted all the wreckage and debris from a flattened casino and hurled it against a wall covered in flypaper.

Part of the wall was covered in scaffolding and there were five or six industrious young people quietly working away at restoring the gold leaf. They were extremely cordial to us and quite happy to discuss what they were doing. This had the effect of making the space feel more museum-like than church-like, and so we felt a little less like the crass, gawking tourists we were, and a little more like the connoisseurs of fine art we wanted to be.

I was staring intently through my camera viewfinder at a newly-leafed section, where a cluster of tiny cherub faces were bubbling to the surface like little puffball mushrooms, when I heard Bob's voice calling from up near the altar.

"Stephen, you've got to see this!" he whispered loudly.

I clicked the shutter and went up to where he stood.

He walked me over into the north transept (the transept is the section of a church that on the floor plan makes a cross design by crossing with the nave), and took me right up to the far wall. We were thus standing directly under an eighty-foot-high wall of golden baroque madness, much of it literally hanging over our heads.

I think I saw Bob's eyes roll back up into his head and his jaw slacken as he seemed to be on the verge of entering another of his mystical states of pure bliss.

Then he said to me, "When you look up . . . it moves."

Well, it did appear to move if you rocked your head back and forth, but that was about the extent of it for me.

"Amazing," I said. Better to say something like that than what actually came into my head, which was, "You're a bit of a nut case, aren't you Bob?" if I wanted to get a ride back home.

I went back and got the others, and they were quite bowled over by our discovery. For the pièce de résistance, Bob took each of them, one at a time, to the north transept for their own special moment of communion with Bob's World, for which Florence and

Barney were obsequiously grateful. At last, replete with having seen enough gold ornamentation to fill three Hadassah Bazaars and still have enough left over to furnish a mausoleum for Liberace, we headed back to the van and began the trip home.

We were about halfway back to San Miguel, and Florence and Bob were having a heated discussion about whether a Waldorf teacher could possibly be worth $150 an hour for psychological counselling, when Bob said, "You know what I've always thought was the main weakness in Christianity, Florence? We give it away for free."

No. The main weakness in Christianity is that it produces pantloads of really terrible drivers. At that very moment, Bob was driving his all-dressed, supercharged, monster-sized minivan with his foot pressed to the floor, on the wrong side of the road, headlong into the oncoming traffic. There was a wall of tractor-trailers on our right that was very effectively keeping us from re-entering our own lane and it went on into the dusty distance as far as the eye could see. We were totally hooped. Headed straight for the organ-donor clinic. And that's the trouble with Christians, you see. They don't give a damn about us agnostics. It's no problem for them. They're looking forward to death! They're going to heaven! And some of them will get to drive Harleys!

We lived. It's almost enough to make a guy believe in the power of prayer, especially the hysterical, no-holds-barred, any-god-who'll-listen variety.

Chapter 18

Knowing we were down to our last two weeks suddenly brought an incredible focus to everything. The friendly faces of the local shopkeepers that had become such a valuable part of our daily routine would soon be only memories from the past. Odd as it must sound, they had become like aunts and uncles from a faraway land to us, and it was saddening to think we might never get back here to see them again. I think the old fruit man with the parrot across the street could sense we were leaving – he'd probably seen the same quiet melancholy in others before. Robyn wanted to get photos of the sort of little details that would remind her of day-to-day life in San Miguel. She wanted one of the two policewomen whose mannish attire of white shirts and black pants did nothing to hide the fact that their beauty was so striking they could have passed for fashion models on the runways of Milan; and she wanted one of the beautiful brass sign outside the Colmena Bakery – because it had a bee design on it and she thought a copy of the photo might be of interest to a friend of hers back home called Honeybee, who'd sent us more English Breakfast tea when our supply had run out. I went out and bought my only real souvenir of our trip – one of the dangling-hand doorknobs that were everywhere in San Miguel.

One of the strangest things I noticed in those last two weeks was that people in the street began to speak to me spontaneously in Spanish, something they'd never done before. One of my daily routines while we lived in San Miguel was to make the long trek up the steep, winding maze of streets to the open cactus fields at the top of the town, and then to cross over them to do a little shopping at a little supermercado called Gigante. The air was clearer up there and the view out over San Miguel was glorious. These last two weeks, it seemed to me I never stopped chatting with folks along the way. An old man would stop part way up the gruelling flight of steps, clearly exhausted, and then proceed to chat with me about the trials and tribulations of getting old. When I reached the top, there would be two or three workmen standing around and they'd ask me about the weather. A lady crossing the field carrying bundles of laundry would smile and say good afternoon.

At first I just thought it was because local folks got used to seeing me around. But then even English-speaking newcomers to town started asking me for directions in their phrasebook Spanish. Visually, I'm sure I looked the same as when we first arrived, so all I could figure was that something subtle in my bearing must have changed. I felt as though, sometime when I wasn't aware of it, I had penetrated a thin membrane that had been separating me from the Mexicans. I wasn't one of them, of course, but for the first time, it felt as if we were at least all together in the same place. Maybe all it took was for me to finally lose that frenetic gringo tension that most of us carry with us wherever we go. Maybe when your body language finally slows down to a relaxed lope and starts to walk in harmony with theirs, you don't look so scary to them anymore. And after five months in Mexico I was certainly moving more slowly. Much, much more slowly.

We started to get a lot of lunch and dinner invitations from the various friends we'd made during those five months, and I found myself urgently pressing them all to tell us more of their stories, to fill us up so full with them that they'd spill out behind us when we left San Miguel, and act like markers on a trail to help us find our way back.

Katherine, our Laughing Muffin friend in her seventies with an over-the-phone healer in L.A. and a fondness for left-wing political raves, shared a few of her stories with us over breakfast one morning at the Villa Jacaranda.

She told us about the time in the early Sixties when she and Dixie, a gorgeous blond friend of hers, drove her convertible out to a crummy old stock-car racetrack just outside of town for a bit of a lark. When they got to the entrance, they were greeted by a giant cloud of dust hovering over the entire area and by the deafening roar of suped-up cars from out on the track. There was a guy on the road near the gate directing them to the parking area. He couldn't take his eyes off Katherine's beautiful friend and he kept waving them on and waving them on, pretty much oblivious to what he was doing, and they just went where he said, and before they knew what had happened they were right out there on the track in the middle of a race with a bandstand full of hysterical Mexicans egging them on to go mas rapido. Their convertible was still zooming round the track, with their long hair trailing out behind, when Katherine started into another one of her stories.

One day, she and Dixie decided to go to the bullfights in Morelia. Apparently when they got there, the place was jam-packed full of people – a famous toreador was fighting that day – so the only space left was on the very top row of the bullring on the sunny side. (At a bullfight, the cheap seats are always on the sunny side.)

After a while they started to get absolutely scorched by the sun, so Dixie headed down to ground level during one of the fights to get a couple of beers. Gorgeous, blond-bombshell Dixie squiggled her way through the crowds and finally made it to the bottom, and there she got two beers and two bags of chips for her and Katherine. Then, both arms full of chips and beer, she looked up through the packed stands and couldn't possibly imagine how she was going to squeeze herself through that mass of bodies to get back up to the top. She was starting to wilt from the heat. The gallant gentlemen standing nearby could see her difficulty right away, and took immediate command of the situation by taking the chips and beer from her and putting them onto a human conveyor belt of hands that moved them gradually up to the top row, where they were cordially received by Katherine. The four little parcels marched as if they had legs of their own above the heads of that vast sea of humanity.

But Dixie still had a problem. She still had to get herself up there. She paused to consider what to do. It was a brief pause however, because in an instant those gallant men of Morelia came to her rescue once again and, in the politest way possible I'm sure, hoisted her up over their heads like a voluptuous sack of beans and proceeded to pass her from one to the other just like with the chips and beer. According to Katherine, Dixie enjoyed every second of it. The toreador, however, was less impressed. When he became distracted momentarily by all the commotion in the stands, the bull sensed this was an opportunity not to be missed and cashed in by leaving the toreador a little something to remember him by.

We pumped Florence for stories as well. She told us about a guy who threw tequila onto his ex-wife's chest and then set it on fire; a charismatic cellist who put a contract out on Florence's mother to have her killed and then died of AIDS himself; and the most famous San Miguel story of all, about the man who murdered the same person twice: the first time with a bash to the head, and the second time by throwing him down one of the mine shafts at Pozos. Just the usual small-town stuff, I guess.

With ten days to go, Robyn and I decided to make one last trip to Guanajuato to have a look at a couple of things we'd missed on our first time through.

The Cervantes Museum in the heart of old Guanajuato was simply extraordinary. It included work by Picasso and Dalí, and every single nook and cranny of the place was packed full of sculptures and artwork based on the trials and tribulations of the intrepid old adventurer himself, Don Quixote. Many of them were comical, some were tragic, and others were just plain bizarre. But what the exhibition really made me realize was what a remarkable writer Cervantes must have been to have created in one character someone who was able to draw out not only our laughter, but also our pity and our respect as well. Those emotions whirled like a diaphanous dust devil around Robyn and me as we were pulled from room to room by the barrage of mesmerizing images. Sometimes Don Quixote's pathetic attempts to achieve conquests of heroic proportions filled me with sadness and pity for an old man suffering from delusions; and other times his exploits delighted me, because, no matter what else you might say about Don Quixote, he strove for lofty goals, and he did so not for the fortune or fame they might bring him, but to defend the noble principles in which he believed. Don Quixote created a world that was larger than life, as large as he could possibly make it, and in doing so, he made life richer for those around him. Florence did the same thing, with her town of giants and her glowing tributes to the magnificence of erosion. I, for one, am all for it.

Our eyes were glued to a large detailed porcelain sculpture sitting in a glass display case in the centre of one of the rooms, when two gringos walked in. They looked like Abbott and Costello.

"So, uh, Neil, tell me. Most of these pictures have a tall, skinny guy on a horse and a short, fat guy on a donkey. But were they real people these guys?"

"Oh, yeah," said Neil, "they were real the way Davy Crockett and Daniel Boone were real. The skinny guy, that was Don Quixote. And that short guy there? That was his sidekick, Cervantes."

From there we hopped onto a little local bus and went straight out to the Ex-Hacienda San Gabriel de Barrera.

It's never possible to enjoy walking around an old hacienda without feeling a little guilty. The blood of the poor peasants that built and supported these things has left a stain on them that can never be completely washed away, and just like African-Americans, Mexicans remember well their days of slavery. But if you can get past that for a moment, these beautiful structures can be wonderful places to wander around in for an hour or two. They're a little like churches that way, in that they seem to settle down our minds and put a temporary halt to the incessant yammering that goes on inside.

As we walked across the grounds, there were a few labourers resting on a bench, and I sensed resentment there, resentment mixed with a sad futility. The expression on their faces seemed to be saying, "Look, after all Mexico has been through, there's still a leisure class, represented by tourists like you, with the time and money to travel, and a working class like us, who must work and be poor till the day we die." Throughout Mexican history, the people have had to stand by and watch as the ownership of the land has moved from the wealthy to the poor and back to the wealthy again. In fact, that's exactly what happened at the San Gabriel hacienda. It was confiscated from its owners in the aftermath of the 1910 Revolution, a revolution all about land reform, but by the 1970s, it was back in private hands again. Today it is back in the government's possession, but the wealthy still lay claim to it, being the only ones who can afford to rent it for their weddings and other events.

I hadn't felt resentment like this in the little rural towns of Mexico – places like San Luis de la Paz or San Martin – and yet the people in *those* towns were probably not nearly as well off financially as these labourers working at the hacienda. But after a little reflection, I realized that country living is very different from town living. It's probably easier to be poor in the country, where at least the sky and the hills and the winds are shared equally by all.

I've always had a certain knack for doing nothing. I like to do nothing while sitting beside the sea; I like to do nothing in a sunny jardín; I like to do nothing while walking with Robyn; and I would very happily spend an entire afternoon doing nothing in that hacienda in Guanajuato. Even in this day and age, it succeeds at being a sanctuary from the chaos of the everyday world. Robyn and I lost track of one another while we were there, so when I reached the main house, I stepped inside and started to do a little prowling on my own.

It was full of that dark, Spanish, richly carved furniture of the seventeenth century. Stiff, Rembrandt-like portraits of the family were placed with military precision in each of the rooms, but the overall effect of all those dark serious faces was softened and made more human by the warm, friendly terra-cotta colour of the walls, against which they were displayed. Filling the open archways above the large, heavy, wooden doors were long, ornate, iron spindles that fanned out over the arches like the spokes on half a wheel. Delicate iron filigree decorated the wall space around windows, lending them an air of femininity like lace on a pretty blouse. Chandeliers and lamps on long chains dangled down from tall, elegant ceilings; candlesticks were four feet tall; balconies were big enough to serve dinner for twelve. A deep, rich essential oil of graceful living had seeped right down into the marrow of this place – like port poured into a round of Stilton – and there was a slow and continuous release of that essence back out into the air of every room and hallway in the hacienda. It felt as if the owners had just stepped out, and would be back any minute. The historian in me was uncomfortable with this place, but the romantic was enthralled.

The haciendas were noted for their hospitality. A report written in

1828 stated: "We arrived about three o'clock . . . and the leftovers from lunch were brought for us . . . We spent the afternoon in the shade on the terrace, chatting and smoking cigars with the Marqués de Santiago and his sisters, as well as miners, soldiers, lawyers, and priests . . . We made the number of guests twenty-four, and for the most part they had come – like ourselves – au hasard, uninvited and unexpected, but sure of a hearty welcome and good fare."

For a couple of hours we wandered about fancying ourselves genteel, and then, to try and continue the illusion just a little bit longer, we sat down at the hacienda bar to have a drink. The illusion, however, was abruptly shattered when, having taken a look at the prices, we ended up ordering just one beer for the two of us, and had to try and look dignified while passing the bottle back and forth.

During our final week, we got to know a guy called Grant. We misjudged Grant badly when we first met him. He looked about fifty, and we thought he was probably a murderous psychopath in the tradition of Jeffrey Dahmer, or, if not that, at least an arrogant con-man who had befriended Isadora just to gain day and night access to her computer and Internet connection.

Well, one night while I was helping him polish off a pretty good bottle of Mexican wine he'd bought, the two of us proceeded to ramble on at some length, each trying to explain what we thought made Mexicans tick, and I got to like him quite a lot. (Of course, Jeffrey Dahmer was apparently quite charming as well.)

By his own admission, Grant didn't have a "real" job. He lived for part of the year with his mother in Boston, and kept a cheap apartment in San Miguel for the rest of the time. When he was in San Miguel he liked to help organize murder-mystery dinners in local restaurants. And regarding Isadora, it turned out he was actually quite protective, helping her whenever he could. Four days before our departure, he invited us up for dinner. Hopefully, we wouldn't be the main course.

Like ours, Grant's apartment was right in the centre of old colonial San Miguel. We'd never been to his place before, so we walked slowly along his street keeping our eyes peeled for the number of his building. We went past an old man resting on a step, past a team of burros now carrying sacks of earth for spring gardens instead of firewood like back in December, and then spotted his number on the outside of an old, crumbling building. Our jaws dropped as we gazed up at it. It was a three-story, eighteenth-century building like all the rest in the area – except that this one was only eight feet wide.

Feeling a little as if we were entering a Toontown house from Disneyland, we sallied forth.

Grant's was the topmost flat in the building, so we simply headed up any flight of stairs we came to. The building seemed deserted to me, as if the place had been condemned, which wouldn't have been surprising judging by its condition. The hallways we progressed along were only wide enough for one person and only then if you hunched your shoulders in. The occasional empty room we passed was big enough to be useful as a closet and not much else. It seemed the sort of place where you might stumble on mad scientists wearing lab coats conducting bizarre experiments on homeless people. But eventually we made it to the top and were greeted not with a thump on the back of the head, but by Grant and two glasses of wine.

Beaming from ear to ear, he opened his arms wide towards a wall entirely filled with windows and said, "Welcome to the best view in all of San Miguel."

It felt as if we were standing in one of those glass elevators that go up the sides of tall buildings, except, in this case, the rest of the building had fallen down, leaving only the elevator standing. After crawling down from Grant's arms into which I had inadvertently leapt, I could see what he meant. The whole quaintly medieval town of San Miguel, as well as the misty plains beyond, lay out before us. But even better than that, he was located right above the bullring – a swan dive would have landed me right in the ring itself.

Shortly thereafter, his dinner date, Deborah, arrived. She was an intelligent, attractive woman in her late forties, with the kind of youthful and seductive appeal that one more often associates with someone in her twenties. Until recently she had been a lawyer, but it seemed that she had now joined the ranks of the ever-swelling, independently wealthy, global-wanderers' club – having just returned to San Miguel after taking a tango tour of Argentina. She was beguiling but inscrutable, that charming but deadly combination so wonderfully portrayed by Audrey Hepburn when she played the role of Holly Golightly in *Breakfast at Tiffany's.*

"As you can see," said Grant, "I have no room for a table. So I thought we could just go out somewhere for dinner after a leisurely drink on my rooftop terrace. Sound good?"

After nods of approval all around, the four of us climbed a flight of treacherously steep steps that led outside and onto the top of Grant's roof. Drinks in hand, we sat down at seats right up near the edge of the roof and gazed out over the magnificent bullring.

"So have you ever seen a bullfight, Stephen?" said Grant.

"I saw part of one on TV and that was enough for me. Anyone who thinks it's a test of heroism for a human to fight an animal that is so stupid it can't even tell that there's nothing behind that red cloak is greatly deluded if you ask me. I think it's terrible."

"But it's so much a part of the Mexican psyche. Can you ever get to the heart of the Mexican mind without attending a bullfight? What do you think, Deborah?"

Try to imagine a feisty, sophisticated, Audrey Hepburn replying.

"I think they're absolutely wonderful," Deborah said. "They're primitive and basic and theatrical. They're like life stripped of all pretence. They symbolize life as a battle, which is what I think it is. Besides, I totally adore those costumes the matadors wear."

I turned to Grant, "Do you actually enjoy watching them, Grant?"

"Well, not exactly enjoy, but I do watch them with interest," he replied. "Hey, Canadians play team boxing with sticks and call it hockey, Americans settle parking disputes with semi-automatic handguns, and the English eat bread crusts fried in bacon fat. Who are we to say what's barbaric and what isn't?"

And there I was, right back where I started five months ago when we went to the rodeo and had to leave because we couldn't stand the brutal treatment of the animals. Since then I had found so much to admire about Mexicans. I found them to be polite, gentle, loving, and generous. But occasionally, like at that moment gazing out over the bullring, I also felt an uneasy divide between us. After all was said and done, the country and the people still remained a mystery to me.

Around six in the morning on Sunday, April 1, just two days before our departure from Mexico, Grant came over to our place, and the three of us went over to the neighbourhood of San Rafael to meet up with the crowds of pilgrims who had walked through the night carrying the statues of the Virgin Mary and Our Lord of the Column on their annual journey from the Sanctuary of Atotonilco to the Church of San Juan de Dios in San Miguel.

When we arrived at Independencia Avenue, there was only a small scattering of people about, all of them Mexicans. Some were involved in the little last-minute tasks of decorating the street, and others were quietly laying claim to their chosen spots for viewing the procession. The sun was not yet high enough for making shadows, and the absence of the visual clutter they cause made the street feel particularly clean and fresh. We could see our breath, so we knew it was cold, and were glad that we'd worn our toques and gloves.

Across the street, there was a small brass band of men wearing shabby clothes and playing lovely, muted, solemn music. It was beautiful compared to the discordant mariachi/jazz-improv/oom-pah-pah stuff that they usually played in the jardín on Sunday nights. They sounded a little like a Salvation Army band at Christmas time, only their music was more melancholy. The decorated street, the sense of anticipation, and the sharp, cold nip in the air reminded me of the Eaton's Santa Claus Parade my parents used to take us to in Toronto in the 1950s, except that this parade had a deep spiritual reverence associated with it – more like Santa Claus's funeral than his parade.

We stood on the sidewalk, and just in front of us, lying flat in the middle of the street was a luxurious carpet made entirely of marigolds and bougainvillaea in the design of a yellow cross against a purple background, purple being the colour of Easter. All along the side of the street, the lampposts had colourful crepe-paper flowers and bundles of palm leaves tied to them. To our right, row after row of pink, orange, green, and white punched-tissue-paper squares were strung out above the street from one side to the other like napkins on a clothesline. To our left, a purple and white canopy made of balloons and streamers festively spanned the street making it look like a momentary portal to some magical fairy kingdom.

Some sort of fragrant grass had been scattered about everywhere and it cleansed the air of the usual stale city odour, replacing it with a wonderfully pungent, earthy scent that was like a mixture of camomile, mint, and fennel.

"So, is Deborah coming?" I asked Grant.

"Actually, she decided to do the pilgrimage with an elderly Mexican woman she's befriended – I think she's become a kind of surrogate grandmother to Deborah. They set out with the others from Atotonilco last night around midnight. I suppose we'll see them as they go past."

"Is Deborah religious?"

"No, I don't think so, but I think since coming to Mexico she's started to get a little more into the spiritual stuff. I'm a little worried about her really, she's starting to live like a nun. She came here eighteen months ago and she still lives in a place that's basically a dorm. I think she's getting stuck, losing her zest. She really wanted me to go on the pilgrimage with her, but you know, how can I retain my cynical edge and go on a thing like that? Besides, I'd feel like I was intruding. Standing here is as close as I care to get."

I nodded and watched the growing activity on the street. No one took any notice of us. It felt as if we were ghosts . . . utterly invisible. Apparently when the Aztecs first saw white men, their pale skin made some think they *were* ghosts.

"You know, Grant," I said, "I really envy Mexicans for believing in heaven. It's such a beautiful, comforting idea, and it really ticks me off that it's become lost to me. How lucky is that, to be able to have something like heaven to believe in?"

"Mm. All we have is the Great Void. Oh yeah, that sounds like fun. They're an amazing people. You can't get your sink fixed in Mexico, but they'll put on these terrifically well-organized parades three times a week like it was nothing."

And that started me thinking about something Florence had said earlier in the week when we were over there for dinner. I'd been telling her that I felt more alive here than at home; that there was an intensity to experiences here that was lacking at home.

Florence had replied, "Years ago, when I was living in Stratford, Ontario, they put a play on . . ." She was obviously delighting in the opportunity to recall a fond memory. "It was a play based on

Orwell's *1984*. The city council had permitted them to carry the play out into the streets, so that every day as you walked around town, you would encounter actors who were living out the drama right there in the midst of everybody's regular routine. Now, the play on the stage was okay, but this taking-the-drama-into-the-streets idea was amazing. It had an incredible effect on everybody. At one moment you'd just be shopping for milk and bread, and in the next it was as if you'd been whisked up onto a stage. It seemed to suddenly give meaning to things, and it also made life seem more like a fun game to be experimented with. I just loved the way I was forced to flicker back and forth between reality and make believe. That seems to me to be what happens here in Mexico too, because you know, it's not really real for us here either. Our reality is back home in Canada. But here we get to spend our time in what is really a fantasy world for us. And isn't it fun?"

When the procession arrived, it swept along like an unstoppable lava flow, filling up all the space between the buildings that lined both sides of the street. The number of spectators had swollen to such large numbers by this time that they were crowded onto the tops of walls and the roofs of houses. As movement on our part was practically impossible, we just stood our ground and watched the spectacle as it moved past.

Serious young choir boys in red cassocks and white surplices walked slowly past us carrying long white candles on tall brass candlesticks. Priests appeared from behind clouds of incense, swinging their censers and dressed in elaborate robes. The mournful music of the band droned on.

The statue of Jesus was borne on its huge, glossy wooden funeral bier by about ten men who, in spite of being dressed in their everyday jeans and windbreakers, looked thoroughly imposing – not even the hint of a smile on a single one of their faces.

I muttered quietly to Robyn and Grant, "For a country that virtually outlawed the Catholic Church in the 1917 Constitution, there is incredible passion here."

"This has nothing to do with the Catholic Church," Grant whispered. "This is all Indian."

Two more statues followed, one of the Virgin and another of a Saint, and then the molasses-like movement of the crowd became too powerful to resist, and the three of us were absorbed into it.

I lost sight of Robyn and Grant; it was as if we'd all three fallen out of a canoe while travelling down a mighty river's rapids. Being separated was a bit frightening for a moment. And then I realized I wasn't actually going to sink, and that the river wasn't actually a threat – it was simply that the river was in control and I wasn't. My job was simply to stop resisting. Bodies were unintentionally pressing into me from all sides and this resulted in my having unusually intimate contact with a whole host of complete strangers, but nowhere were there any giggles or embarrassed looks. There was only that same calm, focussed, spiritual passion that seemed to permeate the whole event.

I was carried over a little bridge, briefly worrying about it's possible collapse, and then landed on the other side, where the street-serpent in which I had become firmly imbedded decided to come to a complete stop.

Before me there stretched a tightly packed sea of Mexican heads – black hair and brown necks were everywhere. They were all looking towards the top of the street where a giant crown of thorns, fifteen feet high, had been placed. Underneath the crown was the statue of Our Lord of the Column. A priest with a loudspeaker, somewhere beyond that point, began to speak in Latin.

At six feet, I towered above the people standing around me, sticking out like the proverbial sore thumb. Still, no one took any notice of me. If I caught someone's eye, I read only gentle acceptance there.

The people started to sing softly. The soothing sounds were reminiscent of a lullaby sung by a kindly grandmother. Except for the singing, there was complete silence and stillness.

I had come to Mexico to try and get deeper into the culture. Now, I was literally up to my neck in it. Yet, at that moment, all my thoughts and theories just fell away from me like the skin off a snake. Understanding Mexico didn't seem important anymore. It was willing to warm me, like a fire or a womb – and so I let it.

Sources

Baum, Vicki. *Headless Angel*. London: Michael Joseph, 1948.

Chatwin, Bruce. *In Patagonia*. London: Penguin Books, 1988.

Cummings, Joe, and Chicki Mallan. *Mexico Handbook.* Chico, California: Moon Publications Inc., 1996.

Franz, Carl. *The People's Guide to Mexico*. Santa Fe: John Muir Publications, 1987.

Hudson, W.H., *Idle Day's in Patagonia.* London: 1893.

Lawrence, D.H. "Mornings in Mexico." *Reader's Companion to Mexico.* Ed. Allen Ryan. Harcourt Brace & Co., 1995.

MacLachlan & Rodriguez. *Forging the Cosmic Race.* University of California Press, 1990.

Paz, Octavio. *Labyrinth of Solitude: Life and Thought in Mexico.* New York: Grove Press, 1961.

Riding, Alan. *Distant Neighbors: A Portrait of the Mexicans.* New York: Vintage Books, 2000.

Robbins, Tom. *Half Asleep in Frog Pajamas*. New York: Bantam Books, 1995.

Sánchez, Alberto Ruy and Margarita de Orellana. *Guía del Tequila.* Mexico, D.F: Artes de México, 1998.

Street-Porter, Tim. *Casa Mexicana: The Architecture, Design and Style of Mexico.* Stewart, Tabori and Chang, 1989.

Von Hagen, Victor W. *Aztecs: Man and Tribe.* Scarborough: New American Library.